Harnessing the Bohemian

ARTISTS AS INNOVATION PARTNERS IN RURAL & REMOTE COMMUNITIES

Harnessing the Bohemian

ARTISTS AS INNOVATION PARTNERS IN RURAL & REMOTE COMMUNITIES

PETER SKIPPINGTON

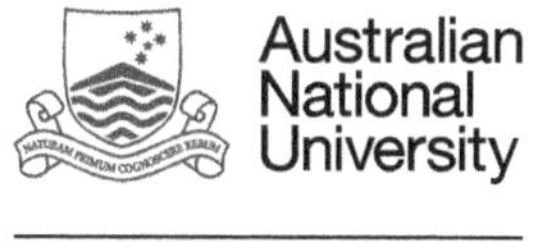

PRESS

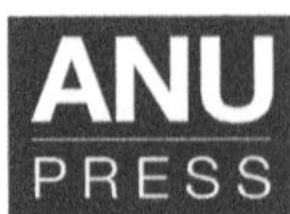

Published by ANU Press
The Australian National University
Acton ACT 2601, Australia
Email: anupress@anu.edu.au
This title is also available online at press.anu.edu.au

National Library of Australia Cataloguing-in-Publication entry

Creator:	Skippington, Peter, author.
Title:	Harnessing the bohemian : artists as innovation partners in rural and remote communities / Peter Skippington.
ISBN:	9781760460525 (paperback) 9781760460532 (ebook)
Subjects:	Community development--Social aspects. Creative ability--Social aspects. Creation (Literary, artistic, etc.)--Social aspects. Diffusion of innovations.
Dewey Number:	307.1

Cover design and layout by ANU Press.
Cover photograph adapted from flic.kr/p/peUNrT by _TC Photography_.

CASS PhD Publication prize
This publication was originally submitted as a PhD thesis and awarded a College of Arts and Social Sciences publication prize for the best thesis in the College between 2010–2015. The prize is awarded on the basis of examiners' reports, a recommendation from the Head of the relevant School and the author's outline of changes to the thesis in preparation for publication. The prize covers the cost of professional copyediting.

Contents

Figures

Tables

Acknowledgements

Stories, poems and songs about the Australian Outback abound. They often assume almost mythical proportions as they celebrate the unique, the eccentric, and the exceptional to the extent that it is sometimes difficult to determine the real from the hyperbole. The hospitality of outback Australia is, however, never questioned and this research has benefited significantly from the friendliness and openness of the people of western and remote Queensland. I am enormously grateful to all the people living and working in the many remote/rural communities who have contributed to the research reported in this book with great generosity and honesty, through surveys, interviews, and site visits over several years.

I would also like to thank Diana Davis, who has been an inspirational teacher, a thoughtful collaborator, and caring friend. Her wisdom and insight has always left me engaged and enthused; her advice and guidance has been astute but moderate, allowing me to make my own mistakes but to also learn and grow from them. She has helped me identify and corral countless insights and opportunities, some of which have been incorporated into this book, while others are for the future.

Foreword

Dr Skippington's book offers a fresh, highly accessible, and interdisciplinary perspective on the intractable problem of shrinking populations and resources in rural and remote Australia. His research not only challenges the conventional wisdom of community development theories and practices, but envisages more central roles for the creative disciplines in revitalisation and futures planning. It speaks to a broad church of relevant stakeholders — policymakers, artists, arts workers, community and business leaders as well as academics — as part of the author's conceptual recognition of what one commentator described as 'the underpinning and essential essence and pervasive value of creative inputs in the milieu of factors and influence that can determine community survival and growth'.

This book is refreshing in that it does more than tilt at the problem; it is all too easy to dismantle what is there, to breathe the air of negativity over work that precedes one's own. He recognises the inherent problems in the application of urban-derived solutions to rural and remote contexts. His approach is both positive and proactive. He proposes a new model of community development — the Creative Communities Development Pyramid (CCDP) — which does not rely for its efficacy on the external wisdom of *experts*. It is a self-help tool designed to assist communities to identify and consolidate their idiosyncratic existing strengths — and then to use these as the basis for developing a planning platform for the adoption of integrative community-wide practices to set and achieve a sustainable outcomes stream for rural and remote communities. In demonstrating the use of the model across a range of scenarios, he demonstrates it to be a highly original framework with significant potential for broad national and international application.

Professor Diana F. Davis
Adjunct Research Fellow
ANU Centre for European Studies

Preface

Australia is revered in her folklore for being a land of wide open spaces, a 'wilful, lavish land'.[1] However, in the change climate of the twenty-first century, those wide open spaces are the most vulnerable; they must measure up to the challenges of change or face virtual extinction. Our most rural and remote communities are shrinking in population and their traditional agricultural bases are ever eroding. While technological changes (e.g. the National Broadband Network (NBN)) are integral to the nation's egalitarian strategy, the harsh reality remains that these communities face idiosyncratic challenges, ones that will never be confronted by their urban counterparts. Sadly, given its almost exclusive focus on urban contexts, the now vast community development literature has very little to offer those in rural and remote communities in terms of strategic direction. There is an urgent need to redress the balance and to provide relevant options for people living in and committed to these communities and their further development.

The research described in this book derives from the principles of the creative economy; it questions whether a focus on such principles might create potential affordances for such communities. Specifically, this book examines the links between the arts and robust, sustainable, and inventive communities capable of meeting the challenges of an increasingly globalised society. The potential of the arts to contribute to social, cultural, and economic development in rural and remote communities has not yet been fully explored, let alone realised, since the arts are not commonly integrated with community life. Indeed, traditionally, community artists and arts workers have not been fully

1 According to Dorothea Mackellar's iconic poem, *My Country*.

apprised of or engaged with community-wide issues and problems, the natural consequence of which has been that there have been few opportunities for cross-disciplinary projects or initiatives.

In this volume, the literature pertaining to conventional community development theories and practices is scoped, backgrounding an environmental scan of documented lighthouse projects in the area. Arguing from the concept that the creative economy impacts on multiple aspects of community life and growth, and is proving to be broader, deeper, and more all-encompassing than current conventional approaches to community development, the study explores the potential links between the skills and processes inherent in the artistic crucible of creativity, and those skills and attitudes required to build robust, sustainable, and inventive communities capable of meeting the challenges of an ever more globalised society. Underpinning methodologies include environmental scanning (surveys, interviews, and site visits) in regional, rural, and remote communities to sample the current role of arts in the social, cultural, and economic development of communities, followed by case studies.

The resultant picture of a significant disconnect between the arts and their communities leads to the proposal of a new model for community development that identifies the arts as a community asset to be considered and utilised in conjunction with other community assets. The model encourages communities to develop a focus on creativity and innovation across all sectors of the community, and to embrace the development of community partnerships in anticipation of new synergies, leading to more divergent and innovative solutions to community problems. The relevance of the model is demonstrated through application to a range of recognisably intransigent problems that confront such communities in order to demonstrate how it might stimulate and guide integrated community development. The challenges to the arts and artists to become less insular and more connected with community issues across the spectrum, thus relinquishing a monocular focus on artistic products towards a new focus on creative inputs to other disciplines and community sectors, will doubtless require a disciplined harnessing of the Bohemian — therein lies a significant, albeit intriguing challenge.

1

Struggling to Survive

With every year the rural/urban divide fissures more deeply as contemporary economic and technological pressures challenge communities in many ways, often to the precipice of existence. Indeed, the continuum from urban to rural has become more rainbow-like as urban identity escalates and the *real* rural becomes seemingly even more remote. In particular, rural and remote communities are being increasingly challenged to move from primary industries and manufacturing to knowledge-based services; they are also being pressured to respond in new ways to the globalisation of national economies and the consequent emergence of more complex and competitive economic environments. In addition, they are being confronted by information and communication technologies that transcend concepts of distance and place, thus requiring communities to participate more actively in communities of interest rather than only primarily communities of place. In this context of rapid change, rural and remote communities struggle to maintain identity, preserve historical, cultural and environmental distinctiveness, and achieve genuine economic competitiveness. In essence, they struggle to survive.

The Need to Transform Rural and Remote Communities

The sharp and profound changes currently impacting on communities in rural and remote areas are not limited to economic and technological transformations; they arise also from mounting ecological concerns and evolving social attitudes. A growing number of environmentally responsible people in Australian society are progressively questioning the farming and grazing practices of rural Australia and, in the process, raising issues about agricultural sustainability, land degradation and the destruction of waterways. Metamorphosing social mindsets are prompting a much closer scrutiny of rural Australia's relationship with Indigenous peoples and a growing concern about poverty and inequity in rural towns, with research focusing on the high rate of youth suicide in rural communities, especially for males.

New levels of ecological and social awareness, combined with an ever more dominant urban mindset, have stimulated an emerging perception of the functional insularity of rural living — parochialism, circumscribed viewpoints, reluctance to change, and a fettering unwillingness to innovate. The success of rural and remote communities in responding to current economic, technological, social, cultural and ecological pressures thus depends not only on the ability to maintain infrastructure, employment and income, but on the capacity of local people to anticipate, accept and manage change, to develop and apply analytical, critical and problem-solving skills, to communicate effectively, to provide social, cultural and economic leadership, to develop and use effective community networks, and to think strategically and creatively beyond both real and apparent restraints.

Extant abilities, attitudes, skills and resources available to rural and remote communities provide the key to improving their economic and social situations. Indeed, they constitute the very platform on which these communities can mobilise and build capacity to creatively solve problems and develop innovative opportunities for growth and community renewal. However, worryingly, several key questions remain unanswered. To what extent are existing community development programs in rural and remote communities viable? How effective have they been in developing and sustaining creative and innovative approaches to change in communities? What have been the effective change agents in these programs? To what extent have social, economic and cultural potentials been harnessed? What stimuli exist for creativity and innovation? What roles do the arts play in such programs? Might there be further potential for the arts in community development? How might this most effectively be harnessed? Answers to such questions require an initial appreciation of the scope and nature of extant community development programs in rural and remote communities.

The Landscape of Efforts to Help Communities

Over the last two decades, there have been many efforts to help communities to address the challenges and opportunities arising from identified social, economic and technological changes. While such efforts have been described in various ways and marketed under various umbrellas, the most common and pervasive has undoubtedly been community capacity building (CCB). This is a contemporary term used to describe strategies and approaches available to communities in responding to the rapid changes impacting on their futures. Currently there is a bewildering array of definitions and descriptions of CCB in the contemporary literature, a selection of which is provided in 'Appendix A: Chronological Review of CCB Definitions'. These variations arise mainly from the differing contexts in which CCB programs have been designed and implemented (Chapman and Kirk, 2001; Craig, 2007). For example, many such programs are government sponsored and focus on utilising external skills and resources to strengthen community decision making and control over the delivery of government services, including health, welfare, child protection, energy, environment and primary industries (McGinty, 2003; Smyth, 2009). Other CCB activities are community generated and supported from within communities; they build on local knowledge, skills and resources to create local innovative opportunities (Craig, 2007).

Regardless of their context, CCB programs and initiatives, whether developed and applied by governments or communities, share a single aim: to counterbalance the dual and sometimes conflicting pressures to respond to changing economic and social imperatives while conserving and maintaining community historical, cultural and environmental distinctiveness. In such environments, which are increasingly concerned with economic and social survival, cultural products, practices and processes often take a back seat to initiatives focused either on more traditional rural activities, such as horticulture, agriculture and animal husbandry, or on the provision of critical government services such as health, welfare and education. Ironically, however, the cultural industries and the knowledge, skills and understandings underpinning creative practices may offer unique opportunities for meaningful community-based learning and growth. Creative decision making and problem solving, critical analysis, presentation of alternative viewpoints, as well as collaboration and networking are some of the skills inherent in artistic processes. Such skills are also relevant, if not critical, in building a community's ability to manage change. Therefore, the potential of arts practices and processes might be found in their prospective ability to stimulate and accelerate community development, to assist communities in generating a critical analysis of their strengths and weaknesses, and to build on community strengths and eliminate community weaknesses. Such potentials warrant further formal exploration and analysis.

The identified potential of the arts to support community development is based on the concept of the arts connecting with broad community agendas and contributing across a range of community products and services. However, recognition of this potential must also take into account the strong historic connection between the arts and community over many decades. The concept of community arts, for example, has been based on the belief that cultural meaning, expression and creativity reside within a community and the sense that the task of community artists is to assist community members to 'free their imaginations and give form to their creativity' (Goldbard, 1993, p. 2). This tends, however, to be about artists making art in partnership with community members and most often takes the form of one-off projects based on short-term processes and products (Evans, 2005). While these are commendable activities often leading to important social and cultural gains for both individuals and communities, they are essentially short term and lack a developmental framework to underpin aims and provide meaningful outcomes across a range of community concerns (Evans, 2005). The focus on small-scale, time dependent, narrowly conceived projects has thus limited the impact of community arts and kept the cultural industries at the periphery of community life rather than at its centre.

A more recent iteration connecting the arts and community development is the concept of Community Cultural Development (CCD). While analogous with the aims of CCB, CCD narrows its focus to build community capacity solely through the arts. CCD has extended the foundation provided by the community arts movement to connect arts-based approaches more broadly with community development agendas and to respond to contemporary community issues (Sonn, Drew & Kasat, 2002). It supports the development of local leadership, and the establishment and maintenance of networks and partnerships; it recognises that community initiative, control and ownership are critical to sustainable growth and development (Goldbard & Adams, 2006). The strong emphasis on process and community engagement provides a philosophical platform focused on creating social value through lessening social isolation, developing community identity and pride, and prompting action on social justice issues. However, the adoption of a sociopolitical reform agenda with social justice as a core aim has served only to contribute to CCD's insularity and its failure to contribute broadly to community development across social, cultural, environmental and economic areas.

Yet the contribution of the arts to community development may be potentially more significant than current approaches. If artistic processes are to be more fully integrated with the social and economic goals and interests of the wider community, then artistic/creative processes need to be harnessed as key contributors to the development of contemporary rural and remote communities. Successful community responses to current pressures depend on their ability to develop innovative revenue opportunities, apply technology in creative and productive ways, maintain social cohesion, develop and apply innovative problem-solving skills, provide social and cultural leadership, and develop and utilise effective community networks. In this context, the arts and the foundations on which their practices are based may offer a new framework in capacity building in rural and remote communities to facilitate a comprehensive examination of the complex interconnections between the arts and the social, cultural and economic development of rural and remote communities.

Table 1 hypothesises a potential framework based on the identification of potential connections between the arts and community capacity building under five broad categories: community leadership; community growth and development; community cohesion; community problem solving; and partnership building.

Table 1. The Potential of Arts Practices and Processes for Community Capacity Building.

Category	Arts practices and processes	Potential for capacity building in rural and remote communities
Community leadership	Artistic decision making and creative problem solving.	Enhancement of leadership skills enabling communities to manage change and sustain community-led development.
	Reflection on and critical analysis of artistic processes and products.	Adoption of continuous improvement, quality processes and critical evaluation.
Community growth and development	Technical mastery of art processes and technologies.	Provision of additional avenues for economic and social development. Creation of a vehicle for local people to express and act on existing concerns.
	Synthesis and translation of intellectual and sensory ideas into creative outcomes and products.	Provision of new community product and potential community revenue. Empowerment of individuals within the community to explore new options and possibilities.
	Conceptual and research skills.	Provision of new development pathways and reduction of barriers to participation. Facilitation of the adoption of technology by the community. Provision of information to the community. Support of the practice of art in the community. Assistance in keeping abreast of contemporary developments, including the application of technology.
Community cohesion	Artistic ethics.	Promotion of community sensitivity to cultural, historical and environment issues. Promotion of community sensitivity to change and development.
	Visual literacy.	Promotion of the social, historical, cultural and environmental distinctiveness of communities. Appreciation of the opportunities arising from community distinctiveness.

Category	Arts practices and processes	Potential for capacity building in rural and remote communities
Community problem solving	Interpersonal, verbal and written communication.	Linkages between art and learning and community social and economic well-being. Promotion of inquiry and dialogue within the community. Provision of opportunities for economic and cultural development through the visual arts. Promotion of a community appreciation of the interconnectedness of the arts with community history, local economy, and regional culture. Facilitation of the integration of art practice with the wider community.
Partnership building	Participation in collaborative artistic ventures (group participation and team building).	Promotion of partnerships and network development within and between communities. Promotion of collaboration within and between communities. Promotion of individual development and the role of the individual within community.

Source: Author's research.

In identifying some of the potential associations between the arts and capacity building in rural and remote communities, the conceptual framework provided by Table 1 is built on the assumption that arts practices and processes can be applied in rural and remote communities to add depth to and broaden community planning and development in order to promote alternative solutions and pathways, advance recognition and appreciation of cultural and environmental opportunities, and balance the sometimes conflicting demands of economic survival, and social and cultural development. While these associations and the assumptions on which they are based demand further exploration and testing, Table 1 nevertheless provides a starting point for a more comprehensive examination of the interconnectedness between the arts and community development.

Taking the Initiative

The tensions for strategic community building in sparsely populated areas are clear. The relative impotence of current programs is, alas, also a matter for concern given goals for sustainability and social/

economic development. Creative decision making, problem solving, critical analysis, presenting alternative viewpoints, collaboration and networking are recognised as skills and processes inherent in artistic practice. Whether these skills and processes might be better exploited in assisting rural and remote communities to address the challenges in creative and innovative ways, offers hitherto unexplored possibilities. A significant expansion in the current range and scope of capacity-building approaches and strategies available to remote/rural communities is overdue and urgent. The development of new arts-based models, strategies and approaches has the potential to provide a framework for the development of practical strategies for use not only by communities but also by artists and arts organisations in the achievement of economic growth, social cohesion and cultural development in remote/rural communities.

This book seeks to:

1. Examine the viability and sustainability of existing approaches to community development with a particular focus on rural and remote communities;
2. Scope the current and potential role and function of the arts in supporting community development approaches;
3. Probe the nature and scope of specific roles and functions of the arts in community development through contrasting case studies; and
4. Use the data derived to develop a new conceptual model for community development in rural/remote communities.

The particular focus of this book is rural and remote communities. In order to appreciate the particular issues facing these communities it is necessary to examine the scope and nature of their contemporary challenges; this is provided in Chapter 2. An examination of conventional approaches to community capacity building is provided in Chapter 3, while the contemporary literature relating to creativity and innovation is examined in Chapter 4. Chapter 4 also explores contemporary concepts of creativity and innovation and examines how these might influence new approaches to arts-based community building. Chapter 5 draws on national and international literature to showcase current approaches to arts-based community development. Chapter 6 identifies the unique challenges inherent in investigating rural and remote communities, and Chapter 7 reports on the results of investigations of the impact of the arts in these communities. Chapter 8 further explores the impact of the arts on these communities through three major case studies. Chapter 9 draws together key findings of the research to propose a new model for the arts in community building. Finally, Chapter 10 explores scenarios for the application of the proposed new model and elucidates directions for further research and development.

2

Combating the Uncertainty and Timidity of Isolation

Almost 70 per cent of Australia's 22 million people live in major cities, mostly oriented towards the coast. By contrast, just 491,560 people, or 2 per cent of the total population, live in remote or very remote areas of Australia; the remaining 28 per cent live in rural and regional areas of the continent (Australian Bureau of Statistics, 2008). In geographical terms, 70 per cent (over 14 million people) of the population live in a combined area of just 11,500 square kilometres, while the remaining 30 per cent populate over 7 million square kilometres (Infrastructure Australia, 2010). Australia ranks as one of the most highly urbanised countries in the world, with an urban density comparable to that of Japan and the United States of America. Contrary to the romantic image of Australians living and working in a wide, brown land, Australians are more likely to live and work in a city than their compatriots in France, Greece or Ireland. Figure 1 shows the percentage of Australia's population living in urban areas compared with other selected Organisation for Economic Co-operation Development (OECD) countries.

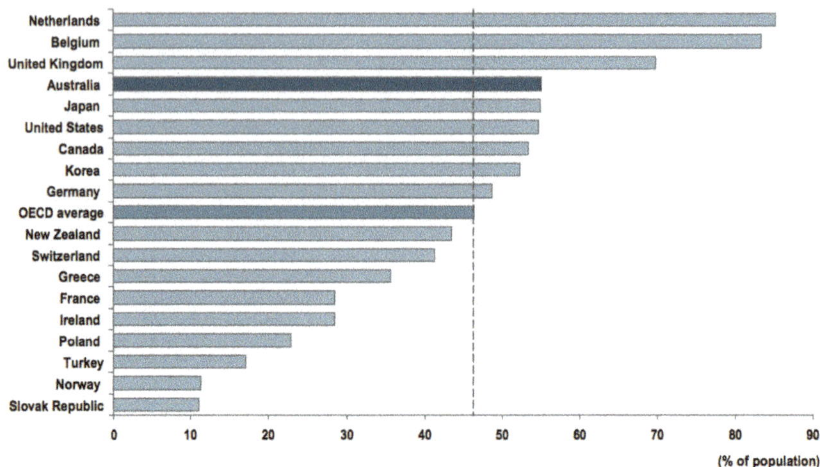

Figure 1. Percentage of National Populations of Selected OECD Countries Living in Urban Regions.

Source: OECD, 2007.

While Figure 1 uses population data to highlight the urbanisation of the Australian population, Australian poet A.D. Hope's *Australia* questions our ability to comprehend and appreciate the vastness and mystery of the continent equally compellingly but more imaginatively:

> They call her a young country, but they lie:
> She is the last of lands, the emptiest,
> A woman beyond her change of life, a breast
> Still tender but within the womb is dry.
>
> Without songs, architecture, history:
> The emotions and superstitions of younger lands,
> Her rivers of water drown among inland sands,
> The river of her immense stupidity
>
> Floods her monotonous tribes from Cairns to Perth.
> In them at last the ultimate men arrive
> Whose boast is not: 'we live' but 'we survive',
> A type who will inhabit the dying earth.
>
> And her five cities, like five teeming sores,
> Each drains her: a vast parasite robber-state
> Where second-hand Europeans pullulate
> Timidly on the edge of alien shores.
>
> (A.D. Hope, 1955)

While Hope observes the overwhelming tendency of the Australian population to hug tenaciously to the coastline, his sense of the Australian psyche is that, historically and culturally, the primarily immigrant population of Australia remains uncertain, perhaps even afraid, of the vast interior emptiness of the continent.

While neither numerous nor populous, Australia's small, inland communities remain diverse and complex, each community possessing unique characteristics deriving from history, population, geography, size, demographic composition, economic and social infrastructure, and remoteness from the products and services of larger population centres. While the recognition of this diversity prompts caution against assumptions that all rural and remote communities share the same or even similar characteristics, there are nevertheless generic socioeconomic and demographic trends readily identifiable across many rural and remote areas of Australia. Firstly, rural populations tend to have more children but fewer young adults than urban areas (Argent & Walmsley, 2008). Secondly, people in rural and remote communities tend to have lower levels of education, partly because there is a limited range of professional opportunities in many rural areas as well as limited access to resources and higher education (Hossain et al., 2010; Reid et al., 2008). Thirdly, household incomes in rural and remote areas are generally lower than in metropolitan areas (Athanasopoulos & Hahid, 2003; Woodhouse, 2006).

As well as being geographically isolated and distant from services, many rural and remote communities have been affected by ecological threats and economic downturns. The impact of recent severe droughts in Australia, as well as other ecological threats such as flooding, salinity and fire, has placed significant financial stress on rural and remote communities. Public infrastructure and service closures, and restructuring of farming businesses, have resulted in further economic uncertainty (Cavaye, 2001), all of which contribute to population decline, making it even more difficult for rural and remote communities to sustain services and businesses (Beer et al., 2003). Inevitably, this leads to a cycle of decline with consequent unemployment and out-migration, particularly among young people (Cavaye, 2001). Limited entertainment, employment and further education opportunities exacerbate the likelihood, even inevitability, of young people leaving the area. Evidence also suggests that people living in inland rural and remote areas are overburdened and challenged by higher rates of injury, diabetes, coronary heart disease, alcohol and tobacco consumption, and suicide (Bourke, 2003; Rajkumar & Hoolahan, 2004). Such social and economic difficulties lead to an erosion of confidence and the sense of community that has traditionally existed in and sustained many rural and remote areas. It is worth noting, however, that not all rural areas are experiencing decline; some coastal and mountain environments and urban fringe areas, for example, are experiencing real growth (Charbit, 2009). Those rural and remote areas more commonly affected by economic and population decline tend to be inland agricultural and pastoral regions, mainly because farming and grazing are no longer the sole pillars of rural economies (Macadam et al., 2004), although some of these are now experiencing consequential growth through expanded mining activity in rural areas.

Despite these challenges, there are also significant new opportunities for rural and remote communities. Increasingly, Australian rural economies of the twenty-first century draw heavily upon three key assets: natural amenities for tourism and recreation; cultural and historical heritage; and natural resources for farming, forestry, and mining (Macadam et al., 2004). Those rural communities currently experiencing growth tend to have successfully accessed or built upon two or more of these assets. Successful rural economies are necessarily diversified, rendering traditional economic development strategies less relevant as enterprising communities apply new business strategies to apply innovative approaches to meet changing market conditions (Chaston, 2008; Haggblade, Hazell & Reardon, 2010; Herbert-Cheshire, 2000). Such communities have overcome uncertainty and timidity to develop and apply innovative marketing of natural amenities, cultural heritage and other income-generating strategies to attract people and jobs (Blakely & Leigh, 2010; Woodhouse, 2006). They are developing new ways of generating income by building not only on their natural resources but also on newly identified community capital in the forms of historical heritage, cultural uniqueness, artistic capital, geographic distinctiveness and human talent (Daskon, 2010; Johnson, 2009; MacDonald & Jolliffe, 2003). In this way they diversify their economies, attract new businesses, and sustain their successes to provide a strong platform for continuous, ongoing growth. The appeal of new businesses using community assets in innovative ways also leads to a greatly enhanced view of rural communities as places to live, retire, and holiday — all of which, in turn, enhance the quality of life for existing residents (Adams, 2009; Lee, 2010; Wolff, 2010).

Increasing Community Involvement, Confidence, Power and Control

Contemporary evidence suggests that the strong and active involvement of constituent communities in development and growth processes has become a critical prerequisite to success and sustainability (Moscardo, 2008; Taylor, 2000; Wood, 2001). There is also strong agreement that communities must be involved in the development process from the outset (Campbell, Wunungmurra & Nyomba, 2007; Fagin, 1997; Geddes, 1995; Gregory, Hartz-Karp & Watson, 2008: Taylor, 2000). Specifically, they need to be involved in designing programs, creating priorities, contributing to management, and controlling budgets (Buikstra et al., 2010). The creation of strong and vibrant communities requires a powerful, knowledgeable and vocal community at the centre of the decision-making process. Real influence in decision making has been demonstrated to confer a sense of purpose and control on communities (Taylor, 2000), meaning that communities are consequently empowered in their relationships with external stakeholders and moved to exercise authority over key resources and assets in ways that have enhanced potential to sustain cohesive growth (Wood, 2000).

Researchers seeking to identify the specific benefits of community involvement have also amplified the message that successful and sustainable community growth can only occur when local people are not only involved in the process but also equipped with the skills to achieve a positive and sustainable outcome (Chaskin, 2001). The specific benefits of increased community involvement and enhanced community skills and expertise may include: (i) unique community perspectives to the specification of problems and the clarification of issues (Jupp, 2000); (ii) maintenance of focus on community needs to ensure that programs meet the needs of local people in comprehensive ways (Carley & Kirk, 1999); (iii) a higher level of acceptability in the community, with improvements having greater longevity because of higher levels of ownership (Taylor, 2000); (iv) the development and application of new community skills applied across a range of activities and problems (Purdue et al. 2000); and (v) revitalisation of local democratic and participative processes (Newman, 2005).

Despite the strong and unequivocal emphasis on community involvement and empowerment evident in the literature, confusion nevertheless exists as to how these approaches might be implemented most successfully. A major concern is that many community developments over the last decade have been designed to support public policy, with the result that initiatives are controlled and managed by external agencies, usually government (DeFilippis, 2001). While external agencies have often provided opportunities for limited community input into planning and development, essentially they have exercised majority control over development agendas and exerted power and influence over communities (Cavaye, 2000). Other researchers also recognise that community initiatives designed, sponsored and governed by external agencies are unlikely to engage and fully involve community members in sustainable approaches to growth and development (Taylor, 2000; Wood, 2000). In a specific instance, Harvey and Shaw (1998) reviewed government processes in the United Kingdom and found that community groups were highly critical of the short time frames involved in the development of applications for projects as the pressure to meet tight deadlines actively worked against meaningful community consultation and planning.

Wood (2000) provides a further insight into the potentially negative impacts of the involvement of external agencies and, indeed, suggests that extreme care should be exercised by agencies and organisations engaged in working with communities, as local people may find the assumption that they need to increase their capacity insulting and patronising. Agencies and organisations supporting communities often assume that the infusion of training and support from the outside will automatically strengthen community participation (Henderson & Mayo, 1998). Such approaches underestimate the wealth of knowledge, skills and expertise extant within communities. Over the longer term, processes that seek actively to ensure that communities gain and retain influence, control and ownership must be adopted:

> Unless communities feel a sense of ownership and control, benefits tend to be short lived … Involving residents throughout the lifetime of the project was both time consuming and resource intensive.

> But their involvement, based where necessary on providing tailored training and other support to those wanting to contribute to the process of regeneration, was critical (Barr, 1998, p. 6).

The problem of capacity-building agendas being controlled by external agencies is also evidenced in the literature through a critical mismatch between rhetoric and practice in the areas of community control and empowerment (Cavaye, 2000; Harvey & Shaw, 1998; Henderson & Mayo, 1998; Taylor, 2000; Wood, 2000). The balance between the capabilities of communities and those of external agencies has been tipped in the favour of external agencies, an imbalance that raises significant questions about the sustainability of many current community development initiatives and programs. Contemporary literature appears to have failed either to acknowledge or adequately explore the power relationships extant between external professionals and local residents. This is a complex process based on the development and maintenance of meaningful partnerships but, in many cases, the community's role in partnership development has been restricted to a very menial role focused only on meeting externally imposed criteria (Wood, 2000).

Developing New Partnerships and Networks

The current community development literature reveals a lack of emphasis on the nature and scope of relationships between external agencies and local people in communities, which has led several researchers to observe that the role of community partnerships has often been overly narrowly focused and to have operated merely as an adjunct to the achievement of community objectives and outcomes, usually predetermined by external funding agencies acting as controllers rather than facilitators or partners (Chanan, Gilchrest & West, 1999; Harvey & Shaw, 1998; Taylor, 2000). While Wood (2000) stresses the need for strong and equal partnerships, the literature documents little in the way of specific partnership-building strategies. The best strategies on offer are limited to generic calls to overcome past failures and build meaningful, long-term partnerships as a way of ensuring that development is sustained once the initial stimulus for a project has subsided. Chanan, Gilchrest & West (1999) emphasise this fragility and argue for stronger and more balanced community partnerships, but fail to provide a detailed examination of the complex issues involved in partnership building between groups or organisations with vastly different experiences, skills and power bases:

> When the regeneration scheme ends, many of its initiatives will be at risk of disappearing with it. A scheme that has built up community involvement is more likely to be able to hand some of its components on to be maintained by viable, independent local organisations. Also if the community has been widely involved, it will be in a better position to help devise new programmes and press the local authority to keep the momentum of development (Chanan, Gilchrest & West, 1999, p. 8).

While the development of meaningful partnerships based on equal power, control and responsibility is stressed by many researchers, it is also the case that limited recognition of the importance of those partnerships is likely to place considerable new demands and responsibilities on communities and the external agencies involved in the community development process. Moreover, much of the literature focuses primarily on the demands and responsibilities of external agencies rather than on community organisations *per se*. It might be argued that such a focus serves to strengthen the power imbalances in partnerships by implicitly acknowledging a primary role for external agencies. For example, Duncan & Thomas (2000) point out that, in order to achieve sustainable development in communities, there is a strong argument in favour of developing the institutional capacity of external agencies and stakeholders, including government departments, partnership agencies and the private sector to integrate community-based approaches into their organisational and decision-making cultures. While such an approach has certain merit, it argues for action by stakeholders only on one side of the equation and, *ipso facto*, ignores the talent and skills to be found in communities. Chapman & Kirk (2001) present a more balanced approach by arguing that principles of conjoint working, common purpose and shared responsibilities are essential to the success of any multi-agency partnership. Nevertheless, currently the literature fails to detail principles that might usefully guide the development of community partnerships.

The primary economic emphasis on the roles and influence of external stakeholders seems to result from local community organisations coming to the partnership table without substantial financial resources. This is often compounded by a local community's failure to acknowledge in any explicit way the breadth, depth and value of the resources it contributes to the partnership in the form of local knowledge, skills and expertise (Hounslow, 2002). As a consequence, the local community can become complicit in its potential marginalisation and exclusion from decision making. Henderson & Mayo (1998) are representative of mainstream community development researchers in their recognition of the problems associated with partnerships, focusing almost exclusively on changes to the behaviour of external stakeholders and organisations. They argue that external stakeholders need training in how to listen to and work with communities and gain the confidence to work in new and unfamiliar ways (Henderson & Mayo, 1998). There is certainly evidence in the literature to show that the majority of external stakeholders do not undertake any initial training with communities and have varying levels of commitment to working with communities on equal terms (e.g. Chapman & Kirk, 2001). A stronger and more explicitly articulated acknowledgement in the literature of the challenges associated with establishing balanced, productive partnerships is sorely needed.

Cavaye (2000) and Broughton & Chambers (2001) have recognised, against the trend, some of the problems in partnership building arising from within communities. Acknowledged community leaders whose power derives to some extent from existing institutional arrangements may not necessarily be welcoming of new ways of operating (Cavaye, 2000). In some instances, local people are reluctant to take control, expressing a wish to depend on external experts (Broughton & Chambers, 2001). In other cases, local people whose 'lives are already overburdened with responsibilities are afraid of what new responsibilities will fall on them if they become involved in the regeneration process' (Broughton & Chambers, 2001, p. 9). The key message from the literature is that the local community can become isolated from decision making due to the exercise of power and influence by external stakeholders, or the fear, unwillingness and reluctance of community members to engage with development processes. It is, however, noteworthy that the current literature gives unfair emphasis to the importance of the roles and behaviours of external stakeholders over the functions and responsibilities of people in local communities. In essence, the literature fails to address mechanisms to circumvent unequal power relationships and build mutual respect between external agents and communities.

Networking has also attracted attention as a significant strategy to build relationships and stimulate collaboration within communities, and between communities and external agencies. Some researchers perceive networking to be a core process of community development (Gilchrist, 1995; Gilchrist, 2009; Howe & Cleary, 2001; Littlejohns & Thompson, 2001). Robinson & Green (2010) predict that the recent widespread adoption of the technologies of social networking will provide new and powerful tools to assist community networking. It is widely seen as an important strategy because it allows information and ideas to flow to and from all those directly involved in the process of community building, thus enabling participants to share information, experiences and best practice, and to draw upon the experience of others in similar circumstances (Gilchrist, 1995; Gilchrist, 2009). The importance of networking as a strategy to facilitate partnerships has, however, been largely overlooked in the literature. Those researchers who have examined the role of networking have focused solely on the roles and responsibilities of external agencies and have not given equal attention to external stakeholders and communities. For example, Chapman & Kirk (2001) argue that external agencies have an important role in developing and supporting community networks, and identify two key aspects: improving access to information and networking opportunities, and helping communities to manage information.

However, the literature remains silent on the roles of communities in supporting and maintaining networks. Chapman & Kirk (2001), however, do argue that the information sharing and networking potential of information and communications technologies (including the internet) provides significant potential for communities and they point out that external agencies need to work with communities to reduce the digital divide and technological disadvantage. Successful networks evolve only when local people are involved in the process and equipped with the skills needed to have an impact. Researchers have identified the value networks as follows: (i) communities develop a direct perspective on relevant issues (Jupp, 2000); (ii) community involvement helps to deliver programs that accurately meet the needs of local people (Carley & Kirk, 1999); (iii) projects are more acceptable to community members, with improvements having longevity, because of community ownership (Taylor, 2000); (iv) active involvement helps communities to build valuable organisational skills applied across a range of problems (Purdue et al., 2000); and (v) community involvement helps to revitalise local democracy (Putnam, 1993).

Building Human and Social Capital

In his landmark book, *Bowling Alone*, Robert Putnam (2000) identifies a decline in social capital in the United States of America by analysing quantitative data measuring civic engagement and social connectedness. He argues that this decline in social capital has resulted in a measurable decrease in the quality of everyday life. Over the last decade, perceived declines in social capital in communities have become a major concern for governments and community organisations, based on the premise that social capital is the bedrock on which communities can build and grow as, without a strong core of social capital, communities face a tangible cost to community well-being, health and wealth. As a result, the concept of social capital has grown in both breadth and depth and now dominates the community development literature. This has resulted in a concept characterised by many overlapping and related issues, including theories and practices of community development, community capacity building (CCB), social cohesion, community empowerment, and community well-being (Woolcock, Renton & Cavaye, 2004).

Social capital's connection with other theories and practices has resulted in a myriad of definitions rooted in specific purposes and approaches (e.g. Dolfsma & Dannreuther, 2003; Edwards & Foley, 1998). However, the similarities and commonalities across definitions focus primarily on social relationships that have productive benefits for both communities and the individuals that work and live within them (Knoke, 2009; Woolcock, 1998). Commonalities in the now extensive literature on social capital centre on how the accumulation of networks, skills, expertise, resources and confidence collectively facilitates the process of empowering individuals and communities (Fukuyama, 1995; Putnam, 2000). While the commonalities are strong, different authors focus on the diverse aspects of social capital and the different contexts for social capital. Such foci have resulted in a range of perspectives on the real and potential impacts of social capital on individuals and communities. Table 2 categorises social capital theories in terms of their major foci and exemplifies selected theorists' views on the role of social capital.

Table 2. Scope of Social Capital Research in the Literature.

Authors	Date	Perspectives from social capital research	Key observations
Research focus: Social capital focusing on the role of individuals in networks			
Baker	2000	Social capital is the application of resources available to community members through personal networks including information, ideas, leads, and opportunities. Resources are not personal assets but can be used by individuals to pursue their interests. Access to social capital depends on who you know not what you know (human capital).	Social capital depends on the size, variety and quality of personal and business networks. Opposite of individualism but strongly connected with individual achievement.
Belliveau, O'Reilly & Wade	1996	Social capital is formed through an individual's personal network especially those that have elite professional affiliations.	Social capital is based on personal networks and professional affiliations.
Research focus: Social capital focusing on institutionalised relationships and networks			
Bourdieu	1986	Social capital is the aggregate of the actual or potential resources available through membership of institutionalised networks or relationships.	Social networks are a product of investment strategies to establish institutional relationships for short- or long-term gain. Networks are based on social obligations that are convertible into tangible benefits.
Bourdieu & Wacquant	1992	Social capital is the sum of the resources, actual or virtual, that accrues to an individual or a group by virtue of possessing a durable network of more or less institutionalised relationships of mutual acquaintance and recognition.	Sustainable networks and institutionalised relationships are important.
Research focus: Social capital focusing on support and brokerage			
Burt	1992	Social capital is a network of friends and colleagues (and other contacts) through whom opportunities are provided to use individual, financial and human capital.	Stresses the brokerage opportunities of social networks. Networks to support individual achievements are important. A facilitator is recommended for the development of human and financial capital.

Authors	Date	Perspectives from social capital research	Key observations
Research focus: Social capital as a process to gain access to information and resources			
Knoke	2009	Social capital is the process by which social actors create and mobilise their network connections. Connections operate within and between organisations to gain access to other actors' resources.	Based on strategic corporate interactions and benefits. Focused on professional and business outcomes.
Portes	1998	Social capital is the ability and aptitude of actors to secure benefits by virtue of membership in social networks or other social structures.	Social networking for professional or personal benefit is stressed.
Research focus: Social capital as a process for collaboration and cooperation based on trust			
Fukuyama	1995	Social capital is the ability of people to work together for common purposes in groups or organisations.	Based on unwritten or informal rules that allow and facilitate cooperation. Based on trust, not legislation or laws.
Inglehart	1997	Social capital is based on a culture of trust and tolerance, in which extensive networks of voluntary associations emerge.	Cultural focus on trust and tolerance. Volunteerism.
Putnam	2000	Social capital involves networks, norms, and social trust that facilitate coordination and cooperation for mutual benefit.	Strong focus on trust as the foundation of social capital. Communal cooperation and coordination. Community rather than individual benefit.
Woolcock	1998	Social capital is the information, trust, and norms of reciprocity inherent in one's social networks.	Reciprocity introduced as a key concept along with trust. Informal processes inherent in social networks.
Research focus: Social capital as good will, empathy and neighbourliness			
Duncan & Thomas	2000	Social capital is an intangible web of relationships that stimulates participation in communities and community organisations. Social capital is essentially good will, empathy and neighbourliness between the individuals and households who make up social units.	Intangible relationships as strong as formal networks. Focus on qualities of good will and empathy.

Authors	Date	Perspectives from social capital research	Key observations
Research focus: Social capital as a process for collaborative resolution of civic problems			
Brehn & Rahn	1997	Social capital is the web of cooperative relationships between citizens that facilitate resolution of collective problems.	Focus on citizenship and political action. Social capital as collaborative, cooperative action at community level.
Thomas	1996	Social capital is formed through means and processes developed within civil society that promote development for the collective whole.	Focus on collective citizenship. Processes are both formal and informal. Emphasis on collective action and cooperation.
Research focus: Social capital as a variety of different entities			
Coleman	1990	Social capital is not a single entity, but a variety of different entities having characteristics in common.	Variety in the functions of social capital.
Research focus: Social capital as an influencer of economic growth			
Pennar	1997	Social capital is a web of social relationships that influences individual actions and thereby affects economic growth.	Focus on the links between social and economic capital.

Source: Author's research.

Much of the contemporary literature on community development is defined primarily through the language of social capital researchers who emphasise concepts of community cohesion, trust, collaboration, reciprocity and tolerance. Duncan and Thomas (2000), for example, define social capital as an intangible web of relationships that stimulates participation in communities and community organisations. For them, it is essentially goodwill, empathy and neighbourliness between the individual and households who make up social units. Its most common definition, however, is in terms of the 'features of social organisations such as networks, norms and trust that facilitate coordination and cooperation for mutual benefit' (Putnam, 1995, p. 66). The issue of social capital has become extremely popular in the community development literature, frequently being used as a catch-all phrase to address perceived core issues of community cohesion, networking and community empowerment. However, this tends to overlook issues relating to economic development, innovation and change management. Indeed, there is currently little evidence in contemporary community development literature of researchers exploring the links between social and economic capital.

Somewhat detrimentally, the community development literature also draws selectively on the arguments of social capital theorists primarily concerned with the degree of social cohesion extant in communities, the levels of cooperation and collaboration between people in communities, and the sense of empowerment and control felt by people in communities (Williams, 1995). In addition, community development also emphasises the social capital values of trust, collaboration, reciprocity, volunteerism and civic engagement (Hulse & Stone, 2005). Social cohesion and community empowerment are concepts that encompass the social connectedness developed through meaningful and sustainable interrelationships between the inhabitants of a community (Hulse & Stone, 2005).

From the 1960s and 1970s, such concepts have been utilised to focus on 'fostering the ability of people to take control over their lives and environments through working together for common goals' (Hounslow, 2002, p. 20). Consequently, the literature strongly suggests that existing community assets in the form of skills, knowledge, understandings and experiences provide the basic building blocks of community development, the inference being that communities need increasingly to identify and strengthen their own skills and capabilities, and recognise these as the essential scaffold from which community growth and development can be stimulated. Indeed, Hur (2006) suggests that ever since the Brazilian educator Paulo Freire first introduced the term 'empowerment' into the English academic discourse in 1987, social scientists have used it to describe processes of community building.

Laverack & Wallerstein argue that 'the importance of community empowerment as a central theme in community development has been overshadowed since the mid-1990s by discussions about community capacity, community competence and community cohesiveness' (2001, p. 179). They also suggest that an advantage of empowerment as a key concept in community development is that it recognises the importance of power and authority residing within the community rather than just with external stakeholders. While some definitions of community development allude to the distribution and control of power, few give it specific attention. Yet a central concern of community development is based on ensuring that communities not only have the resources, skills and experiences to take action, but also have the power to make decisions, manage resources, and control outcomes (Taylor, 2001).

While the strong connection between community development and social capital provides many potential benefits, there are also significant challenges. The strong emphasis of social capital on networking and relationship building may actually strengthen exclusivity and contribute to the development of anti-social subcultures in communities (Hawe & Shiell, 2000; Ross, 2009). The literature suggests that some social capital studies focus too specifically on relationships while overlooking the structural conditions that impede effective community actions, such as the accessibility of resources (Wallerstein, Sanchez & Verlarde, 2005). Thus its usefulness in considering the physical, financial, technological and ecological aspects of community development may be seriously limited. For this reason, Wallerstein, Sanchez & Verlarde (2005) argue for a broader concept of social capital, which addresses the multiple dimensions involved in building capacity in communities. Hawe & Shiell (2000) have also cautioned that the concept of social capital may even dilute initiatives already in place under the various names of community development, regeneration, community empowerment and capacity building. The arguments of Wallerstein, Sanchez & Verlarde (2002), Hawe & Shiell (2000) and others point to the need to develop new approaches to community development that recognise its dynamic complexity and multifaceted nature.

These issues aside, social capital nevertheless draws strong attention to social relationships as a key aspect of capacity building and, in doing so, offers a vital lens through which to examine those relationships. As one of the first authors to use the term to refer to those difficult to quantify aspects of community life that make some communities safer and more enjoyable places to live, Jacobs' (1961) concern was that much urban planning over-emphasises physical, financial and cultural capital, and ignores the valuable role of social capital in contributing to quality of life. It is interesting to note than Jacobs' (1961) concern to balance the social with the more tangible and measurable aspects is now in reverse; the emerging argument is in favour of rebalancing the social with the economic and cultural aspects of community development, reflecting the rapid rise over the last 40 years of social capital as a dominant trend in social science and public policy, a trend that has made it central to community debate and discussion to the exclusion of other forms of capital (DeFilippis, 2001).

Interestingly, Chenoweth & Stehlik (2001) argue that social capital provides a way of understanding the social ties between the state, private and non-government sectors within society. Social capital theories offer a 'challenge to current structural, more traditional, and economic rationalist approaches' (Chenoweth & Stehlik, 2001, p. 49). They provide a starting point to conduct more rigorous examinations of the interconnections between the social and the economic, rather than considering them as separate and unrelated. Additionally, a social capital framework provides an opportunity to recognise and analyse the effects of government policy and practice on people in communities (Lyons, Smuts & Stephens, 2001). This is important as a great deal of policy making can inadvertently subvert community growth and development. For example, Lyons, Smuts & Stephens (2001) discuss the damaging effects on community growth and social cohesion arising from the widespread introduction of competition policy in social and community services.

Responding to New Economic Development Opportunities

The community development literature also stresses the impact of economic pressures on communities and the resulting potential for significant disadvantage in communities (Cavaye, 2000; Fowler & Etchegary, 2008, Hounslow, 2002). Cavaye (2000) especially sees economic forces as primary drivers of change in communities, citing as evidence the challenges being faced by rural communities in terms of pressures to shift from primary industries and manufacturing to knowledge-based industries. Other researchers also recognise the challenging effect of the rapidly developing trend towards the globalisation of national economies and the emergence of more complex and competitive economic environments on rural and remote communities (Herbert-Cheshire, 2000; Watkins, 2006).

Given the strength of the concern with economic restructuring as a major driver of community development, it is surprising that few researchers have seriously examined the potential of economics to provide genuine solutions to the problems facing communities. Those researchers who have considered economic development as part of the broader agenda have usually done so from the perspective of social capital (Duncan & Thomas, 2001; Healy, 2001; Howe & Cleary, 2001; Williams, 1995). However, while it is important to recognise the potential impact of improvements in social capital on economic growth and development, it is equally important to consider the potential for communities emanating from improvements in human and economic capital, especially in the forms of physical infrastructure, fiscal policies, and employment policies and programs. A more useful and equitable way to examine community development might be to consider it as the interplay of all forms of capital with the emphasis on particular forms of capital increasing or decreasing according to the context of the work under completion. The achievement of an integrated view of community development as the interplay of all forms of capital is necessarily dependent on the development of comprehensive indicators across social, human, cultural and economic dimensions. Yet this has still to be substantially addressed in the research literature relating to community development.

The problems arising in the contemporary literature from the singular emphasis on social capital at the expense of other forms of capital and its role as a key contributor to community building are examined by DeFilippis (2001). He argues that the meanings and uses of social capital as applied in community development are misguided because they fail to understand issues of power in communities and are divorced from other forms of capital, especially economic capital. This is not to argue that social capital is unimportant in community development, but rather that social capital must be 'reconnected to economic capital for the term to have any meaning' (DeFilippis, 2001, p. 798). Elements of social capital such as community networks and relationships are important foundations for economic growth and development, relying, as they do, on the development of trust and reciprocity.

Bullen & Onyx (1998) argue that where high levels of social capital exist, people are not only more likely to feel they are part of the community but also to feel useful and able to make a real contribution to economic development. Social capital also encourages community members to participate actively in local community networks and organisations, to come together in times of crisis, and to welcome strangers and participate in groups (Bullen & Onyx, 1998). These are key foundations for economic development, although definitive linkages remain largely unexamined in the literature. Conversely, Bullen & Onyx (1998) note that, in cases where communities lack social capital, there are limited opportunities for people to come together and work for the common good of the community.

The paucity of social capital is often linked to a number of interrelated factors including the lack of core community building blocks such as individual self-esteem, trust, and community communication skills. Compounding these can be inadequate material well-being in a community, inadequate physical infrastructure, and the lack of opportunities to develop networks between people (Bullen & Onyx, 1998). In short, economic factors such as material well-being and the provision of infrastructure are arguably preconditions for the development of social capital. To reconnect social capital with economic capital, mechanisms to allow communities to build networks to recognise the importance of achieving greater control and power over the flows of capital that shape communities must be developed

(DeFilippis, 2001). Many struggling communities have strong social networks and active community organisations but lack the power and related economic capital.

The current strong emphasis on social capital may also provide insights into the heavy reliance on anecdotal evidence regarding community development outcomes. While such information is not without value and can offer clues as to the identification, construction and analysis of more formal statistical information, anecdotes tend to be selective and hence convey a 'false message about the success or failure of programs' (Greenspan, 2005, p. 2). Since community-building initiatives often focus on traditionally underserviced populations (which inevitably include rural and remote communities), formal, well-structured economic indicators, underpinned by anecdotal information, may improve the measurement and reporting of community development programs and offer new insights into the influence of programs. Indeed, the consistent and reliable measurement of economic and social outcomes is critical to a comprehensive understanding and reporting of community successes so that they can be emulated and failures reduced:

> In the quest to do good for our society's most vulnerable populations and communities ... analysts must embrace the challenge to develop objective and quantifiable standards for assessing community development programs. Ultimately, research is the only means for determining whether we are making advances ... by improving access to economic opportunities for traditionally underserved populations (Greenspan, 2005, p. 4).

Enhancing Cultural Developments in Communities

While many community development programs from previous decades have focused primarily on the social aspects of community development, thus reflecting the domination of social capital theory, recent research has extended the concept to include cultural aspects of community growth. New terms such as 'cultural capacity building' and 'community cultural development' have emerged in the literature and focused interest and research on the cultural and social outcomes of community development (Goldbard & Adams, 2006;

Grodach & Loukaitou-Sideris, 2007; Matarasso, 1999). The processes associated with these new terms are centred on strengthening organisational capacity and community skills/talent to enable community cultural and artistic growth. Their goal is to stimulate new practices, policies and approaches through which communities can adapt dynamically to the ever changing conditions of producing, presenting, and preserving arts and culture (Matarasso, 2001). The emerging literature on cultural capacity building is important as it assists in broadening the scope of understanding about community development. However, there is an inherent danger that it may fail to recognise the relationship between cultural capital and other forms of capital. If it is to have ongoing relevance, research needs to take a fully integrated view of growth, based on the interplay of all forms of capital.

Responding to and Managing Change

For many researchers, successful community growth and development is based on the premise that the 'community has the potential to cope with change' (Niland, 2000, p. 87). While a link between community development and change management theory has been identified in the literature (Blakely & Leigh, 2010; Robinson & Green, 2010), further work is required to explore the nature and extent of potential connections. However, it should be noted that the contemporary community development literature suggests that communities often struggle with the same kinds of problems as those identified in the literature of change management (Beer & Nohria, 2000; Hamel & Valikangas, 2003). These include:

- Changes take more time than allocated;
- Competing and unexpected crises distract attention;
- It is difficult to coordinate implementation activities;
- Those involved in implementing change often have insufficient capabilities and skills and have limited access to adequate training;
- Uncontrollable external factors can have a major adverse impact;
- Expectations and objectives are not defined clearly enough; and
- Those affected by change are not sufficiently involved in the planning and development processes.

The problems include several that could be described as unanticipated or unexpected, and thus reflect what is described in the change management literature as the random nature of change (Bridges, 2007). Despite this, there are some key aspects of success that have been identified as having influenced community development theory and practice. These include the formation of guiding coalitions, the creation and communication of vision, the empowerment of people to act and take control, and the maintenance and embedding of new approaches (Bridges, 2007).

The change management literature reports that, in successful transformations, a guiding coalition often comes together and develops a shared commitment to improvement and renewal. Community development literature reflects this strategy in terms of its emphasis on the importance of bringing together key people from within and outside communities to work collaboratively to manage and influence change (Henderson & Mayo, 1998). Another major mechanism for engaging communities in a change effort strategy is through the communication of a clear and compelling vision of where a change effort is required (Bridges, 2007). The change management literature also stresses that such a vision must show how individual projects and initiatives fit into the broader picture (Bridges, 2007; Stace & Dunphy, 2002). Without a comprehensive vision, change can easily dissolve into multiple confusing and incompatible projects that may have a negative impact on communities (Bridges, 2007).

While the community development literature stresses the importance of communication and community empowerment (Healy & Hampshire, 2002), vision development has not been a significant feature. A more detailed examination of the linkages between change management and community development may result in the adoption of new vision-setting strategies and approaches. The issue of sustainability is also important in the literature of change management (Hamel & Valikangas, 2003). In particular, the dangers associated with short-term achievements must be considered in relation to their active and strategic consolidation in a broad change framework so that changes become embedded and are less subject to degradation as the initial pressures for change subside. In stark contrast, the community development literature, while stressing the importance of sustainability, nevertheless still struggles with the identification of strategies and approaches that monitor and evaluate programs and initiatives over the long term in order to embed change within communities and focus on long-term growth. There is little evidence in the community development literature of attempts to develop frameworks through which activities might be analysed and evaluated. However, research undertaken for the Victorian Government on community-building strategies by Howe and Cleary (2001) identified five key success factors for community development initiatives:

1. A focus on education and training and the development of human and social capital
2. A linked approach involving collaboration and coordination across all stakeholders (including government, business, community, and philanthropic sectors)
3. An emphasis on local democracy whereby bottom-up initiatives take priority over solutions imposed from outside, as well as the importance of local identity, leadership, knowledge and management being recognised as critical components
4. Flexible approaches that take account of the multifaceted nature of problems facing particular communities and emphasise the importance of continuous reflection and development
5. An emphasis on sustainable strategies, rather than one-off projects, in tandem with approaches that recognise the ongoing interdependency of social, economic and environmental connectedness.

A decade and a half later, there remains a strong need for further effort to build on the work of Howe & Cleary (2001) and develop strategic frameworks for the long-term evaluation of community development projects.

The literature on both community development and change management stress the importance of involving and empowering people in the change process. However, higher levels of engagement with change management processes and strategies have the potential to assist communities to not only better understand the change process but also to adopt and adapt useful strategies to manage change associated with community growth and development. Of particular relevance are: (i) understanding the perceived risks associated with change; (ii) understanding and appreciating the inherent uncertainty around the outcomes of CCB approaches; and (iii) awareness of the costs and benefits of change to the community (Stace & Dunphy, 2002).

Recognising Community Creativity and Innovation

Innovation has been one of the dominant preoccupations of enterprises throughout the world for the last 25 to 30 years. However, its importance in community development has not been widely recognised. Hawkes (2001) stresses that successful community development programs must be underpinned by a strong focus on creativity combined with optimism that supports innovative practices. While the importance of innovation in community development initiatives is limited in the current literature, there is relevant research emerging from the agriculture industry. For example, the Australian agriculture industry generates substantial economic value for the country; innovation, along with environmental sustainability, is seen as the key to continued export competitiveness. Gaining returns in investment in innovation in agriculture has been facilitated through a long-standing tradition of promoting and sharing best practice through the work of extension officers (Dickie, 2005). The agricultural extension officer is a combination of consultant, researcher, knowledge manager and educator — a person whose job is to find innovative and good practice, promote change, teach farmers how to implement new practices, and share the body of knowledge about effectiveness and efficiency (Dickie, 2005).

Recent research has generated statements of principle that appear to underpin the success of agricultural extension workers in encouraging farmers and graziers to adopt innovations (Fulton et al., 2003; Stone, 2005; Macadam et al., 2004). Dickie (2005) summarised these principles into 10 key statements that may well be applicable more broadly to the challenges faced by whole communities in adopting innovation and innovative practices in community development. Table 3 applies the 10 innovation principles summarised by Dickie (2005) and tests their application more broadly by substituting the term 'community' for 'farmer' and 'community development' for 'farming'.

Table 3. Proposed Principles for the Adoption of Innovation in Community Development.

Innovation in agriculture	Innovation in community development
Farming is a sociocultural practice.	Community development is a sociocultural practice.
Farmers are not all the same.	Communities are not all the same.
Adoption of change is a sociocultural process.	Adoption of change is a sociocultural process.
Profit/direct tangible benefit is not necessarily a driving force.	Profit/direct tangible benefit is not necessarily a driving force.
Doing the right thing is a motivational factor.	Doing the right thing is a motivational factor.
Farmers don't always distinguish innovation from good practice.	Communities don't always distinguish innovation from good practice.
There is a strong desire to leave a legacy.	There is a strong desire to leave a legacy.
Farmers' attitudes are not the problem.	Community attitudes are not the problem.
Farmers construct their own knowledge.	Communities construct their own knowledge.
Farmers have legitimate reasons for choosing not to adopt some innovations.	Communities have legitimate reasons for choosing not to adopt some innovations.
Top-down promotion of innovation is often not appropriate.	Top down promotion of innovation is often not appropriate.
Representation is not participation.	Representation is not participation.
The best method for sharing new practices is multiple methods.	The best method for sharing new practices is multiple methods.

Source: Adapted from Dickie, 2005.

Table 3 demonstrates that the principles for innovation derived for the agriculture industry are broadly applicable to innovation across the whole of community. This is particularly relevant when it is considered that the original principles were derived from the work of leaders/champions working as agricultural extension officers. Their potential relevance to community-based individuals or leaders who must perform broader but similar roles to agricultural extension officers must be considered. The role of community champions and leaders is discussed briefly in the community development literature (Duncan & Thomas, 2001); such individuals are usually self-employed activists who are trained to work with communities to support new and existing initiatives. They have practical skills and experience in tackling local problems and are appreciative of the sensitivities in communities. However, experience has shown that, where residents are trained and employed as local facilitators for their own communities, tensions can arise (Chanan, Gilchrest & West, 1999). Nevertheless, if the principles presented in Table 3 hold true for communities participating in development programs, it may be possible to use them as a checklist for programs seeking to promote innovation and encourage adoption of new practices.

Challenges and Opportunities for Rural and Remote Communities

For each challenge identified for rural and remote communities there is a corresponding opportunity, which, if taken, will allow communities to prosper and grow well into the future. This chapter has outlined major challenges for rural and remote communities, especially those arising from social, demographic, economic, political and technological change. It has provided a synopsis of the issues and opportunities arising from change, including the need for rural and remote communities to take control of change agendas, to identify existing community resources that may provide a platform for programs to address change, and to become active participants in planning and implementing change processes. The conclusion is that the major opportunity for rural and remote communities derives from the development of holistic community approaches that integrate all forms of capital (economic, human, social and economic capital) so that approaches span and incorporate the concerns of all community stakeholders. Such responses will provide significant and important opportunities for communities to grow and learn, and build approaches to ensure their future viability and sustainability. The next chapter identifies and examines major current approaches to community growth and development, and explores how these approaches have attempted to address the issues identified in this chapter.

3

A Maelstrom: Theories, Concepts, Models and Movements

The Vortex of Community Development Initiatives

Over the last two decades, deriving from the melange of evolving community development theories, concepts, and practices in response to pressures for communities to adapt to and manage change, there have been multiple and diverse attempts to assist communities in addressing the challenges and opportunities arising from social and economic shifts and developments. Yet the contemporary literature has, at best, been indiscriminate in its description, categorisation and evaluation of these diverse approaches to support community building and, as a result, reflects a lack of clarity and definition, and is a conceptual jungle.

With a primary focus on communities that are increasingly being challenged by new ways of understanding and interacting with the world, especially those that emphasise creativity as a primary stimulus for the generation of healthy, sustainable economies and communities, this chapter explores the viability and sustainability of the main species inhabiting the jungle. The first, and perhaps most significant of these, is community capacity building (CCB), which is a broad, all-encompassing approach to community development built on (i) community empowerment, (ii) the development of skills, knowledge and resources, (iii) strong social relationships, and (iv) the development of strong networks within and between communities and organisations (Verity, 2007). CCB operates across many community services, including health, social welfare, family services, community services, environment, agriculture, tourism, local government and education (Hounslow, 2002). While the arts have not so far been explicitly linked to CCB, there have nevertheless been parallel arts-based approaches aimed at community development and capacity building. This chapter also probes the potential of the arts in community development in the context of three arts-based movements: (i) the community arts movement; (ii) community cultural development (CCD); and (iii) the evolving concept of creative communities. It concludes with a critical examination of CCB and the specific arts-based movements in terms of their potential for supporting contemporary community development.

Community Capacity Building (CCB)

What does CCB Mean?

Over the last two decades in particular, there has been a significant growth in interest in CCB and its potential role in supporting communities to develop, implement and sustain actions through which they can exercise control over their ongoing social, cultural and economic environments (Chapman & Kirk, 2001; Craig, 2007). The term, however, is an expansive one, which has been almost randomly applied to a diverse range of activities conducted in different settings for multiple purposes. It has been described as 'elusive, slippery, shifting, contested, muddled, ill-defined' (Chapman & Kirk, 2001, p. 8). CCB has also been described variously in the literature as a concept, a strategy, a process, and a value in and of itself; each approach provides part of the jigsaw that defines CCB (see Figure 2).

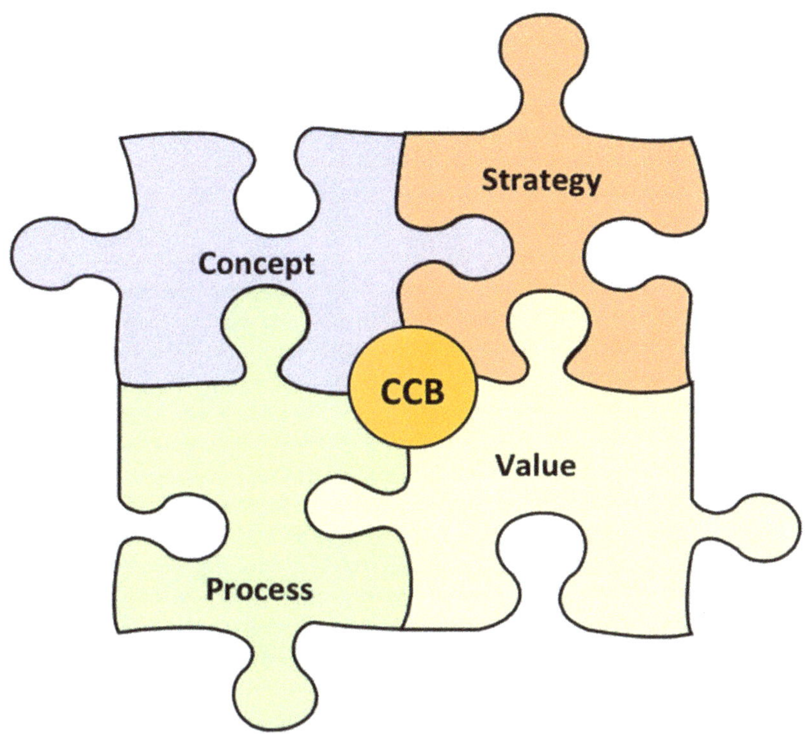

Figure 2. The CCB Jigsaw: Many Meanings for Different People.
Source: Author's research.

Using Figure 2 as a framework for a more detailed examination of extant CCB definitions, Table 4 draws on contemporary literature to encapsulate the range of definitional characteristics (see Appendix A).

This selection of definitions serves to illustrate just how loosely and broadly the term has been applied. Attempts to clarify and render the definitions of CCB more specific have typically involved the articulation of the characteristics and features of specific projects and activities. The contextual diversity of CCB projects and activities, including projects in health, community services, primary industries, government services and tourism, has further exacerbated the problems inherent in attempts to identify the core aspects of CCB (Hounslow, 2002). Rather than adding precision to definitions, the development over the past decade of a comprehensive practice-based literature that largely reports on individual projects and programs loosely characterised as CCB has served only to add a further layer of confusion and vagueness.

Table 4. Definitional Characteristics of CCB.

Focus of CCB	Authors	Primary definitional focus of CCB
Concept	Jackson (1999)	CCB as a holistic balance of community assets to which the community has access.
	Duncan & Thomas (2001) Eng & Parker (1994) Hounslow (2002) Howe & Cleary (2001) Littlejohns & Thompson (2001)	Community empowerment concept.
Strategy	Cavaye (2000a)	Strategy for governments working with communities.
	Thompson & Pepperdine (2003)	Equity strategy to redress imbalances arising from change.
Process	Healy (2001)	Process to develop and strengthen social networks that can be applied to support disadvantaged communities.
	Healy & Hampshire (2002)	Problem-solving process for communities.
	Bryden, Watson, Storey & Van Alphen (1997)	Project management process.
	Henderson & Mayo (1998)	Education and training process.
	Purdue, Razzaque, Hambleton & Stewart (2000)	Skill analysis process.
Value	Hawkes (2001)	A value in and of itself based on innovation, creativity and optimism.

Source: Author's research.

While fuzziness surrounding the meaning of a key term is unhelpful in many ways, certain positives can nevertheless be identified. Firstly, the scope and diversity of activities grouped under the CCB label reflect a rapidly growing interest in mechanisms to develop and sustain viable and dynamic communities that is no longer limited to researchers and practitioners but has extended to government agencies, not-for-profit organisations, and communities themselves (Chapman & Kirk, 2001; Craig, 2007). There is also a growing recognition of the limitations of interventionist and paternalistic approaches in sustainable development of communities resulting in new arguments for the adoption of more inclusive practices, because community growth and development strategies must be contextualised and flexible enough to cater for the diversity that characterises individual communities (Mowbray, 2005). Lastly, and more significantly in terms of this research, problems with the specificity of CCB point to the multidimensional complexity of CCB — a reality that remains largely unacknowledged.

The current lack of precision in the application of the term may reduce the understanding and appreciation of linkages between projects and initiatives and thus limit the potential for collaboration and learning across and between projects. Although not yet acknowledged in the literature, it can be argued that the absence of clear purposes and directions may create significant barriers to the process of evaluating potential outcomes of CCB projects because performance indicators can seldom be specified.

Such diversity and complexity in both concept and practice suggests that, rather than seeking an overarching single definition, it may be more useful to tease out the concepts implicit in the term as a basis for action. To that end, it is possible to educe from the literature the key characteristics of CCB. As a starting point, CCB's five key areas of influence on communities can be identified:

1. Community empowerment
2. Partnerships
3. Change management
4. Social capital
5. Economic empowerment.

Table 5 draws from the work of the major contributors to CCB research to identify key characteristics of each of the five spheres of influence.

Table 5. Domains and Characteristics of CCB.

Spheres of influence	Community empowerment	Change management	Partnerships	Social capital	Economic empowerment
Defining characteristics	Community ownership and control.	Change management strategies and processes.	Inter- and intra-community partnerships.	Community networking, coordination and cooperation.	Community empowerment through economic development.
Unique characteristics	Community ownership. Sense of community. Community competence. Community assets. Participation. Leadership. Resources. (Knowledge and skills.) Ongoing learning.	Community champions and leaders. Community values. Problem solving. Resources. Knowledge and skills. Critical reflection. Social networks.	Balance of assets (community and external). Role of external agencies. Role of government. Collaborative problem solving. Joint leadership.	Community structures. Equity. Resource mobilisation. Participation. Leadership. Problem assessment. Human and social resources. Program management.	Sense of community. Change management. Community assets. Business development. Financial capability.
Shared/common characteristics	Community involvement and empowerment. Addressing community disadvantage. The interplay between social and economic capital. Collaboration and cooperation. Recognition of community assets. Recognition of the need for innovation. Management of change.				
Key exponents	Duncan & Thomas (2000), Eng & Parker (1994), Hounslow (2002), Howe & Cleary (2001), Littlejohns & Thompson (2001)	Chanan, Gilchrist & West (1999), Hawkes (2001)	Cavaye (2000a), Henderson & Mayo (1998), Jackson (1999)	Healy (2001), Healy & Hampshire (2002), Laverack (2001), Thompson & Pepperdine (2003)	Purdue, Razzaque, Hambleton & Stewart. (2000)

Source: Author's research.

The shared or common features identified in Table 5 may be further compressed to distil seven key principles of CCB.

Key Principles of CCB

Seven identified key principles of CCB are presented in Table 6, referencing the identified five spheres of influence.

Table 6. Seven Key Principles of CCB.

CCB spheres of influence	CCB key principles
Community empowerment	1. Communities should be empowered to control their own futures. 2. CCB values equal opportunity and greater social equity.
Partnerships	3. CCB emphasises collaboration and the active participation of all stakeholders.
Change management	4. CCB focuses on the management of change in communities.
Social capital	5. CCB recognises and builds on existing community assets. 6. CCB values innovation and creativity.
Economic empowerment	7. CCB addresses the economic development needs of communities.

Source: Author's research.

Issues implicit in these seven principles distilled from the literature can be elaborated as follows.

Principle 1: Communities should be empowered to control their own futures

CCB recognises that solutions to problems are best developed and implemented by those closest to the problem as they have a detailed understanding of it as well as an acute appreciation of the potential and workability of solutions (Healy & Hampshire, 2002; Howe & Cleary, 2001; Mowbray, 2005).

Principle 2: CCB values greater social equity

CCB acknowledges that some communities have been or are in danger of being disadvantaged by economic, social and political change, and that action needs to be taken to redress imbalances arising from such changes. However, it also implicitly endorses the value of equal opportunity and the desirability of greater social equity (Cavaye, 2000; Cavaye, 2000a; Cavaye, 2001; Hounslow, 2002; Thompson & Pepperdine, 2003).

Principle 3: CCB emphasises collaboration among all stakeholders

CCB emphasises active participation by all sectors of the community and a collaborative approach between communities and external stakeholders (Cavaye, 2000; Chapman & Kirk, 2001; Murphy & Thomas, 2002).

Principle 4: Effective change management approaches are crucial to CCB

CCB focuses on the management of change in communities and uses a range of change management processes to support communities (Chanan et al., 1999; Hawkes, 2001).

Principle 5: CCB recognises and builds on existing community assets

CCB is predicated on the conviction that all communities have tangible and intangible assets in the form of skills, knowledge, understandings and experiences. It respects these assets and recognises that approaches deriving from existing community capacities are more likely to be successful than those that adopt more traditional top-down, paternalistic and interventionist approaches (Cavaye, 2000; Howe & Cleary, 2001; Littlejohns & Thompson, 2001).

Principle 6: CCB values innovation and creativity

CCB values innovation, imagination, creativity and optimism (Hawkes, 2001; Williams, 2000).

Principle 7: CCB addresses the economic development needs of communities

CCB balances social capital with economic capital with an emphasis on particular skill requirements for communities, emphasising economic development and business development and drawing attention to the interplay between financial capacity, physical resources and assets, and human and social resources (Healy, 2001; Purdue et al., 2000).

While the seven principles provide a concise description of the platform on which CCB theories and practices are based, the following examination of the factors influencing CCB will highlight the continuing confusion surrounding its use and application in communities.

Operational Issues Influencing CCB

While it has been possible to distil these seven key principles of CCB, the strong theoretical underpinnings implicit in the principles have been substantially eroded by the association of the term with a myriad of diverse activities and initiatives. In fact, the term has been used in so many different ways by dissimilar groups to suit such a variety of purposes that the concept of CCB has become confused and convoluted. This threatens and undermines both the purposes and viability of many initiatives and programs. For example, it has been used by government departments responsible for funding community projects aimed at regeneration and growth in which little power and control may actually reside with communities (Cavaye, 2001; Cavaye, 2008). It has also been used by public, private and not-for-profit agencies seeking to work with communities to access specific funding sources to address issues that may or may not have originated from community demand (Chaskin, 2001). Thus the CCB principles relating to community control and empowerment have been seriously jeopardised. Laverack & Wallerstein (2001) have argued that the importance of community control and empowerment as a central theme of CCB has been overshadowed and eroded since the mid-1990s by a growing fascination with a plethora of related terms and concepts, such as community capacity, community competence, and community cohesiveness. The central message that communities should be able to exercise the power to make decisions, manage resources and control outcomes has been lost through an emerging preoccupation with skill development, resource allocation and intervention.

Further anomalies between the theoretical underpinnings of CCB and its application in various settings are evidenced by the current focus of projects and initiatives on social outcomes. These include improved community cohesiveness, the reconciliation of community diversity, the development of shared community values, and the development of community partnerships (Williams, 2000). The now pervasive links between the social sciences and CCB indicate that the current dimensions of CCB have been strongly tipped in favour of social outcomes at the expense of economic outcomes (DeFilippis, 2001; Shaw & Carter, 2007). Some contemporary researchers have focused on the underlying tensions inherent in CCB programs. Hounslow (2002), for example, draws attention to several tensions and ambiguities. Firstly, there are not always local solutions to local problems, regardless of the strength of the community's capacity; some problems require state- or national-level changes in policies and resource allocation. Secondly, community is not a single or homogeneous entity as, within any community, there will be different viewpoints and interests potentially leading to conflict. Thirdly, there are sometimes significant tensions between the goals and outcomes set by government and other external organisations and those central to and preferred by local community organisations.

However, it has also been argued that CCB is an evolutionary theory subject to continuous development and refinement (Green & Haines, 2011; Li, 2006). For example, it has recently captured the attention of public policymakers and program planners as a strategy to complement a range of public policy directions and initiatives (Cavaye, 2008). Consequently, the language of CCB has been used to support objectives in government services including health, crime prevention, primary industries and community services. While this has added to confusion over the meaning and purpose of CCB, it has also expanded the term (Cavaye, 2008; Shaw, 2008). The most significant impact of this development has been the acceptance of a view of CCB that integrates the social and the economic:

> community capacity building is about providing communities with the tools to help themselves, adopting a way of thinking that will add value to the social, economic and human resources that exist in each community. It is a bottom up, long-term process that integrates the various aspects of community well-being (economic, social, environmental and cultural) and improved quality of life is its main outcome (Smith, Littlejohns & Roy, 2003, p. 22).

Broadening the Concept of CCB

Arguments for the integration of social and economic objectives in community building highlight an interest in broadening the concept of CCB and developing a new framework for understanding, implementing and evaluating CCB. However, as demonstrated, much of the contemporary literature lacks specificity and extensive work is required, especially regarding the interplay between different forms of capital, not just social and economic but also cultural, environmental and other forms of capital. Some researchers argue that most of the work undertaken during the last 30 years under the banner of CCB has simply involved recycled social insights and theories from 1960s community theory (Broughton & Chambers, 2001; Williams & Durrance, 2008). However, other researchers believe that, while there is a continuum, a qualitative shift has nevertheless occurred over the last decade (Green & Haines, 2011; James, Wrigley & Lonnqvist, 2009).

Researchers have identified three characteristics that differentiate current CCB approaches from earlier community development theories. Firstly, contemporary CCB places a far greater emphasis on collaborative approaches to tackling social and economic issues (Howe & Cleary, 2001). Secondly, contemporary approaches stress the explicit demands for place management rather than program-focused management and for a bottom-up approach to solving community problems (Howe & Cleary, 2001). Thirdly, current CCB places a far greater emphasis on the community itself in terms of needs identification, defining outcomes and initiating actions, rather than being mobilised to act solely by external agencies (Littlejohns & Thompson, 2001).

New Directions for CCB

The significant growth in interest in CCB over the last decade and the associated explosion in practice-based literature has created complexities and tensions that produce difficulties in (i) understanding and appreciating the connection between CCB projects, thereby limiting the potential for understanding and learning across and between projects (Craig, 2007), and (ii) setting benchmarks and performance indictors against which CCB programs can be successfully measured and evaluated (Laverack & Wallerstein, 2001; Smith et al., 2003). After a decade of intense activity, critical questions remain unanswered in the CCB literature. What long-term community outcomes from CCB can be identified? To what extent might CCB consolidate the power of government agencies and other institutions rather than serving the goal of empowering communities themselves? How might communities exercise more control over the activities of external CCB stakeholders?

Such questions lead to further questions about how communities might become self-sustaining. Who will judge if/when they become so? By what criteria? How will power be exercised in communities? What are the factors affecting the capacity of communities to meet their needs and resolve issues?

Unanswered questions coupled with continuing confusion and ambiguity around CCB suggest an urgent need for a new framework to underpin a fresh logic for planning, supporting and sustaining CCB. Such a logic might provide renewed energy around the why of CCB; clarity about the what of CCB; a rethink of the who of CCB; and a revolution about the how of CCB. It is sometimes the case that CCB programs and projects are narrowly focused and fail to recognise that many programs do not operate in a policy vacuum (West, 2009).

CCB is part of a wider policy agenda supporting civic participation, decentralisation and local service delivery (Taylor, 2000; Wilson, 1997; Yarnet, 2000). However, Duncan & Thomas (2000) believe that the most significant policy factors impacting on CCB have yet to emerge fully. They observe that many current programs are developing in ad hoc and non-strategic ways and argue that, unless programs are more effectively linked to wider policy agendas, they may lead to disenchantment among communities and the consequent waste of valuable resources. Chapman & Kirk (2001) identify a range of policy drivers that support CCB, including the reduction in poverty, the alleviation of social exclusion, the creation of an equal and just society, modernisation of local government, the establishment of balanced, stable and cohesive communities, promotion of effective partnerships, community networking, community economic development, and the improvement of local service delivery. CCB programs and initiatives would benefit from a deeper understanding and appreciation of why and how CCB is important locally, nationally and internationally.

While CCB is a term popular with communities, researchers and governments, its meaning is often misunderstood. As already indicated, the pervasive links between the social sciences and CCB have resulted in the dimensions of capacity building being strongly tipped in favour of social outcomes in terms of improved community cohesiveness, reconciliation of community diversity, development of shared community values, and development of community partnerships. However, over the last five years, CCB has captured the attention of public policymakers and program managers as an overarching strategy to complement a range of policy directions and initiatives. The language of CCB has been used to support objectives in government services, including health, crime prevention, primary industries and community services. The diverse contexts in which the language of CCB has been adopted has, at one level, contributed to confusion over its meaning and function; yet, on another level, it has added breadth and depth to the concept. These developments highlight the continuing evolution towards a framework for understanding, implementing and evaluating CCB.

Given that another key feature of CCB is the interaction needed for building relationships between people and organisations within communities, between separate communities, and between communities and external agencies, clarity around the roles and responsibilities of these people is paramount to successful CCB design and implementation. CCB rarely takes place without some form of facilitation, usually in the form of project officers or community development workers. In their study of sustainable communities pilot projects, Carley & Kirk (1999) found that the role of project officer was vital in supporting CCB. The project officer's ability to act as a catalyst for local action, in coordinating necessary support from alternative sources, and in creating linkages with key agencies was critical to the success of the initiative (Carley & Kirk, 1999).

The use of the project officer or community development worker is also a key feature in the literature on community involvement in rural development (Bryden et al., 1997). While the work of the project officer is well documented in CCB literature, more work is required to clarify the roles and responsibilities of other people and agencies involved in CCB programs, including government officers and agencies, funding bodies, community groups and others. Another key issue around the who of CCB is the potential for disruption of the balance between communities and other stakeholders as a result of the involvement of external stakeholders in CCB activities. There is a critical difference between communities taking action and communities being mobilised to act, which is not always explicitly recognised.

A revolution around the how of CCB must acknowledge the power relationships that exist between external professionals and local residents. In many cases, partnerships in CCB have been forged simply as a consequence of funding opportunities that specify community involvement as a funding criterion rather than due to a strategy for community empowerment. Community involvement has often played a narrow and largely functional handmaiden role, concerned merely with achieving externally imposed criteria. The evolution of CCB has moved from its original emphasis on community empowerment, and later community mobilisation, to a more refined understanding that effective community improvement requires engaging those who are experiencing problems directly — and in ways where meaningful decision making is shared.

CCB has enormous potential to mobilise communities to achieve self-reliance and ongoing sustainable community improvements. As yet, the literature has failed to communicate an integrated view of CCB. There is an ongoing need to research CCB in a more all-encompassing manner to consolidate strategies and approaches that recognise the existing abilities, attitudes, skills and resources available to communities as they provide the key to improving their economic and social futures.

Arts-Based Approaches to Community Building

The Role of the Arts in Community Development and Capacity Building

While the evolution of CCB over the last two decades has intersected with many community services and impacted on several industry sectors, it has not connected with the arts in any discernable way. This may be explained partly because the development and growth of a separate and specific community arts movement has, to a degree, paralleled the growing interest in and application of CCB in communities. However, while CCB has operated from a primary focus on communities and their challenges and needs, the community arts movement places its central emphasis on the value of the arts and artists and their role in communities. CCB has operated across a range of services and industry sectors while the community arts movement has mostly focused specifically on the arts and cultural industries (Hawkins, 1993). The next section traces the evolution of the arts in community development from the community arts movement to the evolution of the concept and practice of community cultural development (CCD) and finally to the newly articulated creative communities. It also examines the ongoing potential of these arts-based movements to support community development and capacity building.

Hallmarks of the Community Arts Movement

The term 'community arts' was first coined during the late 1960s and spawned a movement that grew rapidly initially in the United States and then spread to Canada, the United Kingdom, Ireland, and Australia (Hawkins, 1993). The original community arts movement was centred strongly on the arts and focused primarily on artistic activity in a community setting (Hawkins, 1993). Since the late 1960s, community arts practice has been strongly founded in the belief that cultural meaning, expression and creativity reside within a community and that the task of the community artist is to assist community members 'free their imaginations and give form to their creativity' (Goldbard, 1993, p. 2). While specialist individual artists were vital to the movement, collaboration between artists and others was also considered central to the practice of community arts. Examples of early community arts projects outlined in Table 7 reflect what were, at the time, new and somewhat radical approaches focusing on whole-of-community involvement in the arts by emphasising access and participation. In this way, these examples also reflect the political ideals of the 1970s and illustrate what was essentially a move towards the democratisation of the arts rather than dominantly a movement to support community development (Hawkins, 1993).

Table 7. Overview of Selected Community Arts Projects.

Name of initiative	Date	Country	Background and purpose of initiative	Positioning of the arts	Outcomes	Issues	Source
San Francisco Neighborhood Arts Program (NAP)	1967	USA	Regarded as a founder and exemplar of community-based arts. At a time of social and racial unrest the US Government was keen to fund projects to occupy young people in constructive pursuits — things like creating murals, learning and performing music, putting on street festivals, and so on.	Provided arts-based services to San Franciscan neighbourhoods. Focused on poor and underprivileged neighbourhoods. A key driving principle was to use the arts to provide new opportunities for communities to grow and learn.	Exposure of the arts to neighbourhoods relatively untouched by art. Use of government grant money to support small-scale community projects like murals and street festivals. Provision of arts-based education and training. Increase employment opportunities for artists.	The short-term success of NAP represented an historical moment in time when government agencies saw community arts as a valid tool for engaging communities in self-education and self-activation. Issues included: • Sustainability of activities after government grants subsided. • Seen by government as a highly visible, often effective and always colourful way to achieve community outcomes. • Changing government priorities in mid-1980s meant that funding disappeared. • Project folded.	Goldbard, 1993
Jam Factory	1974	Australia	Established with government funding in 1974 to assist, train, guide, challenge, empower, and promote community artists. Name derives from location in a disused jam factory. One of the earliest examples of art and artists reclaiming an abandoned building.	Art as core activity. A major centre for the design, production, exhibition and sale of work by leading and emerging Australian artists and designers.	The Jam Factory outcomes included: • Provision of income streams for community artists. • Training and employment opportunities for artists and designers. • Provision of funding to support arts and artists from sales, services and creative business initiatives.	Sustainable over more than three decades. Government financial support continues but the factory has moved towards more financially sustainable models. Original aims of empowerment and promotion of emerging artists have been challenged as demands increase for sales and returns on investment.	www.jamfactory.com.au

Name of initiative	Date	Country	Background and purpose of initiative	Positioning of the arts	Outcomes	Issues	Source
Fusion Arts Centre – Oxford Arts Agency	1980	United Kingdom	One of the first community arts organisations in the UK. Originally called Bloomin' Arts, established by three committed people who initially developed a program of participative performance events in the local parks. Organisation grew to offer many arts-based programs at venues across the UK.	Primarily a community arts organisation dedicated to using the arts to support communities in the UK.	Provision of a hub for community artists and community workers through which programs and resources could be communicated and shared. A program of arts activities for adults and children in UK communities. Facilitation of and support for creative arts projects within communities.	Fusion Arts Centre has evolved and changed as government support decreased. Now operates as company limited by guarantee as well as a registered charity and fundraising has become a significant part of its operations. Operates in a much wider environment than community arts.	www.fusion-arts.org
Community arts networks (CANs)	1980s	Australia	Established in several Australian states during the 1980s (Western Australia, South Australia, and Queensland). Evolved from a network of people committed to community arts practice. Committed to empowering communities through community arts.	Focused on supporting communities through community arts. Achieved by linking communities with artists who would work collaboratively with community members on an community art project — such projects were usually murals, theatre productions, etc.	Government funded and provided many community arts programs for Australian communities. Significant outcomes for communities included: • Community involvement in the arts. • Community resources. • Community confidence (new skills).	The CANs build on their early experiences in the 1980s and continued to evolve for the next two decades. Their commitment to social justice increased and they developed a philosophical platform of using the arts to address social inequalities. Many CANs began working with Aboriginal communities and disadvantaged communities in urban and regional areas.	www.canwa.com.au/about/the-organisation/history/

Source: Author's research.

Table 7 provides examples of arts-based projects in communities that were primarily focused on social concerns and the achievement of objectives aimed at promoting community dialogue, communications and social interaction. The majority of community arts projects, during the 1960s and 1970s and over subsequent decades, have been implicitly based on the premise that arts practice is concerned with cultural identity and the expression of cultural values within communities (MacDonald, 2000). Art in the community is also seen as providing an opportunity to communicate individualism, eccentricity, diversity and inspirational example (MacDonald, 2000). The arts are seen, at least by community artists themselves, as a powerful medium through which communities could add value to and create meaning in people's lives.

Community arts programs have always been strongly focused on the development or refinement of values and philosophies based on improving the ability of community members to take action to improve social well-being and respond to community change (Goldbard, 1993). Projects have often been built on visiting artists commissioned to work with communities to achieve specific social outcomes, usually related to community engagement and linked social objectives (MacDonald, 2000). In the sense of tangible outcomes, such projects have often resulted in murals, community sculptures and other public art installations. However, the link between the tangible art products and the less tangible outcomes of art has always been a key characteristic of community arts practice. For community artists and communities, the project is generally as much about the journey as the product, providing a strong focus on the development of grassroots involvement that is characteristic of the arts over this period.

Guiding Principles of the Community Arts Movement

Many studies claiming that the arts contribute positively to the development of social capital and community cohesiveness have been based on an examination of community arts programs. Generally these have been supported and operated by organisations desirous of using the arts as a tool for human and material development (Lowe, 2000). While there is huge diversity in the approaches and methods adopted by community arts projects and initiatives, it is possible to identify a common set of guiding principles underpinning the community arts movement. Firstly, almost universally they involve community members in a creative activity leading to a public performance or exhibit (MacDonald, 2000). Secondly, community arts involve professional artists and community members working in a collaborative creative process resulting in collective artistic experience (Williams, 1995). Thirdly, these projects provide a way for communities to express themselves and enable artists, through financial and other supports, to engage in creative activity with communities (Goldbard, 1993). Lastly, community arts values the creative process as of equal importance to the artistic outcome (Macdonald, 2000).

These guidelines provide a platform for what has been described as the transformative potential of community arts (Williams, 1995). It is argued by Williams (1995) that community arts build social capital by boosting individual or group ability and motivation to be civically engaged. Others argue that it also builds organisational capacity to support effective community action (Guetzkow, 2002). This may be accomplished by creating a venue that draws people together who would otherwise not be engaged in constructive social activity and contributes to fostering trust between participants, augmenting their generalised trust of others (Lowe, 2000). Effective community action may also be achieved by providing an experience of collective efficacy and civic engagement, which spurs participants to further collective action (Hawkes, 2001). Community arts events may be a source of pride for residents (participants and non-participants alike), increasing their sense of connection to community (Williams, 1995). They may also provide experiences for participants to learn technical and interpersonal skills important to collective organising, increasing the scope of individuals' social networks and providing an experience for community organisations to enhance their capacities (Matarasso, 1996).

Key Problem Areas Characteristic of Community Arts

Successful community arts projects such as festivals, art exhibitions, community plays and other arts-based events have demonstrated how cultural activities can energise people to contribute to a range of positive social outcomes (MacDonald, 2000). These include improving the image of a region or town, reducing offensive or antisocial behaviour, promoting interest in the local environment, developing communal self-confidence, building private and public sector partnerships, enhancing organisational capacity, supporting local independence, and exploring visions for the future (Williams, 1995). The concept of social capital and the premise that art plays a vital role in building cohesive and ultimately viable societies has thus been fundamental to the community arts movement (Williams, 2000). However, one of the problem areas for community arts has been its reluctance to grow its influence across other areas of community development and to move towards more integrated, whole-of-community approaches to growth and development.

While the strongest voices supporting community arts have been the community artists themselves, government agencies have also begun to see community arts as a valid tool for engaging communities in self-education and self-activation, perceiving it to be a highly visible, often effective and always colourful way to achieve community outcomes (Goldbard, 1993). However, by the mid-1980s, government priorities had changed and, as a consequence, funding for community arts quickly disappeared, resulting in failure for many projects. At this time, the rhetoric around the community arts also began to change through attempts to link the movement more strongly with community development. Arguments increasingly embraced the arts as a vibrant and dynamic way to build community capacity, increase social capital, activate social change, and develop human capital (Williams, 2000).

Thus when funding for the community arts began to subside, the philosophical and political principles on which the community arts movement had originally been based were incrementally seen as providing a platform for cultural development through encouraging cooperation, acknowledging and celebrating the strengths and unique qualities of communities. The movement was seen as a means for communities to be recognised and nurtured through a range of arts and cultural activities (MacDonald, 2000). At this time, the term 'community cultural development' (CCD) emerged to describe how communities could advance their artistic, social and cultural aspirations.

Key Features of Community Cultural Development (CCD)

As with the community arts movement, CCD is a community-based arts practice, which can embrace any art form. CCD is often described as the work of artists, arts workers and other community workers 'collaborating to express identity, concerns and aspirations through the arts ... it is a process that simultaneously builds individual mastery and collective cultural capacity while contributing to positive social change' (Goldbard & Adams, 2006, p. 20). The Australia Council for the Arts (2006) funding guidelines argued that there are, in fact, many variations of community-based arts processes and, as such, there is no single correct model; however, the guidelines then proceed to define the process narrowly as primarily the collaboration between professional artists and community members to create art (Australia Council for the Arts, 2006). While Goldbard & Adams' (2006) definition encapsulates many of the key features of CCD, it is by no means a widely accepted one for, like CCB, the theory and practice of CCD is highly contested. Artists, arts workers, CCD practitioners, community workers and researchers/commentators argue about what constitutes CCD and the ways in which it differs from CCB and the community arts movement. Some suggest that its distinguishing feature is work that is motivated by social justice outcomes, while others argue that it includes any activity that assists human beings to engage in conscious reflection on their life experiences.

Goldbard & Adams (2006) argue that, while CCD is a well known theory and practice, it has attracted neither public attention nor the adequate resources to support its widespread adoption. They illustrate their argument by drawing on recent experience in the United States where an active CCD field has been well nigh invisible to those not directly involved. They argue that, because CCD employs the same forms as conventional arts disciplines, 'work in the field has mostly been treated as a marginal manifestation of mainstream arts activities' (Goldbard & Adams, 2006, p. 20).

Key Principles

The absence of an agreed definition in the CCD literature has not limited the breadth of work undertaken under its auspices and, over time, artists and arts workers have agreed to and adopted key principles to guide and explicate their work. The following seven key principles are derived for Goldbard & Adams (2006):

1. Active participation in cultural life is an essential goal
2. Diversity is a social asset, part of the cultural commonwealth, requiring protection and nourishment

3. All cultures are essentially equal and society should not promote any one as superior to the others
4. Culture is an effective crucible for social transformation, one that can be less polarising and create deeper connections than other social change areas/disciplines
5. Cultural expression is a means of emancipation rather than an end in itself; the process is an important as the product
6. Culture is a dynamic, protean whole and there is no value on creating artificial boundaries within it
7. Artists have roles as agents of transformation that are more socially valuable than mainstream art world roles — and certainly equal in legitimacy.

An analysis of these seven principles provides an insight into the strong ideological platforms on which the theory and practice of CCD is based. All are powerful ideological statements expressed in highly emotive language to stake a claim for what is perceived to be a key role of the arts in social and cultural development. However, it could be argued that words and phrases such as 'cultural commonwealth', 'crucible for social transformation', and 'means of emancipation' suggest a special, privileged role of the arts in providing higher order social and cultural outcomes, especially at the expense of community economic outcomes such as new businesses and employment.

Perhaps most contentious of the principles derived from Goldbard & Adams (2006) is the observation that artists have key roles as change agents who must engage socially and culturally with community issues. Without exception, 'they must recognise an obligation to deploy their gifts in the service of greater social aims as well as individual awareness and transformation' (Goldbard & Adams, 2006, p. 58). While this may constitute a noble role for artists, Goldbard & Adams (2006) illustrate the principle by arguing that the mainstream version of this issue is the ongoing controversy over Hollywood activists whose qualifications to speak out on public issues are often questioned. Goldbard & Adams (2006) use this analogy to raise implicit questions about the nature of artists and their often unquestioned access to celebrity and status. To what extent does their comparison of Hollywood activists with community arts workers suggest that artists might reasonably expect to exercise an intrinsic right to express social, cultural and political views? Such a suggestion implies an inherent superior or leadership role for community artists simply as artists. Such a privileged or special role for artists is a key implied theme in much of the CCD literature. This implication needs to be explored further in order to determine the appropriate position and role of the artist in community development. Further work is also required to identify and evaluate the potential artistic contribution to community development in the context of other community occupations and talents. While the role of the artist in community development may be significant, it may deserve neither special status nor privilege.

Related to issues of the role of the artist are principles relating to emancipation through cultural expression, culture as a crucible for social transformation, and active participation and authentic citizenship through cultural life. While these are admirable principles and the associated social and cultural outcomes should remain important goals for all communities, there is an inherent problem in the almost exclusive, perhaps single-minded, focus of CCD on the social and cultural. The seeming failure to consider the potential of the arts and culture in the economic development of communities may limit CCD from working with communities in an appropriately holistic and integrated way.

Key Problem Areas

There is evidence in the literature of the significant differences that CCD has made to people's lives, the development of community identity and the strengthening of community cohesiveness (Hawkes, 2001; Hawkes 2003; Ruane, 2007; Sonn, Drew & Kasat, 2002). However, as intimated previously, they are almost exclusively related to social and cultural outcomes and CCD's role in the promotion and acceptance of diversity and inclusiveness. It has also been recognised that the people who work in CCD sometimes pioneer arts and cultural activities through governments, organisations and institutions sceptical of the relevance of artistic processes to community outcomes and unsympathetic to the potential of the arts in civic life (Mills, 2006). Nevertheless, alongside these acknowledged important outcomes, CCD has been challenged by the increasing exposure of its limitations in terms of addressing the escalating complexity of community life.

Firstly, the language and philosophy of CCD is neither understood nor appreciated within the communities it purports to support (Goldbard & Adams, 2006). The resulting confusion in communities about CCD's purpose and function may well represent a serious limitation to its potential for meaningful partnerships between artists and other community member organisations. The purpose of CCD seems to be misunderstood even within the arts and cultural industry and remains marginalised within the sector as too few artists, arts policymakers and arts funding bodies comprehensively understand the term (Dunn, 2006). Consequently, CCD artists and arts workers all too often operate at the periphery of mainstream arts sectors and find a career in CCD difficult to sustain. Throsby & Hollister (2003) report that, over the 10-year period from 1993 to 2003, the total average income of a CCD artist declined in real terms by $5,000 while the income of other artists increased by $7,000. Throsby & Hollister (2003) estimate that there are 2,500 artists working in CCD in Australia, representing less than 6 per cent of all artists. This figure had decreased during the 10-year period of the study from just over 3,000, indicating a significant decline in the number of practising CCD artists.

A further problem identified in the literature has been the apparent inability of CCD to embrace a sufficiently comprehensive range of community projects and activities because of narrowly defined parameters for supporting CCD activities. While the community arts movement has included a range of visual, theatrical, musical, textual and other art forms, CCD has adopted a narrower approach that focuses only on the role of the arts in formulating and enhancing the future social and cultural aspirations of communities (Sonn et al., 2002). Typically, community arts harnesses active community involvement in the art-making process to produce images, symbols and other resources for community appreciation and use. CCD, however, utilises a more complex approach involving cultural planning and mapping, usually with local governments, to identify strengths and resources in communities that can be used to enhance community functioning (Sonn et al., 2002). Benefits are considered in terms of empowerment, community identity, community cohesiveness and sense of community rather than the artistic merit of products and outcomes.

Cultural planning and mapping is a process aimed at interpreting what makes up a local identity, and assessing what cultural resources can be developed to improve community well-being and quality of life

(Grogan, Mercer & Engwicht, 1995). However, there exists no clear systemic framework to determine how cultural planning and mapping links to and influences individuals and communities. This has seriously limited the effectiveness of CCD in influencing broader community development, especially in terms of economic development and environmental planning (Sonn et al., 2002). In order that CCD artists and arts workers might address both perceived and real problems, there is a need to engage more broadly with communities and support the integration of the arts in all aspects of community development so that CCD artists and arts workers might address perceived and real problems, there is a concomitant need to broaden approaches to include the full range of community activities that may benefit from the involvement and support of the arts. Broader and more active engagement not just with government but also with community organisations and private sector agencies is essential to promote the potential of the arts across a range of community services that lead to the achievement of economic, social and cultural outcomes.

Creative Communities: A New Umbrella

Prior to 2006, CCD had been the official label used in Australia to describe those arts programs and activities that (i) emphasised collaboration between artists and other community members, and (ii) linked artistic work to community development practices and community empowerment (Goldbard & Adams, 2006). Until that time, the Australia Council for the Arts had been a strong advocate for CCD and was committed to supporting the concept through funding and policy development. However, in 2006, the Australian Council commissioned a review of CCD and, as a result, adopted a new term, 'creative communities', to describe arts-based funding for communities. The findings of this review recommended that the Australia Council adopt 'a Creative Communities Strategy that integrates policy, planning and delivery through strong leadership and effective partnerships to facilitate the growth of culturally vibrant communities' (Dunn, 2006, p. 2).

One of the key premises on which the recommendation was developed was the finding that the 'ownership of, and identification with, arts in communities is broader than the community development sector' (Dunn, 2006, p. 1). However, rather than quantify the scope of ownership, explore the breath of community activity or outline a strategic approach to guide future practice, the review chose instead to articulate components of a vision for the achievement of stronger, more self-directed and culturally vibrant communities in Australia. Such a vision, argued the review, would be grounded in the common goals of economic viability, social equity, environmental sustainability and cultural vitality (Dunn, 2006). The review thus resonated with a broader contemporary move, both ideological and practical, to recognise the potential commonalities of economic, social, environmental and cultural goals (Phillips, 2004).

While the Dunn (2006) review stops short of defining what is meant by the term 'creative communities', it does provide four strong statements to support its vision of artists and communities working collaboratively on the achievement of community goals:

1. Arts and cultural practices are valued as an integral part of everyday life
2. Communities are valued as creators and active participants (not just consumers)
3. Cultural diversity is valued as a foundation of innovation, creativity and artistic excellence
4. Creativity and innovation are valued as means of engaging communities, building capacities, responding to issues and generating change.

Others have attempted a definitional framework by observing that the term describes the 'broad spectrum of arts and cultural development activity in and across communities in Australia' (Mills, 2006, p. 12). While such attempts deliver some precision, they do little to explain either the scope or nature of activities that might be undertaken under the label or identify the philosophical or ideological premises upon which the term is based.

The adoption of the term 'creative communities' by the Australia Council may be seen as a deliberate policy approach to ensure the arts are better placed to support communities in facing contemporary challenges. Indeed, a speech made by the Chief Executive Officer of the Australia Council at the time of the adoption of this term would substantiate this view:

> Art agencies do see a role for themselves in the rejuvenation process — with good reason. The impact of the arts can be far-reaching … the arts are more concerned about how people in communities connect — or, in some cases — why they fail to connect. We aim to do something about that, by promoting social cohesion and reconciliation; as a window onto deep-seated problems and how communities can start to resolve them; in boosting economies; and especially, and critically, in helping sustain local and regional identity (Bott, 2006, p. 2).

It is noteworthy, however, that the rhetoric of the Australia Council is yet to be matched by a significant change of direction or improved outcomes for communities. While the new rhetoric connects with the concept that 'creative capital — new ideas and innovations, new designs, new ways of working and playing — is the fuel for the twenty-first century economic engine' (Bulick et al., 2003, p. 34), there is much still to be achieved if creative communities is to be more than just a different, albeit catchy, new term to describe the same old practices related to the community arts and CCD.

CCB, Community Arts, CCD and Creative Communities Compared

Thus far, the major community development and capacity building programs have been examined. Drawing on key issues facing rural and remote communities identified in Chapter 2 and cross-referenced to the stated aims of contemporary community development programs, it is possible to generate key desired features and potential outcomes of various approaches to community development and capacity building as presented in Table 8. The resultant checklist is aligned, as appropriate, with CCB, the community arts movement, CCD, and creative communities. A star rating system has been used, with five stars indicating that there is substantial evidence in the literature to demonstrate a theoretical platform for addressing the key area of concern and evidence in the practice literature of outcomes being achieved. At the other end of the spectrum, a one-star rating indicates that there is little or no evidence in the literature to demonstrate a commitment to the key area of concern, either theoretical or practical.

Table 8. CCB, Community Arts, CCD and Creative Communities Compared.

Key outcome areas	Desired features and impacts of community development and capacity building programs	CCB	Community arts	CCD	Creative communities
Community involvement	High levels of active community involvement across all community sectors.	* * * * *	*	*	*
	A strong focus on the creation of strong, sustainable, and cohesive communities.	*	*	*	*
	The community and its members are at the centre of the decision-making processes.	* * * * *	*	*	*
	Focus on the development of community skills, knowledge and expertise.	* * * * *	* * * * *	* * *	*
	Strong expectation on sustainability of development process.	* * * * *	*	*	*
Community empowerment	Empowers communities to gain a sense of ownership and control over the processes that influence their day-to-day lives.	* * * * *	*	* * *	*
	Activities are inclusive of all community stakeholders/interest groups.	* * * * *	*	*	*
Integrated, whole-of-community solutions	Recognises that whole-of-community development is a high-risk strategy that takes time and requires investment and resources.	* * * * *	*	*	*
	Provides planned, integrated and holistic solutions reflecting local needs and circumstances.	* * * * *	*	*	*
	Focused on all community stakeholders.	* * * * *	*	*	*
Broad linkages	Operates in a broad policy context.	* * *	*	*	*
	Links with local, state and federal government initiatives and directions.	* * * * *	*	* * *	* * *

Key outcome areas	Desired features and impacts of community development and capacity building programs	CCB	Community arts	CCD	Creative communities
Partnerships	Values and supports the development and maintenance of partnerships (both within the community and between the community and external agencies).	* * * * *	* * *	* * *	* * *
	Partnerships are seen as key outcomes that contribute to the sustainability of initiatives and longer-term community benefits.	* * *	*	*	*
Social capital	Acts as a catalyst to engender stronger social ties, trust and responsibility, while enhancing the social fabric of the community.	* * * * *	* * * * *	* * * * *	* * * * *
	Improves community cohesiveness.	* * * * *	* * * * *	* * * * *	* * * * *
	Strengthens community identity.	* * * * *	* * * * *	* * * * *	* * * * *
Economic empowerment	Places strong emphasis on community economic development.	* * * * *	*	*	*
	Provides a catalyst for business development.	* * * * *	*	*	*
Community needs	Places a strong emphasis on the community itself identifying its needs, defining outcomes and initiating actions rather than being mobilised to act by external agencies.	* * * * *	*	*	*

Source: Author's research.

Table 8 demonstrates that, against the desired parameters, CCB is clearly the most effective method of supporting communities to develop strong and sustainable approaches to contemporary challenges. CCB uses a platform of community empowerment to stimulate development and growth across economic and social domains. It operates across a range of community services and connects with diverse industry sectors. Interestingly, there has been very little connection between CCB and the arts and cultural industries, suggesting that there is considerable potential for further exploration of these linkages. Table 8 also indicates the significant shortfall between the three arts-based concepts and practices and the achievement of desired features and impacts for communities. In many instances such shortfalls are a matter of degree; for example, community involvement in arts-based initiatives and programs is generally quite high but usually limited to specific groups within communities already engaged with or committed to the arts. In other instances the arts programs are exposed as narrow and insular, especially in areas focusing on integrated, whole-of-community outcomes.

Regarding the achievements of social outcomes, Table 8 indicates that CCB, community arts, CCD and creative communities all achieve high levels of connection. While this is commendable, it contrasts dramatically with the key outcome area of economic development where CCB is the only approach to place a strong emphasis on economic outcomes. In summary, there would appear to be significant opportunities for examining the potential for integrating CCB principles and practices with arts-based approaches.

4

Innovation and Creativity as Drivers of Contemporary Society

A New Direction: The Central Role of Creativity and Innovation in Community Building

A key objective of the current focus on creative communities is the forging of new and different linkages between art, commerce and community (Eger, 2003). The desired partnerships between art and commerce reflect a much bigger push by governments and businesses to highlight the critical importance of innovation and creativity to effective competition in a global marketplace. As the knowledge intensity of economic activity rapidly rises, governments are increasingly recognising that innovation and creativity are key ingredients for economic growth (Manley, 2001). Businesses also progressively understand that innovation may offer their sole sustaining competitive advantage, and that future survival depends on their capacity to identify and capitalise upon new ways of thinking, meeting demand and staying ahead of their knowledge competitors (Ireland & Webb, 2006; Mann & Chan, 2011).

While there is a growing recognition of the changing nature of the economy, it remains difficult to characterise the new knowledge economy because, unlike previous economic changes, which have been distinguished by physical symbols such as the heavy machinery of the industrial age or the computer of the information age, the knowledge economy is distinguished more by ideas, interaction and creativity (Martins & Terblanche, 2003). However, these new understandings of the role of innovation and creativity in the knowledge economy have been driven primarily by the technological changes facilitated by the advances of the information age (Martins & Terblanche, 2003).

Of special relevance is the emergence of the internet as a worldwide communications network, now recognised as the primary carrier of 'all communication and financial transactions affecting life and work in the 21st century' (Eger, 2003, p. 5). The internet's dominant application, the world wide web, is now integrated into the marketing, information and communications strategies of almost every major corporation, educational institution, community service organisation, commercial charity and government identity in the western world (Eger, 2003). While communications and information technologies have been important in providing infrastructure and applications to support the evolving knowledge economy, interest is now focusing on business and community developing practical applications for technologies to enhance economic development, create jobs, and improve quality of life. In other words, 'technological propagation in smart communities is not an end in itself but rather a means to a larger end with clear and compelling benefits for communities' (Eger, 2003, p. 7).

In this environment, innovation has become the predominant occupation of enterprises, especially over the last decade (Dickie, 2005b). It is now seen as a key to organisational competitiveness and effectiveness. There is also a growing consensus that innovation is complex and multifaceted and cannot be fully understood without analysis of the personal, organisational, technological and environmental contexts in which it takes place. However, there is agreement both that the foundation of all innovation is the generation of ideas and that it is people who develop, carry, react to and modify ideas towards fruition. The new economy's voracious demand for ideas and innovation has manifested in the emergence of what Florida (2002) has termed the 'creative class'. According to Florida, the main difference between the creative class and other classes is best understood through the kind of work they perform. Members of the creative class are paid mainly to create the plan and subsequently have considerably more autonomy and flexibility than do other classes.

Florida recognises that the emerging creative class is currently significantly smaller than the service class (those who deliver services, currently comprising approximately 45 per cent of the workforce) but that its vital economic role gives it substantial influence that is being felt by organisations, enterprises and communities, primarily because, like the managerial class of the 1950s, the creative class is the norm-setting class in respect of the knowledge economy (Florida, 2002). However, these norms are markedly different as the creative class values self-expression, individuality, and openness to difference (Florida, 2002). The identity of the creative class is also differentiated in that it is not solely defined by salary, organisational status or, indeed, discipline — it is inherently inclusive. It encompasses people in engineering and science, architecture and design, education, music, arts and entertainment (Florida, 2002). Members of the creative class balance financial considerations against 'the ability to act as they wish, set their own schedules, perform challenging work and live in communities that reflect their values and priorities' (Eger, 2003, p. 12).

Economic Drivers

Along with other researchers (Eger, 2003; Markusen & Schrock, 2006; McGranahan & Wojan, 2007; Peck, 2005), Florida (2002) has provided a huge service for communities struggling to redefine themselves for the new economy. Community organisations and governing bodies are increasingly realising that traditional economic stimulus tools such as grants and subsidies are having limited impact; communities are adopting strategies to attract and retain creative workers who have the potential to generate new approaches, new strategies and new products. It is about 'organising one's community to reinvent itself for the new, knowledge-based economy and society; preparing its citizens to take ownership of their community; and educating the next generation of leaders and workers to meet global challenges' (Eger, 2003, p. 4).

Changes in the economy, especially those related to globalisation, digitisation, the rise of the knowledge worker, the boom in intellectual property, and changes in leisure consumption (Tepper, 2002), offer significant challenges to conventional approaches to community development and capacity building. Essentially, the established approaches to community arts, community capacity building, community cultural development, and even the more recent approaches to the development of creative communities are now being challenged firstly by the concept of the knowledge economy and, more recently, by the emergence of the creative economy, the underpinning ideas of which stress the centrality and interdependence of knowledge and creativity in the economy. While the economic value of knowledge is not new and has played a key role in economies for centuries (e.g. knowledge of land management has always been a key resource in agricultural economies, and knowledge and management of natural resources and labour have been key resources in industrial economies (Jaffe & Trajtenberg, 2002)), knowledge in the twenty-first century has become so integrated into economic activity that the primary resources now driving economic growth are knowledge, creativity, innovation and talent (Hawkes, 2005; Jeffcutt & Pratt, 2002; Peters, Marginson & Murphy, 2009).

Increasingly, the knowledge economy relies not only on the creation of knowledge but also on its propagation and use. Economic success depends not only on the capacity of businesses to gather, absorb and utilise existing knowledge but also on their ability to generate new knowledge (Teece, 2010). In this environment, sustained business success is heavily dependent on the ability to innovate, to recognise and exploit new ideas and opportunities ahead of the competition. The ability to innovate, in turn, depends partly on the availability and application of creative skills (Cox, 2005). Among other priorities, businesses need access to the talents of creative people in order that innovation may flourish:

> People with ideas — people who own ideas — have become more powerful than people who work with machines and, in many cases, more powerful than people who own machines (Hawkes, 2001, p. 35).

The Emergence of the Creative Economy

Recognition of the importance of people and their creativity has lead to the coining, adoption and widespread use of the term 'creative economy', with its implication that the success of business and industry, and the consequent prosperity of nations, is dependent on the creativity of workers:

> Creativity, properly employed, carefully evaluated, skilfully managed and soundly implemented, is the key to future business success — and to national prosperity (Cox, 2005, p. 3).

The term has thus not only consolidated the key concepts inherent in understandings of the knowledge economy but has also provided new depth and meaning by linking economic development more closely with human talent. The concept of the creative economy has not only captured our understanding of the importance of digitisation and globalisation as core foundations driving economic change but has also deepened our appreciation of the impact of economic change by drawing attention to four key outcomes:

1. The increase in the value of creativity and the subsequent rise of the creative worker resulting in significant changes in the world of work
2. The increase in leisure time and changes in the way leisure time is used, resulting in an increase in the consumption and demand for creative products and services
3. Recognition of the economic centrality of development of talent and human capital
4. Recognition of the key role of education in stimulating and developing creativity and nurturing human talent.

Changes in the World of Work

The new economy's recognition of the centrality of ideas and talent is impacting significantly on workforce development, as workplaces are progressively requiring not only academic and vocational skills but also less tangible qualities such as flexibility, responsiveness, creative thinking, problem solving and interpersonal skills (Brown, Hesketh & Williams, 2003; Rojewski, 2002). As a result, the older, hierarchical, tightly structured organisations are being replaced by new kinds of working arrangements aimed partly at attracting workers with new skills and contemporary attitudes. Greater decision-making and problem-solving authority rests in the hands of front-line employees as self-managed, cross-functional teams replace bureaucratic structures (Isaksen, Dorval & Treffinger, 2011; Proctor, 2010). Such workplaces need employees with skills in communication, maintaining relationships, problem solving and the management of organisational processes. Psilos's (2002) identification of the skills necessary to acquire and retain a job in today's workplaces is presented in Table 9 in terms of three levels of skills for the new economy.

Table 9. Skills for the New Economy.

Basic skills	Higher-order thinking skills	Affective skills and traits
• Oral communication. • Reading, especially understanding. • Basic arithmetic. • Writing.	• Problem solving. • Learning skills, strategies. • Creative, innovative thinking. • Decision making.	• Dependability and responsibility. • Positive attitude towards work. • Conscientiousness, punctuality. • Efficiency. • Interpersonal skills and cooperation. • Working as a team member. • Self-confidence, positive self-image. • Adaptability, flexibility. • Enthusiasm, motivation. • Self-discipline, self-management. • Appropriate dress, grooming. • Honesty, integrity, ability to work without supervision.

Source: Adapted from Psilos, 2002.

The breadth and depth of the skills identified in Table 9 illustrate that human capital has become the primary determinant of economic viability. This is the case not only for nations and regions but also for rural and remote communities.

The Demand for Creative Products

Over recent years, there has been an exponential increase in the size of the market for creative products, services and new ideas (Caves, 2000; Cunningham, 2006; Tepper, 2002). While there are many factors influencing the growth of the sectors making up the creative economy, recent shifts in leisure consumption and the way leisure time is used have significantly contributed to a massive increase in demand for and expenditure on creative products (Freeman, 2007). This has created an annual growth of the creative economy in OECD countries that has been twice that of the service industries and four times that of manufacturing (Howkins, 2002). The creative industries in the United States alone have been 'estimated to be worth over $360 billion making them more valuable than the automobile, agriculture or aerospace industries' (Robinson, 2001, p. 42). The British, Americans and Japanese all spend more on personal entertainment than on clothing or health care (Howkins, 2002). However, creative products are, in economic terms, luxury goods and, inevitably, the demand for them rises and falls as income levels rise and fall. Thus, creative products are victims of cyclic shifts in the disposable income of populations (Freeman, 2007) and, consequently, such trends must always be considered in light of broader patterns of economic growth.

The link between leisure, disposable income and demand for creative products is further evidenced by an analysis of sources of income for creative products in the United Kingdom (Freeman, 2007). Freeman (2007) estimates that the creative industries sell 61 per cent of their products to households, suggesting a strong consumer-led market demand. This strong consumer-led demand has contributed to profound shifts in the nature of the arts and the artistic world (Morato, 2003). The demand for technology-based, audio-visual creative products is growing rapidly, particularly in terms of games, music, film, video and publishing. The demand for interactivity in these products is strongly influencing the nature of creative products. Technological innovation is enabling new relationships with consumers who seek greater control and influence over products so they can adapt and customise them to suit their personal needs and circumstances. Interactivity, convergence, customisation, collaboration and networks are now key criteria for creative products (Cunningham, 2004). While still controlled by major publishing and broadcasting systems, global film studios, and flagship arts companies, the response to this new demand for interactive, digitised products is being met primarily by micro and small enterprises (Cunningham, 2004). The emergence of micro and small creative enterprises relating to and operating with large established distribution and marketing organisations provides new opportunities for creative business development in rural and remote communities as technology has reduced reliance on size and place. Small enterprises can create or contribute to the creation of product from any location.

Talent and Human Capital

Shifts in consumer demand are also having significant impacts on labour markets and workforce development, as previously held ideas and beliefs regarding productivity are being reassessed, reshaped and realigned (Psilos, 2002). Human capital, especially in the form of individual creativity and talent, is now being recognised as a primary determinant of economic vitality and sustainability (Atkinson & Easthope, 2009; Storper & Scott, 2009). The flatter and more flexible organisational structures inevitably mean that decision-making and problem-solving authority is increasingly resting in the hands of front-line employees (Psilos, 2002). Thus the multiple dimensions of human capital drive both the creation and application of knowledge at the centre of the process of economic growth (Banks, 2010).

As higher levels of human capital have been found to be strongly associated with higher levels of creativity, innovation and productivity (Banks, 2010), growth and development will depend more and more on each community's capacity to invent, innovate and adapt. Success will depend on the skills and attitudes of community residents, and how those skills are utilised by community organisations and businesses.

The Role of Education in Stimulating and Developing Creativity

Communities, workplaces and organisations are not alone in recognising the centrality of creativity; governments are also developing policies and programs on the premise that creativity is a key national resource that must be fostered and managed to stimulate future economic growth through innovation. Nowhere is this link more relevant than in education as schools, colleges and universities seek to stimulate the development of the creative human capital platform on which innovation depends.

Adams (2005) draws on the work of contemporary educational theorists to assert that thinking is the core aspect of the creative process and to identify four aspects of creative thinking:

1. Comfortably disagreeing with others and attempting solutions that depart from the status quo
2. Combining knowledge from previously disparate fields

3. Persevering through difficult problems and dry spells
4. Being able to step away from an effort and return later with a fresh perspective (incubation) (Adams, 2005, p. 6).

While there is little evidence that current curricula or learning approaches address these aspects, Eger reports that creativity can be encouraged and enhanced through the use of thinking tools coupled with an appreciation of the links between 'mind and body, sense and sensibility' (Eger, 2003, p. 19).

Coupled with a growing interest of the potential of education to encourage creative thinking and innovation is an increasing awareness of the specific role of arts education in stimulating creativity and inventive thinking. The arts, after all, represent the curriculum area that explicitly regards creativity as a core element (Davis, 2008). Moreover, original and inventive thinking derives from non-verbal and non-logical forms regardless of field or curriculum area (Eger, 2003). To support the development of creative, inventive thinking people, students 'should learn to abstract, empathise, analogise and translate intuitive forms of knowledge into numbers, words, image, sound and movement' (Eger, 2003, p. 19). That is, in many instances, the arts can provide the most effective thinking tools to encourage creativity.

The Role of the Arts in Innovation and Creativity

At the heart of endeavours to build innovative and creative communities is the dawning recognition of the vital role that the arts play in enhancing economic development. Ultimately, a successful creative community will be one that 'exploits the vital linkages between art, culture and commerce, and in the process consciously invests in human and financial resources to prepare its citizens to meet the challenges of the rapidly evolving post-industrial, knowledge-based economy and society' (Eger, 2003, p. 12). The role of the arts in communities has always been valued, albeit primarily as entertainment and with an underlying assumption that they are an expendable aspect of community life. However, over the last decade, the demand for creativity has outpaced the ability to produce sufficient workers to meet the needs of the growing digital entertainment industry based on the merging of entertainment and information technologies, incorporating games, films and television. It is partly this demand that has stimulated the emergence of Florida's creative class. Florida argues that the individuals who make up his creative class share a common ethos that emphasises individuality, creativity, difference and merit but, most importantly, understand and appreciate that 'every aspect and manifestation of creativity, cultural, technological and economic, is inextricably linked' (Florida, 2002, p. 34).

The traditional contribution of the arts to a region's attractiveness and liveability has been underscored and stressed in recent years by numerous studies that point to the economic success of cities and regions that have lured companies and workers to their areas through the promotion of their arts programs and cultural advantages (Bayliss, 2007; Yigitcanlar, Baum & Horton, 2007). While towns and regions may adopt strategies to attract workers to their areas, arts-based education is also critical to ensuring the next generation of leaders and workers for the knowledge economy. Arts programs serve local communities extensively by 'contributing to the region's innovation habitat, thus improving the quality of life — making them more attractive to the highly desirable, knowledge-based employees and permitting new forms of knowledge-intensive production to flourish' (Psilos & Rapp, 2001, p. 1).

While current understandings of how the social and cultural benefits of the arts impact on communities are reasonably well recognised, less so is an appreciation of how the arts can integrate with and inform other aspects of community planning and development. To develop a vision with the arts at the heart of community development is a bold endeavour only achievable if arts programs and artists operate in a way that encompasses community-wide objectives and builds towards community-shared visions of the future. It requires artists and arts workers to create a fresh dialogue with new community partners who may not previously have been perceived to be collaborators. Similarly, 'creativity' is a term that has too often and for too long been applied almost exclusively to the arts and artists. New understandings of the notion of creativity as a non-domain-specific, multi-discipline area of human activity are influencing approaches to problem solving, planning and implementation of programs and projects (Haufman & Baer, 2005; Haufman & Sternberg, 2006).

Whole-of-government strategies and programs that are now being implemented in certain areas are providing good examples of how different disciplines can work collaboratively to solve problems and deliver services in creative and innovative ways (Gemmel & Clayton, 2009; Miller, Hess & Orthmann, 2010). The push towards whole-of-government approaches has provided an opportunity to position the arts as an integral player in broader and more dynamic policy debates and programs — linking the arts to reconciliation, social cohesion and economic prosperity:

> If the arts are to impact on all Australians, it needs to enter communities of interests — and draw government, media and corporate support. For that to happen, we need to put culture not at the end of the value chain, tacked on if and when funds are available, but right at the start — and the heart — of community building and engagement, where it belongs (Bott, 2006a, p. 4).

Currently, the arts play a central role in urban revitalisation and community renewal; they attract new businesses, visitors and residents and encourage consumer spending, which creates new economic opportunities and increased community revenues (Grodach & Loukaitou-Sideris, 2007; Richards & Palmer, 2010). In turn, new opportunities stimulate the development of new skills and the creation of new ideas (Brault, 2005). The arts also enhance the market appeal of regions and communities and have been identified as a key component in attracting new economy workers and thus encouraging corporate relocation (Florida, 2002; Pratt, 2009; Scott, 2006). The arts are also being more explicitly recognised as a key contributor to workplace innovation (McNicholas, 2004). While workers with arts-related skills have for some time been seen as critical to software development firms, technology companies, advertising firms, and audio-visual and entertainment industries, other industries are now recognising the value of high-level communications and creative problem-solving abilities (Phillips, 2004; Seifter, 2004). Involvement in the arts is now seen by some companies as providing employees, whether scientists, marketing managers, financial managers or business analysts, with opportunities to network, stimulate creative thinking and build team spirit (Birch, 2002). The key issue is the extent to which the arts can help build the skills required by businesses and enterprises so that they can compete effectively in the new economy.

The Need for Arts Education

The accumulation of human capital, like physical capital, requires investment of resources and time, and is a key area for investment in education systems. However, a distinction needs to be drawn between the role of education in giving people the ability to acquire specific skills and vocational competencies, and its role in developing analytical, problem-solving and communication skills (Banks, 2010). The new economic focus on creativity and innovation demands more from education and both categories of skills, the generic and the specific, are important to future growth and development (Banks, 2010).

However, it must be acknowledged that learning occurs beyond schools and workplaces, that learning about and through the arts happens in all kinds of cultural and heritage organisations, including community organisations (Culture and Learning Consortium, 2009). In such environments, learning about the arts, local culture or heritage can inspire community engagement, leading not only to personal, social and community benefit but also to the development of creative solutions to social and economic challenges. Community cultural organisations need to understand and appreciate that learning lies at the heart of all community concerns, and learning about and through the arts may provide a key mechanism for developing creative community solutions (Holden, 2008). Community cultural organisations need to ensure that learning and community development are central to their functions and the 'needs of children, families, and other learners from the wider community are identified and addressed' (Culture and Learning Consortium, 2009, p. 7).

Contemporary scholars and researchers confirm the value of the arts in providing 'authentic learning experiences that engage minds, hearts and bodies' (Fiske, 1999, p. ix), nurturing the development of cognitive, social and personal competencies. However, research has also demonstrated that (i) success in the arts often provides a bridge to success in other areas of learning, (ii) the arts can connect with disengaged students, providing motivation to learn, and (iii) the arts provide new challenges for successful students (Catterall, 2002; Deasy, 2002; Fiske, 1999; Rabkin & Redmond, 2006). The arts have also been shown to connect learning experiences to the world of real work (Fiske, 1999; Larson & Walker, 2006). Research has shown that arts-based learning experiences have a remarkable consistency with the demands and processes of the new economy and workplace. In arts-based learning environments and contemporary workplaces, 'ideas are what matter, and the ability to generate ideas, to bring ideas to life and communicate them is what matters' (Fiske, 1999. p. 12). The arts have been shown to encourage other competencies recognised as important in contemporary workplaces, including self-directed learning, the promotion of complexity in the learning experience by encouraging open debate and discussion, and the encouragement of risk-taking in a managed way (Burton, Horowitz & Abeles, 2000; Catterall, 2002). However, there is little direct evidence of curricula designed to foster the development of creativity leading to innovation. Indeed, the arts still tend to be perceived as isolated from other curriculum areas (Davis, 2008) and the growing awareness of the link between the arts and creative thinking seems to be largely ignored by curriculum designers.

The Rise of Creative Industries

The creative economy values human capital and talent, and recognises that such capital and talent is found in all aspects of society (Mellander & Florida, 2006). Human creative capital is broad and deep, and includes not only writers, actors, singers and other traditional artists, but also advertisers, architects, multimedia developers and others. Creative capital is not limited to the world of the arts and entertainment but is also located in business, technology, the sciences, and many other areas of the broader economy (Hemlin, Allwood & Martin, 2004). The creative economy is 'bigger and broader than we think, and is much more than culture and the arts' (Cunningham, 2006, p. 2). In this context, the relatively new term, the 'creative industries', may be seen to address only one component of what makes up the creative economy. One of the first uses of the term came in the report of the Creative Industries Task Force in the United Kingdom, which defined the creative industries as those activities that have their origin in individual creativity, skill and talent, and that have the potential for wealth and job creation through the generation and exploitation of intellectual property (CITF, 2001). The CIFT report included the following as creative industries: advertising, architecture, arts, crafts, design, fashion, film, interactive leisure software, music, television, radio, performing arts and publishing. If this list is considered indicative of the creative industries, two conclusions can be drawn. Firstly, the creative industries clearly represent just one small component of the creative economy; secondly, traditional roles associated with the arts and cultures are just one cog of the creative industries (see Figure 3).

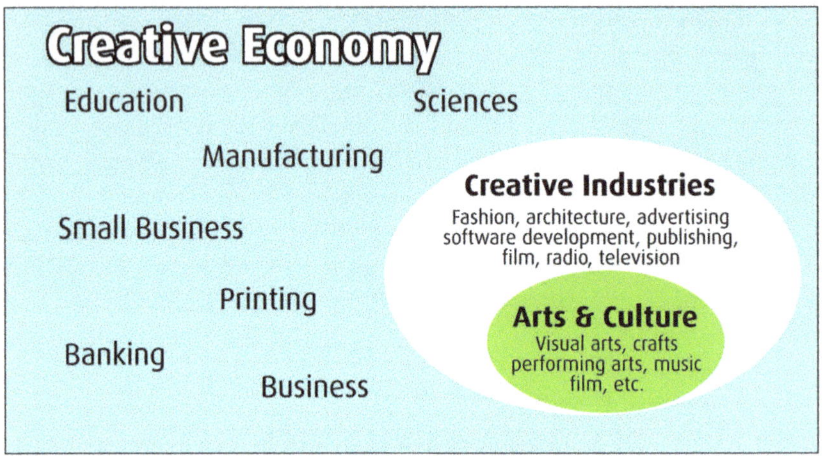

Figure 3. Creative Industries and the Creative Economy.
Source: Author's research.

Figure 3 can only be indicative as the relationships between roles and functions within the creative economy are complex. The key point to be drawn from Figure 3 is that the creative economy is broad and includes many industries, not only those traditionally labelled creative. The special case that has been made historically for the strong link between the arts and creativity is becoming more difficult to sustain in an environment where creativity is increasingly seen as an essential element for all aspects of the economy:

> The 'price' to be paid for a creative economy is that the case for the arts and culture will become less about their special or exceptional difference, and become diffused into the need for creativity across the economy and society (Cunningham, 2006, p. 4).

Hence there is an inherent challenge for both. The arts need to reconsider the alignment of their identity as a special case, while society (and the economy) need to recognise the integral and all-encompassing need for creativity into the future in order to be both sustainable and self-generative.

Reach and Definition

Since the release of the CITF report (2001), the 13 industry sectors identified as comprising the creative industries have been widely accepted, despite their divergent scope. All 13 identified sectors are underpinned by creativity as their prime source of value, a value that is becoming progressively more important for growth in knowledge-based societies (Caves, 2000; Garnham, 2005). Each of the identified sectors has, at its core, individual skill, creativity and talent, and each has the potential for wealth and job creation through the exploitation of intellectual property (Kenway, Bullen & Robb, 2004). The concept of creative industries thus links previously disparate industry sectors and expands significantly what have been traditionally seen as the key components of the creative sector, primarily the arts.

The new concept has corralled the established arts (theatre, dance, music, and visual arts), the established media (radio, film, and television), the design and architectural sectors, and the new media (games, software). This grouping is less coherent than our traditional definitions of the arts, media and the cultural industries, and is little more than an eclectic alliance of activities that have creativity as their core. However, the major purpose of the creative industries umbrella is not definitional; it is the provision of a strategy for linking creativity with economic and industry development policy (Cunningham, 2006). By grouping industries under the creative banner, governments have been able to draw attention to that fact that creative industries are a significant component of gross domestic product and, in advanced economies, have the potential to grow at a faster rate than many other industry sectors (Hesmondhalgh & Pratt, 2005). As a consequence, many countries have developed creative industries strategies aimed at nurturing the development of creative skills and facilitating the establishment of creative enterprises and industries. In essence, the concept 'foregrounds the sector's economic potential and makes the creative industries the sparkplugs of the next generation, post industrial growth' (Cunningham, 2006, p. 14).

The Contribution of the Creative Industries

It has been argued that the creative industries concept may be overhyped rhetoric destined to lose favour along with previous attempts to ramp up the importance of new industries or industry groupings (Hutton, 2008). This view is advocated primarily by those concerned that the new industry grouping might marginalise the traditional arts and cultural sectors by aligning them far too strongly to economic agendas and undermining not only the social and cultural outcomes of the arts but also the higher agenda of the arts to explore the meaning and purpose of the human condition. Such concerns have deepened over the last decade as evidence of the scope of the creative economy has begun to be quantified by government and economists. In 1999, the creative industries accounted for $US2.2 trillion or about 7.3 per cent of the global economy, although the contribution of the creative and performing arts was only 1.7 per cent (Cunningham, 2005; Cunningham, 2006).

There is also a view that industry classifications, including classifications of the creative industries, can never capture the dimensions and trends underpinning the economy of the twenty-first century given its inherent demand for novelty and change, complex and dynamic structures and industry groupings, and complex contractual relationships and networks (Caves, 2000). While a crisis of industry classification is identifiable in all industry sectors, it is likely to be particularly relevant in the creative industries that are arguably subject to more rapid change and greater differentiation and specialisation (Cunningham, 2006). That is, not only is the sector diverse (comprising the traditional arts, established media, design and architecture, and the new media) but the groupings within the sector have vastly different business models, commercial positions, product cycles and revenue sources, and are driven by different philosophies and demands, all of which makes the overall contribution of the sector to social, economic and cultural development difficult to measure in the short to medium term.

There are, however, inevitably contrary views regarding the inclusion of the traditional arts in the creative industries grouping; these opposing views point out that the creative industries may have the positive effect of linking the traditional arts and the cultural industries to the emerging, broader economic agendas of government and industry, thus providing new opportunities and challenges (Galloway & Dunlop, 2007; Potts et al., 2008). As the concepts of the creative industries and the creative economy have gained wide acceptance in contemporary policy and industry debate, they have been well accepted by governments, and have become a key consideration in the development of economic policies and national innovation agendas (Throsby, 2008). What defines creative industries in the new economy is the proposition that 'creativity is their primary source of value, something that is becoming increasingly important for growth in post industrial, knowledge based societies' (Cunningham, 2006, p. 14). In this context, the key contribution of the creative industries concept, at least in policy terms, has indeed been to mainstream arts and culture and connect them to broader economic agendas.

The potential of this contribution is deeper and stronger than simply linking traditional arts and culture with the economic powerhouses of publishing, media and software development. It provides a chance for the arts to engage actively with the new concepts evolving from the knowledge economy, including creative human capital, creative assets, intellectual property and cultural economics (Tepper, 2002). Just as importantly, it provides an opportunity for the traditional arts and culture sector to connect with and benefit from government and business agendas to support industry development and stimulate innovation in business and industry. If the arts can position themselves to take advantage of emerging economic agendas while simultaneously protecting their role in community social and cultural development, their role may become more central in efforts to find solutions to contemporary community challenges.

The opportunities arising from the new focus on economics should not be considered simply in terms of financial transactions. The creative industries challenge traditional economic approaches because their unique and complex organisational structures and contractual processes are more likely to be dynamic and matrix based rather than the more traditional linear client/provider structures (Cunningham, 2006). Challenges also arise because the creative industries are characterised by high levels of experimentation and risk taking, which are often minimised in more established industries (Foord, 2009). What is now required are new understandings and models for arts-based development based on the growing awareness and appreciation of the creative economy. Such models are essential to increase understanding and appreciation of the role of the arts and their contribution to creativity in the economy. They might also provide a framework through which this might be quantified. While the benefits of positioning the creative industries in the spheres of industry development and the broader economy are significant, the new focus on creativity and the economy should not distract from consideration of the well-established social and cultural outcomes of the traditional arts (see Chapter 3). An approach that balances economic outcomes with the social and cultural benefits of the arts provides an opportunity to develop more comprehensive approaches to the integral role of the arts in community development.

The Fostering of Innovation

As indicated above, the concepts of the creative economy and the creative industries have provided catalysts for linking the arts (both the traditional arts and new media) more strongly to the creative economy. They are thus well placed to capitalise on the idea of creativity as an input to the broader economy. This, in turn, has the potential to link with the concepts of design and enterprise that drive innovation and change in the knowledge economy (Cox, 2005). There are, however, significant challenges to overcome before the potential of the creative industries to foster innovation can be achieved. Perhaps the most significant of these challenges arises from the bedrock from which the creative industries have emerged: the notion of creative human capital, which is multilayered and multidimensional, comprising designers, cinematographers, writers, lyricists, artists, crafts people, computer interface designers and many others who operate in different working environments with different reporting structures and economic drivers. Additionally, people operating in the creative industries are driven by a multitude of divergent goals and philosophies (Smith & Warfield, 2008).

While this diversity is an important strength of the sector, it has generated fundamental chasms that divide the sector and render it difficult to establish consensus about its role in supporting innovation. To engage with and benefit from government-sponsored innovation policies and agendas, the creative industries need to articulate a clear, shared vision outlining their real and potential contribution to the creative economy and the innovations that drive it (Cunningham, 2006). There is also a commensurate requirement to specify the roles and contributions of the occupations comprising the sector to the creative economy (Throsby, 2008). Whether a sector as diverse as the creative industries can find common ground remains to be seen but, as Cunningham observes, 'the critical spirit that constitutes the creative community makes me doubt that there would be a robust and enduring consensus … to withstand the processes that contemporary public funding must go through' (2006, p. 43).

Further challenges are the reduction of insularity and the establishment of proactive engagement with other sectors of the economy. The varied elements that comprise the creative industries sector have primarily been focused on creative outputs and products in the form of plays, books, games, films and multiple, diverse other creative commodities. While creative products are critically important and will continue to be a key area of growth to meet increasing consumer demand, it is equally important for the sector, as well as occupations within the sector, to move towards the provision of creative inputs to the broader economy (Potts et al., 2008). Sustained success in the new economic conditions depends on the ability of all industries to innovate to exploit new ideas and opportunities and bring them to market in a timely manner. This ability to innovate depends on the availability and exploitation of creative skills. The link between creative skills and the broader economy is well synthesised by Cox:

> In an enterprise culture, these needs create a virtuous circle: for sustained innovation and growth, companies need to be able to draw upon the talents of a flourishing creative community; for innovation to flourish, the creative community need to be responding to the demands of dynamic and ambitious businesses (Cox, 2005, p. 11).

Currently, there is little practical evidence of acknowledgement that creativity has the potential to be a powerful contributor to economic growth across a broad spectrum of industries and businesses. While there is a theoretical recognition that 'much of the real growth dynamics will be found in this move' (Cunningham, 2006, p. 16), neither the businesses nor the creative occupations comprising the creative industries have demonstrated a willingness to move creativity from the sidelines to the nerve centre of innovative activity.

A further challenge to the fostering of innovation by the creative industries is the dual-edged sword created by the concept of an industry group for creative occupations. On the positive side, the concept emphasises that the creative industries are a significant component of gross domestic product for many of the world's leading economies and contribute to export dollars and domestic jobs (Cox, 2005). The industry grouping also allows the creative occupations to position themselves within broader contemporary policy agendas, especially those related to industry development and innovation, and thus broaden considerably the support base for the arts and associated subgroups. This potential allows occupations within the creative industries grouping to access new sources of state funds and potentially benefit from a strategic move from the periphery of economic activity to recognition as a key player in the creative economy (Cunningham, 2006). The downside of the establishment of the new creative occupations industry groupings is the potential perception of a special category of creative workers focused on the design and production of unique products for a particular segment of the market linked to arts and culture. Such a perception at least partially inhibits the creative industries from linking broadly with the economy and recognising that creativity is integral to business, health, manufacturing and very many other areas of development.

Critical Factors in Innovative Practice

For many individuals and the communities in which they live and work, innovation is a remote concept, focusing primarily on high-end innovations such as biotechnology, stem cell research or new information technologies. Consequently, innovation tends to be seen as something that happens to people, businesses and communities rather than something that is created by people and communities (Dickie, 2005b). However, the Cox Review of Creativity in Business placed primary emphasis on the potential innovative use of creative skills by small- and medium-sized businesses. Cox (2005) argued that the opportunities arising from global economic change to conceptualise innovative products and services, and to produce these and bring them to market quickly, were particularly relevant to small- and medium-sized enterprises. However, these opportunities can only be realised if employers and employees understand and appreciate that creativity and innovation should be embedded across all aspects of business. Creativity and innovation can no longer be perceived as remote from people, their communities and work places; it must be integrated into all aspects of work and community life. This concept of integration of creativity and innovation is well summarised in the Cox Review:

> It is common for those in business to see creativity and the related area of design as largely concerned with aesthetic considerations such as style and appearance. While these are important considerations, they are only a small part of I am talking about here. Creative businesses are creative throughout. As well as being the path to new products and services, creativity is also the route to greater productivity whether by way of higher-value products and services, better processes, more effective marketing, simpler structures or better use of people's skills (Cox, 2005, p. 3).

The challenge primarily revolves around attitudes, understanding and behaviour. Cox drew on surveys of business organisations in the United Kingdom to identify the major obstacles impeding businesses from making greater use of their creative talents to stimulate innovation. Obstacles focused on lack of awareness and experience of businesses and their employees in creative problem solving, lack of confidence and belief in the potential of new approaches and products, and limited ambition or appetite for the risks associated with innovation. Cox (2005) recommends several approaches to stimulate changes in the attitudes of businesses and their employees, including the following:

1. Improving the effectiveness of government support and incentive schemes for research and development
2. Broadening the understanding and skills of future business leaders, creative specialists, engineers and technologists
3. Taking steps to use the massive power of public procurement to encourage more imaginative solutions from suppliers
4. Raising the profile of the nation's creative capabilities by way of a network of centres of creativity and innovation.

While these high-level approaches are important, it is equally critical to encourage active change on the workplace floor and in community organisations.

Engaging the Arts and Artists

There is now a strong recognition that changes in the economy have pushed creative assets to the centre of economic life. The new creative economy has been reported as having a major effect on the arts, which, as previously acknowledged, have now been heralded as the one of the potential new engines of economic growth and development

(Tepper, 2002). However, the arts and artists are not necessarily central to new approaches and 'the creative economy … is bigger and broader than we think, and is much more than culture and the arts' (Cunningham, 2006, p. 2). In the new environment, artists may need to reconsider their roles and determine their positions in relation to new economic approaches, especially their relationship to innovation. Bohm-Parr (2011) examined the contemporary roles of artists and identified a fundamental dilemma for today's artists, which relates to the fundamental tension between sustaining artistic integrity whilst retaining economic viability and engaging more broadly with community.

If, despite the broad acceptance of the key importance of innovation to the new economy, the concept remains remote and perceived as removed from the work habitat of most people, then effort needs to focus on helping people connect in meaningful and practical ways with the role of creativity and innovation in their lives (Sahlberg, 2009). Firstly, the adoption and promotion of simple and straightforward definitions of the key concepts could provide a platform for enhanced appreciation of links with everyday living and working (Cruickshank, 2010). While there are many appropriate definitions of creativity and innovation in the literature, those adopted by Cox are among the most simply stated and accessible:

> Creativity is the generation of new ideas — either new ways of looking at existing problems, or of seeing new opportunities, perhaps by exploiting emerging technologies and changes in markets (Cox, 2005, p. 7).
>
> Innovation is the successful exploitation of new ideas. It is the process that carries them through to new products, new services, new ways of running the business or even new ways of doing business (Cox, 2005, p. 8).

The usefulness of these definitions, aside from their deceptive simplicity, is that they significantly broaden what has been traditionally seen as the support base for creativity and innovation, the arts and the creative industries. Consequently, they challenge artists and arts workers to examine their future roles and potential contributions; artists must articulate their new directions in supporting innovation. While artists need to connect fully with the new concepts, simply stated definitions are only the beginning of the process of connecting artists with these concepts. Practical approaches are needed to help them understand how they can most effectively contribute to new products, services and processes. In the new environment, and as part of the creative economy, artists and arts workers are no different from others (Markusen & Schrock, 2006); all must now work out new ways of connecting and developing practical methods of contributing.

One way to help people connect practically with creativity and innovation is to introduce and stimulate open discussion around the interconnecting concepts of the arts, design and innovation (Rosenfeld, 2004). The arts and the creative industries provide the skills that help to fuel design, which is one of the processes that links creativity and innovation and builds enterprises (Cabrita & Cabrita, 2010; Cox, 2005; Mann & Chan, 2010). The arts not only generate and shape ideas but can also contribute to the formulation of design concepts, the tools through which ideas become practical and attractive propositions for users or customers (Totterman, 2008). While the concept of design in the new economy is not the preserve of the arts and the creative industries, artists may be in a position to lead development, especially if they build on their skills and experiences gathered through working with risky concepts on projects requiring the generation and application of new thoughts and approaches.

Valuing Creativity and Innovation: The Challenge for Communities

Traditional community development models were conceived and developed before communities began to be pressured to respond to the globalisation of national economies with the consequent emergence of more complex and competitive economic environments. They evolved before creativity took centre stage in economic thinking and innovation came to be seen as a key business driver. These models matured before the emergence of the concept of the creative class and precede the view that 'every manifestation of creativity, cultural, technological and economic, is inextricably linked' (Eger, 2003). As a consequence, established theories and approaches to community development, including CCB, community arts, CCD and the newer concept of creative communities, are now being marginalised as newer concepts related to the emergence of the creative economy become mainstreamed. The concept of the creative economy is broader, deeper and bigger than conventional approaches to community development can encompass. Communities are struggling to develop new approaches to build creative capital and are attempting to take 'a fresh look at how cultural development contributes to authentic, vibrant and creative — and economically successful — communities' (Bulick et al., 2003, p. 4).

While the traditional approaches to community development presented in Chapter 3 have made important contributions to the theory and practice of community development over the last two decades, their limitations have become more obvious as communities face new challenges arising from momentous economic and structural change. The new environment demands fresh approaches to community development based on flexibility, agility and responsiveness (Hutton, 2008; Tepper, 2002). Such approaches require greater diversity in community skills, the identification and application of unique community resources, as well as the recognition of distinctive experiences able to be coalesced to build imaginative and inventive responses to new and continuing community challenges. Yet it remains important not to throw out the baby with the bathwater. There may be residual values from these models that can be channelled anew.

5

Concepts in Practice: Initiatives in Action

Themes Arising from Community Development Initiatives

There are many practical examples of how communities have worked to overcome challenges and develop successful approaches to support ongoing growth and development. These examples are presented here to illustrate and add depth to the key themes emerging from the literature: (i) the restoration and revitalisation of communities, especially urban communities; (ii) economic vitality through cultural tourism; (iii) business incubation and the stimulation of new enterprises; (iv) the link between the arts and a creative workforce; (v) the use of the arts in creating vibrant public spaces to enhance community life; (vi) the role of new technologies in supporting community development through the arts; (vii) the role of the arts in enhancing social cohesion and building community image and identity; (viii) the role of the arts in reducing antisocial behaviour; and (ix) the role of the arts in developing self-confidence. Exemplars have been selected from numerous initiatives implemented across the world over the last 20 years and are presented as snapshots to showcase these themes. In a small number of cases, the initiatives are no longer operating but have been included in order illustrate the scope and depth of activities as well as their evolution over time. (Further generic examples covering the 50 years from 1960 to 2010 are provided in Appendix B.)

Restoration and Revitalisation of Communities

Artists and arts organisations have always added vitality and character to communities, especially urban communities; however, as already acknowledged, the arts now play an increasingly important role in community regeneration and revitalisation. Initially, arts-based projects and programs focused on capital works such as the building of arts centres and facilities, but recent developments have focused on the capacity of the arts to support community-led renewal, seeing people rather than buildings as the principal asset through which renewal can be achieved (Landry et al., 1996; Markusen & Schrock, 2006; Yigitcanlar, 2010).

Some 30 years ago, several American cities seeking to relaunch the image of their deteriorating downtown areas responded to opportunities arising from two trends: (i) arts organisations began looking for less expensive urban venues to house new headquarters; and (ii) urban developers started showing interest in city-centre projects. One example of this early activity in urban regeneration is the city of Newark, New Jersey.

Newark, New Jersey

Newark suffered devastating urban riots in the 1960s, which had lasting negative impacts of the growth and development of the city centre for several decades. However, during the 1990s it underwent significant revitalisation after becoming home to the seventh largest arts centre in the United States, the New Jersey Performing Arts Centre (NJPAC). The centre was established with a vision that it would provide a catalyst for the evolution of a major new cultural precinct in Newark, spurring the growth of other institutions and encouraging the development of facilities including restaurants, cafes, retail establishments and office buildings (Psilos & Rapp, 2001). The plan has been successful with NJPAC contributing to the reversal of the prevalent image of Newark as a moribund city. The centre provides a venue for world-class artists and attracts audiences from all over New Jersey (approximately 4.5 million people live within a 35 kilometre radius of Newark). It has spurred an unprecedented revitalisation of Newark with developers and tenants recognising its new potential, and now the city is witnessing the return of several sports teams, new restaurants, the development of an underground high-tech culture and the opening of new small business enterprises (Psilos & Rapp, 2001).

Such early approaches to community regeneration in North America provided a model for future activities around the world. In Europe, on the other hand, the regeneration process was motivated not only by the fiscal objective to stimulate economic development of declining inner-city neighbourhoods but also by the desire to reclaim and protect social traditions and heritage. Spain's Barcelona exemplifies urban regeneration that aimed to stimulate economic growth while protecting and revitalising social and cultural traditions.

Barcelona, Spain

The Ajuntament (Barcelona's city council) aimed to create a lively, dynamic city that valued its social and cultural traditions. It prioritised the use of lands for parks and created temporary orders for the use of specified land as parks. It then adopted the concept of allowing artists and architects a great deal of freedom, thus stimulating creative and imaginative approaches to the design and planning of parks. Coupled with the Catalan tradition of and love for the surreal and the colourful, the concept of temporary parks encouraged artists to design and build quirky, humorous spaces and works in the city's parks. Parks and sculptures now link the whole of Barcelona and the city has the largest public art program of any city in Europe. The city has also secured its place as a new world international capital, while retaining and protecting its distinct regional identity (Landry et al., 1996).

Melbourne, Australia, is a city acknowledged as an international leader in innovative urban design that has recognised the connection between urban design and liveability.

Melbourne, Australia

Over 20 years ago, Melbourne recognised the importance of good urban design when it launched the Save Collins Street campaign. The character of Collins Street, a major city street famed for its unique architecture and Victorian streetscapes, was being threatened by high-rise development. The Victorian Government responded to community concerns by introducing planning procedures to safeguard the street frontage by ensuring new buildings maintain the original Victorian façades. This philosophy has provided the framework to ensure planning sensitivity in other developments including the development of Southbank, which opened up pedestrian access along Melbourne's river, and, more recently, the redevelopment of the Docklands (Landry & Wood, 2003).

However, the impact of regeneration activities is not only experienced by whole cities; it also impacts neighbourhoods and small communities within cities. The Aurora Arts project provides an example of how arts activities can create new productive uses for underutilised neighbourhood spaces.

Aurora Arts, Chicago

Aurora Arts operates in the Chicago neighbourhood of Logan Square and seeks to provide connections between adults and children, and residents and artists through arts activities. To overcome its major challenge, which was to find venues in which to conduct its activities, Aurora Arts forged an alliance with local churches that were, at that time, facing significant declines in the use of their facilities. The partnership served the needs of both the arts organisations and the local church groups. The arts programming bought new people to the church facilities while providing Aurora Arts with the space to fulfil its community mission (Grams & Warr, 2003).

In Manhattan, a park created on an old, crumbling railway line has become a major tourist attraction, transforming the line itself and bringing new life to surrounding areas.

The High Line, New York City

The High Line Park has been created on a heavy, black steel structure supporting an elevated rail line that once brought freight cars into factories and warehouses. Until recently, the High Line was a crumbling urban relic that many residents and public officials wanted to tear down. Early demolition orders were challenged and residents of the neighbourhoods around the line formed a non-profit organisation, Friends of the High Line. They advocated for the line's preservation and reuse as public open space and commenced fundraising to save the line. In total, funders of the High Line Park raised more than $150 million and, as public support grew, the New York City government committed $50 million.

As a result, the old freight line has been turned into one of the most innovative and inviting public spaces in New York City. The black steel columns that once supported abandoned train tracks now hold up an elevated park — part promenade, part town square, part botanical garden. Walking on the High Line is unlike any other experience in New York. You float about 25 feet above the ground, at once connected to street life and far away from it. You can sit surrounded by carefully tended plantings and take in the sun and the Hudson River views, or you can walk the line as it slices between old buildings and past striking new ones (Goldberger, 2011).

The success of the High Line has spawned similar initiatives throughout the United States. One example is in Indiana, where the small city of Bloomington has created the B-line trail along a disused rail corridor. The trail incorporates design features such as street name paver treatments at each crossing, a human/pet drinking fountain, park benches, limestone accents, trees, and landscaping.

Economic Vitality through Cultural Tourism

While almost all approaches to community development recognise and value the economic potential of tourism, some programs focus explicitly on supporting and promoting local tourism. For example, the rural community of Tifton in South Georgia has focused on developing specific venues to attract tourists to spend at least one or two days in the community exploring the local arts and crafts.

Tifton, South Georgia

In a bid to attract tourists, Tifton developed two new venues: the Tifton Museum of Arts and Heritage, and the Georgia Agriama. The Georgia Agriama provides a concrete example of the way the arts can be used to directly stimulate community development through tourism. It was conceived and developed as a living history museum and incorporates exhibits of the traditional arts and crafts of Georgia. It attracts over 60,000 visitors a year to Tifton. Both the Agriama and the Tifton Museum of Arts and Heritage have prompted the redevelopment of nearby properties as galleries, retail outlets, cafes and restaurants and other services to cater for increasing tourist numbers (Phillips, 2004).

The arts and culture, history and heritage are also central to the development of Tasmanian tourism.

Hobart, Tasmania

The Tasmanian Government has supported several interlocking projects including the revitalisation of the Hobart waterfront as a 'cultural quarter', which encompasses the redevelopment of the Tasmanian Museum and Art Gallery and the redevelopment of Princes Wharf as a flexible multi-use arts and events space. The revitalisation has also stimulated the development of luxury accommodation and high-end retail outlets. The government has supported the development of the Glenorchy Arts and Sculpture Park linking the Elwick Bay area of Hobart from Wilkinson's Point through to Montrose Bay and the new Museum of Old and New Art. The government has lead the

World Heritage listing of five of Tasmania's most significant convict sites, including the Port Arthur Historic Site and the Brickendon and Woolmers Estates. While these state-based initiatives in cultural tourism are impressive, there are also some interesting locally managed examples of arts and heritage tourism experiences in Tasmania. For example, the Trail of the Tin Dragon is a major project that celebrates the history of tin mining and the cultural contribution of the Chinese to North East Tasmania (Lebski, 2010).

Perhaps the most significant Tasmanian Tourism initiative is the Museum of Old and New Art, which was officially opened in January 2012.

The Museum of Old and New Art (MONA), Hobart, Tasmania

The Museum of Old and New Art (MONA) is the largest privately funded museum in Australia. The museum presents antiquities, modern and contemporary art from the David Walsh collection. Since opening, Mona has seen 1.4 million people through its doors, 65 per cent of them interstate and overseas visitors. According to Tourism Tasmania, in 2014 it attracted 330,000 visitors, or around 28 per cent of all visitors to Tasmania. Crucially, these tourists are also spending money elsewhere in the state. In the period from its opening to June 2004, visitors to MONA in that period spent $606 million locally during their trip — $244 million on accommodation and $254 million on other items — a 13 per cent increase from previous years. Research conducted for Tourism Tasmania shows that MONA has created a new conversation about Tasmania and what the island state is all about. It has also stimulated the development of a range of new cultural and food experiences in Hobart and throughout Tasmania (Teaque, 2015).

The Queensland Government has also invested significantly in the development of tourism through its Heritage Trails Network.

Heritage Trails Network, Queensland

The Queensland Heritage Trails Networks links important historical and cultural sites throughout western Queensland, allowing tourists to plan their journeys to incorporate key attractions. A major aspect of the network is the Matilda Highway journey, which allows tourists to visit attractions including the Charleville Cosmos Centre, which enables visitors to study crystal clear night skies and learn how Aborigines used them for food gathering and navigation. The centre includes an observatory with four telescopes and a multimedia Indigenous theatre. Another feature is the Australian Stockman's Hall of Fame, which celebrates, through displays and exhibits, the icons of the Queensland outback and their contribution to Australia's pastoral industry. The network also includes the Winton Lark Quarry – Dinosaur Trackways, which is believed to be the only preserved evidence in the world of a dinosaur stampede. A major conservation work has been carried out to preserve this prehistoric marvel for future generations (Cook, 2001).

Not all cultural tourism projects are linked to major government initiatives; the Ulysses Link Pathway Project demonstrates how a small-scale activity managed within a community can have major impacts not only on the promotion of local tourism but also on the development and maintenance of community pride and cohesion.

The Ulysses Link, Mission Beach, Queensland

Named after the brilliant blue Ulysses butterflies that inhabit the area, a 1.5-kilometre Ulysses Link Tourist Walking Track has been created along the foreshore at Mission Beach. The history of the Mission Beach area has been interwoven along the walk with both Indigenous and historical stories expressed through mosaics, carvings and ceramic sculptures created by local artists. Fourteen local North Queensland artists worked together to develop the walkway. The artists worked with fruit farmers, tourist operators, steel fabricators, conservation groups and other members of the local community. The link has become a major tourist attraction and has stimulated further community infrastructure/public art initiatives including a children's playground, a meeting piazza and a sculpture park (Arts Queensland, 2007a).

However, the link between culture tourism, the arts and economic vitality may not always be direct, and the experience of Singapore is instructive in this respect.

Singapore

Singapore's commercial success during the latter part of the last century as a major transport hub and a shopping capital resulted in a significant part of its heritage and culture being destroyed, and there was very little reinvestment in culture and the arts. 'It didn't take long for the government to realise that it had created a city that was super shiny and commercially successful, but lacked soul' (Archer, 2009, p. 6). During the last two decades, the Singapore Government has begun to invest in the arts by renovating galleries and museums; establishing arts grants programs for small contemporary companies and individual artists; assisting companies and artists to find studio space in the city; renovating and building new Esplanade Theatres on the bay; and establishing an international festival of the arts. Now the arts are thriving in Singapore,

> making it again an interesting place to stop over and visitor numbers are increasing. The reclamation of the soul of commercially focused Singapore through the arts demonstrates not only the power of the arts to create ambiance, atmosphere, passion, and a sense of identity and purpose, but also clearly illustrates the link between the arts and economic growth and sustainability (Archer, 2009).

The link between cultural tourism and economic vitality is not, however, limited to the arts. Singapore has also used its scientific and architectural achievements to stimulate tourism.

> **Marina Barrage, Singapore**
>
> The Marina Barrage is considered Singapore's latest downtown icon. It is a 350-metre-wide dam built across the Marina Channel to keep out seawater. This colossal architectural masterpiece allows tourists to walk through the barrage's vast compounds and come face to face with stunning engineering equipment. Tourists can visit the gallery and discover how the Marina Barrage ingeniously prevents flooding to the city's low-lying areas. Or simply stand atop the green roof to take in the sweeping Singapore city skyline. The Barrage combines tourism, architecture, science and education into a unique visitor experience (Singapore Travel Guide, 2012).

Business Incubation and the Stimulation of New Enterprises

Business incubation has become a widely recognised and well-utilised economic development tool designed to foster and stimulate economic growth through new business opportunities. It has been successfully applied by governments and private enterprises. Governments have usually adopted business incubation processes to stimulate the achievement of broad economic goals such as job creation and economic diversification. Private enterprises have used business incubators to test and pilot new products and services not only to check viability but also to facilitate the development of new markets. The approach often includes shared administrative and other services, centralised space and business development assistance provided in a facility where new and experienced businesses operate (Phillips, 2004). While there is little evidence that business incubation has been widely adopted in rural and remote communities as a strategy to support economic development, there are some examples of how the arts have provided a context for successful business incubation. Through business incubation approaches, artists and craftspeople can achieve lower costs by accessing shared services and facilities. More importantly, they can access advice and resources in a way that allows them to develop new business skills and make sound business decisions, drawing on the knowledge and understanding of experienced business people.

One interesting example is the Jubilee Business Incubator, which was funded and operated by a community coalition in Sneedville, Tennessee.

Jubilee Business Incubator, Sneedville, Tennessee

Skilled craftsmanship is a key part of the history and heritage of the small Tennessee community of Sneedville. The Jubilee Business Incubator project emerged as a way to preserve and protect local arts and crafts while addressing broader community concerns. The incubator program provides (i) affordable rent to small arts-based businesses, (ii) access to shared office facilities such as computers, internet, printers and copiers, (iii) the provision of business advice and counselling from experienced business people, and (iv) access to market intelligence including the timing and location of local markets and festivals. The Jubilee Incubator is housed in a centrally located, renovated building and includes a retail store for arts and crafts products, a classroom for small business development programs and a computer training room for business training and market research (Phillips, 2004).

The Entergy Arts Business Centre in New Orleans, Louisiana, which aims to help local artists learn fundamental skills necessary to operate small businesses, is another such example.

Entergy Arts Business Centre, New Orleans, Louisiana

The Arts Business Centre is funded and supported by the Entergy Corporation, local arts councils and revenues generated from centre programs. The goal of the centre is to support the creation and development of arts-based business. It offers rental space and shared office services to small arts-based start-up businesses. Also available are business development programs including business planning, financial management, marketing and legal programs focusing on commercial propriety and copyright law. The centre also provides initial market tests for artists by linking with commercial agents who advise on market demand for new arts products (Phillips, 2004).

Business incubation is simply one mechanism to stimulate and support the development of new enterprises. Other mechanisms include the development of collaborative partnerships, the operation of business networks, the creation of regional hubs and the operation of franchise agreements. One example of a successful collaborative partnership is the venture between Aboriginal artists in South Australia's remote Aṉangu Pitjantjatjara Yankunytjatjara lands, 500 kilometres south-west of Alice Springs, and the traditional craftspeople of Kashmir, in India's north.

Arts Partnership — Australian Aboriginal Artists and Kashmir Craftspeople

Both groups (South Australia's remote Aṉangu Pitjantjatjara Yankunytjatjara people and the traditional craftspeople of Kashmir, in India's north) share not only a love of arts and crafts but also a determination to improve life in their respective communities. From these mutual interests sprung a unique business collaboration through which the Aboriginal artists send their traditional designs to Kashmir where the local craftspeople apply them to handmade rugs, cushions and lacquer boxes. The unique products are sold worldwide and have provided the base for a thriving business. The rugs are sold as limited editions and have been purchased by galleries and museums, including the National Museum of Canberra (Williams, 2005).

As well as incubators, arts cooperatives can be an effective conduit for arts-based business development. These are typically formed by groups of local artists organising non-profit organisations to market and promote their works. The Craftsman's Guild of Mississippi in Jackson provides one such successful example.

Jackson, Mississippi

The Craftsman's Guild of Mississippi was formed to preserve and protect the folk, traditional and contemporary crafts of the Mississippi area. The guild set high standards of excellence in arts and crafts. By ensuring high standards, the guild developed a reputation as one of the best arts cooperatives in the regions. In turn, the guild has impacted on the community of Jackson in positive ways. Their projects have attracted visitors to the areas, generating new revenue streams. The guild has also sponsored community-based continuing education programs, and has created a strong market for local arts and crafts (Phillips, 2004).

Other communities have attempted to use arts-based business development as an overall community development strategy. That is, rather than serving as one component of the plan, the arts becomes the foundation of the plan.

Bellows Falls, Vermont

Bellows Falls was a town suffering serious economic decline. The Vermont Community Development Association sought to redevelop and revitalise the community through creative ideas and the arts. As a result, the Rockingham Arts and Museum Project (RAMP) was developed to stimulate the village of Bellows Falls to take charge of their future. RAMP did not just organise arts events but integrated art into the overall community development plans, including infrastructure development. For example, RAMP renovated an historic building in the community that was considered one the Vermont's most important architectural legacies. The renovation allowed the building to provide affordable space for artists' studios and arts retail places (Phillips, 2004).

Link between the Arts and a Creative Workforce

Another strong theme identified in earlier chapters is the growing importance of the arts and culture to a region's attractiveness to companies and their potential workforces. The success of some cities and regions in marketing their cultural offerings to lure new companies to establish or relocate their operations has been well documented (Florida, 2002; Gertler, 2004; Psilos, 2002). The recognition that the factors in attracting firms and jobs to cities or regions are now much more complex than just bottom line concerns such as office space, transport and tax benefits is well established. The local government of Austin, Texas, recognised at an early stage that its unique cultural environment was a competitive asset to the new economy. Austin has built a world-class high-technology economy on the base of a thriving cultural life (Psilos & Rapp, 2001).

Austin, Texas

Austin adopted a deliberate strategy to grow high-tech industry and employment while preserving cultural vibrancy as a key competitive asset. In order to attract and retain high-tech workers, the Austin community leadership recognised the need to ensure a high-quality lifestyle based on the arts.

The Austin community leveraged state funds to support local arts and raised $3.5 million through a hotel-based bed tax. As a result, overall funding for the arts increased and Austin now has a vibrant and sustainable arts community that contributes to a quality of life that makes working and living in Austin an attractive proposition for new economy workers (Psilos & Rapp, 2001).

Other cities, such as Stavanger in Norway, are working towards creating a vibrant cultural sector as a way of attracting and retaining a creative workforce for the future.

Stavanger, Norway

Stavanger is Norway's fourth largest city and its oil capital. While it has a fairly small population of 110,000 people, it has the youngest demographic profile in Norway and the population includes citizens from over 90 countries. The wages and career opportunities in the oil industry are attractive to many workers.

Stavanger is aware that the oil advantage has a limited time span and the local council is promoting its development as a cultural city. It is deliberately developing a cultural sector to appeal to high-earning global workers as it believes that a vibrant cultural life is a key way to attract a creative workforce to contribute to the long-term future of Stavanger.

Specifically, Stavanger is building a world-class concert hall for its renowned symphony orchestra. The city also hosts the annual Stavanger International Festival of Literature and Freedom of Speech (Landry & Wood, 2003).

Perhaps one of the most successful cities in attracting and retaining creative workers is Portland, Oregon. Portland ranks very high on a variety of creative indices (Bulick et al., 2003) and provides an interesting example of how communities are using culture to attract talent and build creative economies.

Portland, Oregon

Portland has developed a larger and more diverse mix of cultural organisations, artists and cultural projects than any other like-sized city in the United States. There are a high number of small organisations encompassing avant-garde theatre, film, video, new media, new music and contemporary dance. These have added enormous range, interest and quality to the robust and diverse cultural scene.

Portland's public art program, which is one of the largest and most innovative in the United States, has changed the face of the built environment and provided enormous opportunities for artists.

While this vibrant cultural scene is critical in attracting new workers to Portland, another key advantage over other cities and towns is its informal civic culture. People, including newcomers, feel they can get involved and have impact across politics, community development, planning and the cultural scene. Access and participation are welcomed. New community organisations, coalitions and movements are continually developing (Bulick et al., 2003).

The Role of the Arts in Creating Vibrant Community Spaces

Public buildings and spaces are critical to shaping our environments and send powerful messages to communities about values and beliefs. The arts and artists have a key role to play in working with governments to create vibrant public spaces that contribute significantly to the liveability and amenity of communities. There are many examples demonstrating the role of public art in contributing not only to liveability but also to the development of social and economic growth in communities. Indeed, many of the examples already showcased have a public art component to their success (e.g. the parks of Barcelona and the Ulysses Link in Mission Beach). The East Perth Public Art Project provides another example.

East Perth Public Art Project

Claisebrook Cove in East Perth has been transformed from an industrial wasteland into a thriving waterfront community, combining quality residential and commercial development with beautiful parkland, waterways and public art. Five minutes from the Perth CBD, it is an example of how urban designers, landscape architects and artists have created imaginative buildings, street furniture, landscape features and stand-alone works of art.

Many pieces express East Perth's history and some are made from materials found on the redevelopment site or salvaged from old buildings. The area also has pathways and cycleways that provide views of the Swan River and city skyline. It has a unique mix of restaurants, cafés and a variety of great specialty stores (Active Healthy Communities Initiative, 2009).

A more systemic approach to the provision of public art is provided by the Queensland Government's Art Built-in project.

Art Built-in, Queensland Government

The Queensland Government established Art Build-in to stimulate the inclusion of public art in public buildings and spaces. The Art Built-in policy determines that 2 per cent of each capital works building budget over $250,000 will be allocated for the inclusion of public art. In this way, the program integrates art and design into public buildings and spaces rather than simply adding pictures and sculptures after the building project is completed. To achieve this, the project actively encourages the involvement of Queensland artists in the planning, design and development stages of building projects. Such involvement might include the design of gardens and other open spaces, the design of fabric for use in interiors, the creation of murals, tiles or other decorative or functional features, and the creation of sculptures and painting integrated with the building design. Not only do the outcomes enhance people's experiences of government buildings, it also provides opportunities to showcase Queensland artists (Queensland Government Public Art Policy, 2001).

Using New Technologies to Support Community Development

The role of technology in supporting and facilitating growth opportunities has emerged as an important new aspect to community development. Technology can provide opportunities to expand access to markets and support business development in small and micro businesses, especially those remote from major business hubs. This has been demonstrated through a recent project that examined how e-commerce technologies can be used to help small Aboriginal arts businesses in Gippsland and the Yarra Valley region expand their offerings in the Australian mainstream arts market.

Art and e-commerce — Australian Aboriginal Art Businesses, Gippsland and Yarra Valley, Victoria

Aboriginal businesses in rural Victoria face specific difficulties in managing their businesses including limited business infrastructure (e.g. credit card facilities, PCs, telephone lines) and poor customer management skills. Businesses were further disadvantaged in developing wholesale channels because of their distance from metropolitan consumers. This project provided technologies (and training in their use) to Aboriginal art businesses. The project allowed the businesses to expand their markets to include consumers across Australia and overseas at a minimal cost through e-commerce. Sales increased significantly over the term of the project (Choi & O'Brien, 2002).

There are many more examples of how new technologies are being used by communities to enhance their economic competitiveness. However, these examples must be treated with caution, as generalisations of the benefits of technologies in community development may be misleading. Many community-building programs with a focus on the application of technology are seeking to achieve broad objectives relating to economic development, job growth and business development. The technology is not an end in itself but rather 'a means to a larger end with clear and compelling benefits to communities' (Eger, 2003, p. 7).

An interesting example that uses technology to document and record local points of cultural interests is the CHIMER Project involving children living across Europe.

CHIMER Project

CHIMER capitalises on the natural enthusiasm and curiosity of children by using technologies to document items of cultural interest in local communities. Children aged nine to 12 from different parts of Europe build 'digital maps' of cultural points of interest by combining geographical coordinates detected using GPS devices, mobile technologies and digital cameras. Children combine drawings and photographic images with their own comments explaining the significance of the places and items of interest. In this way, the children create a digital archive of their towns, villages and surrounding communities. For example, children create in digital space their own understandings and images of Lithuanian cultural heritage objects, which other children (and adults) throughout Europe (and the world) can access and use (Weiss, 2004).

The Role of the Arts in Enhancing Social Cohesion and Community Building

Since Deidre Williams' (2000) landmark study outlining the significant social benefits of the arts to communities, multiple studies have reported and elaborated on the role of the arts in building social networks, maintaining social cohesion and building community identity (Grams & Warr, 2003).

Arts activities and programs can create a sense of belonging to a community by providing processes and structures for social interaction. They can contribute to the development of social skills such as collaboration and cooperation, as exemplified by the Scrap Mettle Soul project.

Scrap Mettle Soul, Uptown, Chicago

The Scrap Mettle Soul project gathers community stories from diverse people, employs professionals to write scripts, builds sets in partnership with community residents, and produces an annual production featuring residents. The actors are everyday citizens of different races and classes. The productions are also intergenerational, involving people from ages four to 91.

The activity of putting on a play is a way for diverse members of the community to get to know each other in a relatively neutral context. People who start out as strangers, wary of each other, become associates, colleagues and even friends as they work to put on the play (Grams & Warr, 2003).

The potential of art to integrate isolated and marginalised communities is also evident through work undertaken with the community of Northcott in Sydney, which demonstrates how the arts can assist in reducing isolation, challenging entrenched stereotypes, validating individual experiences and encouraging the development of trusting relationships.

The Northcott Narratives, Northcott, Sydney

By 2002, Northcott was a seriously traumatised community; people lived in fear and were seriously disadvantaged. Due to a series of unfavourable press reports, the community and its members were stereotyped and residents were trapped in a spiral of fear, disgust and uncertainty.

The Northcott Narratives project set out to provide community members with an opportunity to make stories based on their experiences living in Northcott. The project resulted in a film, *Can you Hear Them?*, that told the real stories of the Northcott residents. The film was just the beginning and the community continued to tell their stories through text, photos and painting and drawing. More and more community members became involved and, as they did, their expectations of themselves and each other were raised and community trust increased. As confidence increased, community benefits began to flow. While the residents are still disadvantaged, they have built new levels of community involvement and engagement (Mayo, 2005).

Community festivals can also stimulate community pride and lead to higher levels of community cohesion through social networking and the development of a sense of belonging.

The Woodford Folk Festival, Woodford, Queensland

The Woodford Folk Festival is one of Australia's most famous festivals and, falling as it does between Christmas and New Year, provides a chance to review the past and plan the future in an atmosphere of communal celebration. Ritual that draws the community together is a significant part of the festival program. A sense of community arises in the three minutes silence before New Year and the evening processions that weave through the village linking the community in shared experience. The Woodford Folk Festival also maintains a deep commitment to Indigenous themes and issues. Central to Aboriginal culture is a strong sense of family and connection to the land and community, which is something that the festival aspires to create (Queensland Community Arts Network, 2003).

Other projects work to build cohesion by rallying the community to protect its resources. The Bundaleer Weekend seeks to consolidate community effort to protect the Bundaleer Forest, Australia's first plantation of pine trees, which dates back to 1876.

The Bundaleer Weekend, Jamestown, South Australia

The Bundaleer Weekend at Jamestown, South Australia, is an opportunity for a two-day immersion in fine art, music, adventure, heritage and culture. The purpose of the weekend was twofold. Firstly, it was developed to increase tourism to the Jamestown region. Secondly, it was conducted to draw attention to the need to protect and preserve a local environmental treasure, the Bundaleer Forest.

The event takes place in the forest and includes concerts, art exhibitions and performances. A carnival atmosphere is achieved through street stalls, street bands and guided walks through the forest. Participation in the event has increased significantly over the last 10 years and the weekend attracts visitors from all over the world (Murphy, 2004).

The Role of the Arts in Reducing Antisocial Behaviour

The arts provide positive outlets and build new skills that give people, especially young people, a chance at a better life. Arts programs have proved to be an effective intervention strategy for young people who have failed to respond to more traditional education and social services programs (Birch, 2002; Fiske, 1999). Arts learning experiences can alter the perception young people have of themselves and their attitudes toward learning, even among those who have already had serious brushes with the law (Birch, 2002).

Projects such as the Skudda Arts Powerhouse program provide new opportunities for youth at risk to grow and learn.

Skudda Arts Powerhouse Program, Fitzroy Crossing, Western Australia

For Aboriginal youth in Fitzroy Crossing, 'skudda' means 'cool' or 'excellent'. The Skudda Arts Powerhouse is a community arts initiative that connects Aboriginal teenagers with art projects designed to stimulate and appeal but also to connect them with the wider community.

Arts workshops were tailored specifically to connect with the interests of the young people of the community (e.g. designing and printing T-shirts, jewellery making, music-making workshops, dance workshops, etc.). Community relationships have improved, especially between the youth and authority figures, and the local Aboriginal police liaison unit is now involved with the initiative (Murphy, 2004).

Other initiatives target specific problems including homelessness, family breakdowns and mental health problems.

Creative Youth Initiative

Mission Australia's Creative Youth Initiative provides free creative programs for young people facing serious problems in their lives. Typically, the young people participating in the program are homeless, suffering mental health problems or coming to terms with family breakdowns.

With the support of musicians, artists, photographers and social workers, students are assisted and encouraged to use art as an outlet for the issues they are confronting every day (Darling, 2008).

The Role of the Arts in Developing Self-Confidence

The role of the arts in learning and personal development is becoming increasingly important not just to teachers and educators but also to policymakers, researchers and community leaders (Gadsden, 2008; Peppler & Davis, 2010). Research now shows that children who study the arts demonstrate stronger overall academic performance. Arts programs also improve student's self-confidence, build communication and problem-solving skills, and prepare young people to be creative thinkers (Birch, 2002; Fiske, 1999; Rabkin & Redmond, 2006). Exposure to the arts provides positive general learning outcomes, particularly for young people who are Indigenous, in remote or regional communities, or from disadvantaged backgrounds (Bryce et al., 2004).

The *Pardar Kerkar Noh Erpei* Catching a Wave project was an exhibition of works from schoolchildren from the Darnley Island State School in the Torres Strait, where a new cross-curriculum learning focus was reported as dramatically raising literacy levels and the confidence and self-esteem of learners.

Pardar Kerkar Noh Erpei Catching a Wave, Darnley Island State School, Torres Strait

This project was a joint venture arrangement between the Darnley Island Art Centre, the Darnley Island State School, and the Cairns Regional Art Gallery. The core of the project was a children's art exhibition of sea themes produced by 19 Darnley Island students aged between nine and 13. But the main focus was to use the exhibition as a catalyst to support the cross-curriculum literacy initiatives at the school, in this instance through art. Each artwork was accompanied by statements written by the artist explaining the motivation and connection with the art.

While the exhibition succeeded in its intention to introduce Indigenous culture to gallery visitors, the real achievement was in the lives of the Darnley Island community. It was a source of wonder and pride for the children to see their artworks carefully packed in modular containers and stacked on board the barge for Cairns. The need to produce signage and a book for the exhibition motivated the students to higher literacy standards (Murphy, 2004).

Similar arts-based programs have been shown to help students feel more confident about themselves and the contribution they can make, which, in turn, helps them feel more positive about themselves as learners.

Boys Business Program, Northern Territory

Boys Business is a music program that focuses on using music to develop learning skills and enhance self-esteem. While the program is essentially a music and movement program, its influence extends well beyond music. The program is designed to help young men feel good about themselves; there is plenty of time for talking and the program encourages learners to reflect on their strengths and weaknesses. Evaluations of the program have indicated that students participating in the program have improved self-confidence and have developed meta-cognitive skills, such as reflection. There is also evidence that literacy and numeracy skills have improved and that students have a new purpose for learning that is authentic and, as a consequence, they feel good about being at school.

Specific attributes of the program that have been identified as contributing to positive learning include the provision of a positive role model and a learning environment that is non-threatening, where all learners are respected, and where tolerance and self-control are fostered (Bryce et al., 2004).

Broader Impacts of the Arts on Communities

There are many other ways the arts can impact on communities. They can provide a springboard for new skills and new opportunities, they can help communities celebrate place and history, and they can stimulate creativity and diversity in communities.

The Alice Springs Beanie Festival provides an example of how the arts can celebrate and add value to existing community products.

Alice Springs Beanie Festival, Alice Springs, Northern Territory

From humble beginnings, the Alice Springs Beanie Festival now attracts over 3,000 entries. It attracts interest from craft groups and fibre art associations from around Australia. The Alice Springs festival celebrates traditional Indigenous and non-Indigenous women's crafts, as well as bringing together a community of fibre artists from around Australia. While most items are for sale, the festival organisers have worked hard to ensure the festival spirit is not overtaken by an emphasis on retail — a festival celebrating craft rather than a craft market.

The activity started in 1996 as an opportunity to sell excess beanies crocheted by local Aboriginal women and has grown into a significant festival. The beanie has become a fashion statement and a central Australian art form. It grew through commitment and hard work and has not been subsidised. It is run on good will and friendships (Murphy, 2004).

Despite the best intentions, the arts do not always result in positive outcomes for communities. The following example from Santa Ana illustrates how programs and initiatives may lead to community divisions.

Santa Ana, California

Santa Ana is Orange County's largest and poorest city. There is a deep division between the city's poor, Hispanic majority population and its affluent, white minority. Over 10 years ago, Santa Ana proclaimed itself the arts and culture city of Orange County and aimed to use the arts to promote development through the revitalisation of the downtown district, increasing commercial activity, and improving intercultural relations.

The project focused on the development of infrastructure to support and accommodate the arts — specifically, the development of the artists' village and the Bowers Museum. These developments house a range of venues and regularly attract audiences and visitors to the areas. However, many of these visitors are from other towns and cities and the majority are white middle-class people. This generates economic activity that impacts positively on property values and development, and achieves encouraging outcomes. But it further

> isolates the poor Hispanic population and, far from achieving its aim of improving intercultural relations, the project has further divided the community.
>
> The project has not influenced this divide and has, in fact, effectively excluded Hispanics from development efforts. The art programs have further divided the community along class and ethnic lines. (Note that this refers only to those initiatives planned and implemented by the city; the Hispanic population has rich organic, grass roots art practices that contribute to their quality of life.) (Mattern, 2001)

Other projects are novel and provide entertainment and enjoyment while bringing communities together as an audience for special events.

> Bobcat Dancing, Mt Isa, Queensland
>
> The project staged a ballet in the dry bed of the Leichhardt River in Mt Isa, Queensland. The ballet was performed by several three-tonne bobcat machines that spun, twirled and balanced to a live band. The ballet's backdrop was the Mt Isa Mines smoke stacks and was a tribute to the town's lifeblood industry. The project aimed to make music accessible to regional communities. There were three performances that attracted 18,000 people (Queensland Community Arts Network, 2003).

Urban Versus Rural and Remote

The initiatives demonstrate creativity and illustrate how various communities have worked successfully to overcome challenges and develop innovative and often inspirational approaches to support renewal and development. However, the majority are to be found in urban communities. While some may stimulate ideas that could be applied in rural and remote communities, there are few existing models directly applicable to the specific contemporary challenges faced by rural and remote communities.

6

The Unique Challenges of Investigating Rural and Remote Communities

Difference and Distinctiveness

It is demonstrably clear that rural and remote communities are facing significant challenges arising from ongoing social and economic change occurring on a global scale. Extant approaches to community development and capacity building stress the need for communities to address challenges actively by identifying and building on existing community resources, including those deriving from natural, human and social capital. Emerging approaches to the development of creative and innovative communities stress the need for alternative community approaches based on new knowledge and fresh opportunities arising from innovative understandings about the centrality of creativity in human development. In this context, the arts have strong potential to contribute significantly to building creative, vibrant and dynamic communities. However, (i) there is limited direction about potential approaches to the application of the arts in community development, (ii) there are few good practice exemplars of arts-based community development, and (iii) models on which future applications might be based are not available.

More specifically, much of current documented practice is based on traditional perceptions of the arts, often focusing solely on the production of art products or the operations and processes of art producers. A concentration solely on tangible artistic outcomes overlooks the role of the arts in the broader warp and weft of community life, especially in relation to its potential in the development of human and social capital. Much of the current research focuses on the scope and size of the arts market and aims to identify the economic impact of the arts on cities, regions and communities. This approach, while providing some base economic data, contributes little to an understanding of how creative work can help communities change and grow. It also limits understanding of what districts and towns might do to foster more robust, creative communities. Moreover, many current programs focus on the role of the arts in urban regeneration so that there is little documentation of the experiences of rural and remote communities. To compound the problem, there are few case studies from the Australian context; most of the documented experiences of communities emanate from the United Kingdom, Canada and the United States.

In order to broaden and deepen our understanding of the role of the arts in community development, contemporary models and approaches must be re-examined and re-envisaged in the context of rural and remote communities. A strong platform of reinvigorated and remodelled information must be established on which to expand our understanding of the role of the arts in rural and remote communities. Such a platform might result in the distillation of key principles and the development of new models for communities to base future development plans. Hence, the remainder of this book focuses on the rural/remote context through:

1. An examination of the viability and sustainability of existing approaches to community development in rural and remote communities
2. Scoping the current and potential role and function of the arts in supporting community development approaches
3. Probing the nature and scope of specific roles and functions of the arts in community development through contrasting case studies
4. A development of a new model for community development in rural and remote communities.

Challenges in Examining Arts-Based Community Development

An examination of the role of the arts in community development in rural and remote communities presents some specific challenges. The first arises from the fact that arts-based disciplines are multifaceted; the second from the understanding that community development is a broad concept that has relevance to all communities, from urban neighbourhoods to remote Indigenous communities. Lastly, there is a significant definitional problem in terms of how to draw a meaningful line between urban, rural and remote communities.

The Span of the Arts

An examination of the multifacetedness of arts-based disciplines indicates that the concept of the arts might encompass book and magazine publishing, the visual arts (painting, sculpture), the performing arts (theatre, opera, concerts, dance), sound recordings, film and television, multimedia and the electronic arts, even advertising, fashion, toys and games. Likewise, an examination of community development might include urban regeneration, regional and rural development, or the revitalisation of remote communities; it might focus on community health, social services, tourism or agriculture. It is thus necessary to sharpen the focus while maintaining the integrity of the primary task: to determine the potential of the arts, artists and art organisations to contribute to the sustainability and rejuvenation of small remote/rural communities.

Focusing on the arts perspective offers a significant challenge. Contemporary approaches to the creation and presentation of the arts extend well beyond technical mastery and encompass personal development through critical reflection, creative problem solving and decision making, interpersonal effectiveness through collaboration and team work, a dedication to innovation and quality, and a commitment to continuous improvement and lifelong learning.

Selecting one or two of the sectors of the arts that demonstrate these qualities in practice has the potential to focus the examination and make it more manageable. However, such a solution would ignore the importance of collaboration across the arts, the complexity of organisational patterns in the arts sector, the diversity within and across the arts community, the distinctiveness of processes within each subcategory of the arts, and contemporary developments in hybrid, multi-arts, and interdisciplinary approaches to creative endeavours. Additionally, to focus on a single category as a specific perspective would limit any consideration of the particular interests and idiosyncratic talents residing across rural and remote communities.

Consequently, this investigation will encompass the potential of all aspects of the arts from painting to performance, from film to festivals, from drama to dance, and beyond to the ever-expanding new media arts such as digital animation, web design, computer graphics and games. In such an environment, it is essential to provide some parameters to chart the territory for the research. Although all definitions of art are necessarily arbitrary and ultimately problematic, it is necessary to have a framework to guide this investigation of the impact of the arts on community rejuvenation and sustainability. Obviously it needs to be broad and forward looking not only to encompass the traditional arts as well as new and emerging art forms but also to incorporate the arts in their dual role as explorations into the meaning and purpose of human life and creative products and processes adding social and economic value to communities. Consequently, the framework for the investigation is based on the understanding that all arts-based products and processes have their origin in 'individual skill, creativity and talent and each has the potential for wealth and job creation through the exploitation of intellectual property' (Cunningham, 2006, p. 5).

The Overarching Concept of Community Development

While community development, both concept and strategy, has relevance for all communities, its application in and for rural and remote communities must acknowledge that contemporary political, technological, social and economic pressures are impacting heavily on these communities (Cavaye, 2000). In turn, they are being challenged to shift from traditional industries to knowledge-based industries, they are bearing the brunt of pressing ecological concerns and changing social mindsets, and are fighting demographic trends leading to an ageing rural population. Community development programs recognise that these continuing economic and social transformations may result in an ever more divided society with even more deeply entrenched pockets of disadvantage (Healy & Hampshire, 2003). As rural and remote communities increasingly fall into this category, it is vital to address the challenges facing them, which are immediate and require urgent action. The survival of rural and remote communities depends on their capacity to anticipate and manage change, to develop and apply problem-solving skills, and to think creatively and strategically, as key aspects of the application of community development programs (Cavaye, 2000). This book's focus on small rural and remote communities thus serves to magnify the compelling issues surrounding community development and provides an opportunity to examine how community development approaches are applied in meaningful and challenging contexts.

The Rural/Urban Divide: Definitional Issues

Acknowledgement of the important differences between metropolitan, regional, rural and remote communities in Australia is fundamental to this investigation. Yet definitions remain quite problematic. Australia is a vast country characterised by urban concentration and sprawling, widely dispersed population nodes. Clearly, as the distance from the major cities on the edge of the Australian continent increases, population dispersion also increases, health outcomes decline, access to services becomes more difficult and prices of goods and services rise. However, distance from major population centres is only one of many criteria used to classify areas or populations. Many rural/urban classification systems have been developed in Australia and overseas. Wakerman & Humphreys (2000) have identified the most commonly used systems: the Faulkner and French Index of Remoteness; the Griffith Service Access Frame; the Rural and Remote Area classification (RARA) developed and used by the Australian Department of Human Services and Health; the Rural Remote and Metropolitan Areas classification (RRMA) used by the Department of Primary Industries and Energy and the Department of Human Services and Health; the Accessibility/Remoteness Index of Australia (ARIA) used by the Department of Health and Aged Care; and the Australian Standard Geographical Classification (ASGC) used by the Australian Bureau of Statistics. The last three of these systems — RRMA, ARIA and ASGC — are currently commonly used in Australia and have most relevance to this book.

The RRMA uses population size and calculated direct distance from the nearest service centre to determine seven discrete categories: capital cities, other metropolitan centres, large rural centres, small rural centres, other rural areas, remote centres, and other remote areas. The ARIA uses geographical information to define road distance from service centres with a population of more than 5,000, thus producing a sliding scale of remoteness. The scale has also been divided into five classes: highly accessible, accessible, moderately accessible, remote, and very remote. The ASGC is based on a refinement of ARIA and consists of five discrete categories: major cities, inner regional, outer regional, remote, and very remote. Despite the relative advantages of each of these classification systems, the choice of rural–urban classification to underpin this investigation is neither useful nor informative. The communities targeted in this book are at the remote to very remote end of the aforementioned scales. In essence, these formal classification systems prove to be too inflexible to cater for the diversity found in communities across Australia. For example, a small rural community in Victoria located a few hundred kilometres from a major city has very different needs from those of a small rural community in western Queensland located over 1,000 kilometres from a major centre. Yet both types of communities are of interest to this research. To overcome the limitations of current classification systems, this book introduces a new category of remote/rural. This new category includes communities with populations fewer than 4,000 and communities that are more than 400 kilometres from a major centre with a population greater than 10,000. Table 10 contextualises this additional category (remote/rural) with other categories of communities (urban, regional and rural).

Table 10. Categories of Communities by Population, Dispersion and Access to Services.

	Urban	Regional	Rural	Remote/rural
Population	< 100,000	< 50,000	< 10,000	Less than 4,000
Dispersion	Nil	Low	High	Very high
Access to services	High	Moderate	Low	Very low

Source: Author's research.

Surveys, Sites Visits and Case Studies

Surveys and site visits were developed and conducted to interrogate the viability and sustainability of existing approaches to community development in rural and remote communities, and to scope the current and potential role and function of the arts in supporting community development approaches. The nature and scope of the surveys and site visits along with their results are reported in the next chapter.

Three major case studies were identified and developed to provide detailed insights into the application of the arts in rural and remote community development as presented in Chapter 8.

7

Scoping Art in Communities

This chapter reports on an environmental scan conducted to scope the nature and the extent of arts-based activity in regional, rural and remote communities in Australia. Conducted through surveys, interviews and site visits, it aims to identify and document current practices, community perceptions and future directions for the arts in communities.

Survey Distribution and Response Rates

Printed surveys were posted to 500 targeted stakeholders living and working in regional, rural and remote/rural communities. Table 11 provides a summary of the distribution of the responses by six categories of occupation and reports response rates.

Table 11. Survey Distribution Categories and Response Rates.

Respondent categories	Distribution	Response rate	
		No.	%
Local government officials	25	3	12
Local government employees	100	12	12
Artists and arts workers	155	74	48
Community business people	80	13	16
Farmers and graziers	45	4	8
Members of community organisations	95	22	24
TOTAL	500	128	25.6

Source: Author's research.

Overall, the response rate for the survey was just above 25 per cent, which surpassed the objective of a 20 per cent response rate. It should be noted, however, that the response rates across respondent categories were variable, with four of the six categories not achieving the desired rate. Since the response from community artists and arts workers (48 per cent) was significantly higher than all other categories, the subsequent analysis of surveys has examined responses by category to ensure that the views of artists and arts workers are balanced with the views of other categories of community members.

Table 12 examines survey responses by location. Surveys were posted to people living in regional centres (population greater than 10,000), rural centres (population between 4,000 and 10,000) and remote/rural communities (population less than 4,000).

Table 12. Survey Distribution by Location and Response Rates.

Location	Distribution	Response rate	
		No.	%
Regional centres (population greater than 10,000)	70	5	4
Rural centres (population between 4,000 and 10,000)	220	49	38
Remote/rural communities (population less than 4,000)	210	74	58
TOTAL	500	128	25.6

Source: Author's research.

Interestingly, the percentage of responses received from rural and from remote/rural communities far surpassed the anticipated 20 per cent. By contrast, the response rate for the regional centres was disappointingly low. One might speculate that the higher response rate from rural and remote/rural communities may indicate a higher level of interest in community development in these communities and a concomitant satisfaction level in regional centres.

Contribution of the Arts to Communities

Table 13 presents the perceptions of the total group of respondents in relation to the contribution of the arts to their communities.

Table 13. Perceptions of the Contribution of the Arts to Communities.

	Very important		Important		Not important
No.	10	24	62	27	5
%	8	19	48	21	4

Source: Author's research.

Apart from the fact that all the perceptions reflect an almost perfect normal curve, respondents overwhelmingly (75 per cent) endorse the importance of the contribution made by the arts to community development. Table 14 presents perceptions by category of respondent occupation.

Table 14. Perceptions of the Contribution of the Arts by Category of Respondent.

Local government officials (No. = 3)				
Very important		Important		Not important
0%	33.33%	66.67%	0%	0%
Local government employees (No. = 12)				
Very important		Important		Not important
16.67%	25%	50%	8.33%	0%
Artists and arts workers (No. = 74)				
Very important		Important		Not important
8.11%	22.97%	56.76%	12.16%	0%
Community-based business people (No. = 13)				
Very important		Important		Not important
0%	0%	38.46%	46.15%	23.08%
Farmers, graziers and land owners (No. = 4)				
Very important		Important		Not important
0%	25%	50%	25%	0%
Members of community organisations (No. = 22)				
Very important		Important		Not important
9.09%	13.64%	18.18%	45.45%	9.09%

Source: Author's research.

Not surprisingly, 87 per cent of artists and arts workers reported that the arts were important/very important to community development, a perception that was consistent with that of local government officials, farmers, graziers and land owners, albeit with relatively lower percentages. By contrast, relatively few community-based business people and members of community organisations (>40 per cent) perceived the arts to play an important role in community development.

To what extent might location of respondents be a factor in these perceptions? In order to consider this question, the distribution of categories of respondents across regional, rural and remote/rural locations is presented in Table 15.

Table 15. Distribution of Respondents across Regional, Rural and Remote/Rural Locations.

Category of respondent	Regional respondents		Rural respondents		Remote/rural respondents	
	No.	%	No.	%	No.	%
Local government officials	0	0	1	33.3	2	66.6
Local government employees	2	16.6	5	41.6	5	41.6
Artists and arts workers	0	0	30	40.5	44	59.5
Community-based business people	2	15.4	5	38.5	6	46.1
Farmers, graziers and land owners	0	0	1	25	3	75
Members of community organisations	1	4.5	7	31.8	14	63.6

Source: Author's research.

Artists and arts workers are well represented in rural and remote/rural communities. Local government employees, community-based business people and members of community organisations are reasonably well represented across all geographic locations. Local government officials are poorly represented in all locations.

Table 16 presents the perceived importance of the arts to community development by location of respondents.

Table 16. Perceptions of the Contribution of the Arts by Respondent Location.

Regional centres (No. = 5)				
Very important		Important		Not important
60%	20%	20%	0%	0%
Rural centres (No. = 49)				
Very important		Important		Not important
8.16%	34.69%	36.73%	12.24%	8.16%
Remote/rural centres (No. = 74)				
Very important		Important		Not important
4.05%	8.11%	58.11%	21.62%	8.1%

Source: Author's research.

At each location, over 75 per cent of respondents perceived the arts to be important/very important to community development.

Respondents were invited to make additional/expansive comments to support their responses and the following quotations provide examples. Local enthusiasm for the arts in some communities was captured by the following:

> The arts enrich my life and helps put life in perspective and I'm proud and excited about the newer work I'm seeing.
>
> Community artist, rural community

> Our arts groups help to strengthen the community by giving people an opportunity to come together and celebrate the success of the community.
>
> Community arts worker, remote/rural community

Other comments reflect the lack of support for the arts:

> I see very little evidence of the impact of the arts on the community — it's too narrow, only a few people are involved.
>
> Community business owner, remote/rural community

One community arts worker, for example, suggests a disconnect between arts workers and other community members:

> The arts contribute greatly to this community but the contribution is not widely recognised by many people in town and it's not valued by council.
>
> Community arts worker, rural community

Survey respondents were also asked to consider the role of the arts in specific areas of community development, including the impact on (i) the development and maintenance of social capital (including the stimulation of social networks and the achievement of social cohesion), (ii) the stimulation of economic growth, and (iii) the growth, protection and maintenance of cultural capital.

Social Capital

Respondents were first asked to rate their perception of the impact of the arts and arts-based initiatives and projects on the development of social networks in their community. Table 17 presents overall survey responses.

Table 17. Perceptions of the Contribution of the Arts to the Development of Social Networks.

	Very important		Important		Not important
No.	19	46	49	11	3
%	16	36	38	8	2

Source: Author's research.

When asked specifically about the role of the arts in stimulating and supporting social networking, respondents were generally positive, with only 10 per cent reporting that the arts were not very important or unimportant. Table 18 presents these perceptions by respondent category.

Table 18. Perceptions of the Contribution of the Arts to the Development of Social Networks by Respondent Occupation.

Local government officials (No. = 3)				
Very important		Important		Not important
0%	33.33%	66.67%	0%	0%
Local government employees (No. = 12)				
Very important		Important		Not important
25%	25%	50%	0%	0%
Artists and arts workers (No. = 74)				
Very important		Important		Not important
17.57%	52.7%	29.73%	0%	0%

Community-based business people (No. = 13)				
Very important		Important		Not important
0%	0%	46.15%	38.46%	15.38%
Farmers, graziers and land owners (No. = 4)				
Very important		Important		Not important
0%	0%	50%	25%	25%
Members of community organisations (No. = 22)				
Very important		Important		Not important
9.09%	18.18%	50%	22.73%	0%

Source: Author's research.

While the role of the arts in supporting social networks was recognised as important by local government officials and employees and by artists and arts workers, this was not seen to be important by 50 per cent or more of local business people, farmers, graziers and land owners, and over 20 per cent of community organisation members.

Table 19 presents respondents' views on the arts and social networking by location.

Table 19. Perceptions of the Contribution of the Arts to Social Networking by Location.

Regional centres (No. = 5)				
Very important		Important		Not important
40%	40%	20%	0%	0%
Rural centres (No. = 49)				
Very important		Important		Not important
28.57%	59.18%	12.24%	0%	0%
Remote/rural centres (No. = 74)				
Very important		Important		Not important
4.05%	20.27%	56.76%	14.86%	4.05%

Source: Author's research.

Recognition of the role of the arts in the development of social networks was strong across regional and rural centres but less so in remote/rural locations.

The survey instrument also asked respondents to rate their perception of the impact of the arts and arts-based initiatives on the development of social cohesion in their communities. Table 20 presents overall survey results.

Table 20. Perceptions of the Contribution of the Arts to Social Cohesion.

	Very important		Important		Not important
No.	17	48	40	16	7
%	13	38	32	12	5

Source: Author's research.

Again the majority perception is of the arts contributing in important ways to social cohesion.

Table 21 presents the social cohesion perceptions by category of respondent.

Table 21. Perceptions of the Contribution of the Arts to the Development of Social Cohesion by Respondent Occupation.

Local government officials (No. = 3)				
Very important		Important		Not important
0%	0%	66.67%	33.33%	0%
Local government employees (No. = 12)				
Very important		Important		Not important
0%	25%	50%	25%	0%
Artists and arts workers (No. = 74)				
Very important		Important		Not important
21.62%	56.76%	21.62%	0%	0%
Community-based business people (No. = 13)				
Very important		Important		Not important
0%	0%	30.77%	38.46%	30.77%
Farmers, graziers and land owners (No. = 4)				
Very important		Important		Not important
0%	0%	25%	50%	25%
Members of community organisations (No. = 22)				
Very important		Important		Not important
4.55%	13.64%	50%	22.73%	8.09%

Source: Author's research.

While artists and arts workers perceived a strong link between the arts and the achievement of socially cohesive communities (100 per cent), other groups were less convinced by the link with approximately 70 per cent of business owners, graziers, farmers and land owners viewing the arts as unimportant in the achievement of social cohesion.

Table 22 presents respondents' views on the arts and social networking by location.

Table 22. Perceptions of the Contribution of the Arts to Social Cohesion by Location.

Regional centres (No. = 5)				
Very important		Important		Not important
60%	40%	0%	0%	0%
Rural centres (No. = 49)				
Very important		Important		Not important
26.13%	67.35%	6.12%	0%	0%
Remote/rural centres (No. = 74)				
Very important		Important		Not important
1.35%	17.57%	50%	21.62%	9.46%

Source: Author's research.

While the role of the arts in developing cohesive communities was strongly recognised across all locations, 30 per cent of respondents in remote communities did not support its importance.

Economic Development

Respondents were also asked to rate their perception of the impact of the arts and arts-based initiatives and projects on the economic development of their communities. Table 23 presents overall survey responses.

Table 23. Perceptions of the Contribution of the Arts to Economic Development.

	Very important		Important		Not important
No	12	28	38	36	14
%	9	22	30	28	11

Source: Author's research.

While there is quite strong recognition of the role of the arts in community economic development (over 60 per cent), 40 per cent perceived the arts not to be important to economic development. This compares with only 10 per cent of respondents reporting that the arts were not important in the development of social networks and social cohesion.

Table 24 presents perceptions of the role of the arts in economic development by category of respondent.

Table 24. Perceptions of the Contribution of the Arts to the Economic Development by Respondent Occupation.

Local government officials (No. = 3)				
Very important		Important		Not important
0%	0%	66.67%	33.33%	0%
Local government employees (No. = 12)				
Very important		Important		Not important
0%	16.67%	50%	33.33%	0%
Artists and arts workers (No. = 74)				
Very important		Important		Not important
8.11%	21.62%	29.73%	27.03%	13.51%
Community-based business people (No. = 13)				
Very important		Important		Not important
15.38%	23.08%	23.08%	38.41%	0%
Farmers, graziers and land owners (No. = 4)				
Very important		Important		Not Important
0%	50%	25%	0%	1%
Members of community organisations (No. = 22)				
Very important		Important		Not important
18.18%	22.73%	18.18%	27.27%	13.64%

Source: Author's research.

Sixty per cent or greater of each category of respondents regarded the contribution of the arts to economic development as important/very important. However, when compared with responses to the importance of the arts in the development of social networking and social cohesion, the results differ; they seem to indicate that artists, arts workers and government officials and employees view the arts contribution to social development as more important than their contribution to economic development. On the other hand, local business people, graziers, farmers and land owners have rated the contribution of the arts to economic development as more important than their contribution to social development.

Table 25 presents respondents' views on the contribution of the arts to economic development by location.

Table 25. Perceptions of the Contribution of the Arts to Economic Development by Location.

Regional centres (No. = 5)				
Very important		Important		Not important
20%	40%	40%	0%	0%
Rural centres (No. = 49)				
Very important		Important		Not important
6.12%	12.24%	32.65%	40.82%	8.16%
Remote/rural centres (No. = 74)				
Very important		Important		Not important
10.81%	27.03%	27.03%	21.62%	13.51%

Source: Author's research.

While respondents from regional communities indicated that the arts are important/very important to economic development, respondents from rural and remote/rural areas were equivocal — and especially those from rural communities.

Some of these disparities are reflected in the comments made by respondents. A local business operator in a rural community suggests a keenly felt disconnect between arts and economic opportunity in rural communities:

> When it comes to economics, the arts just don't add up. There is not enough demand to warrant any investment.
>
> Business owner A, rural community

Community artists may be unable to see the potential of the arts in community economic development:

> I can't see how it's affecting our economy — we have very few events that raise money.
>
> Community artist, rural community

However, some business operators seemed rather more optimistic about the nexus between the arts and economic returns.

> When the arts council is in town, people get out and spend money — they usually go to dinner before and a few drinks after — it all helps local businesses.
>
> Business owner B, rural community

> Our festivals bring a lot of tourists to town and they do spend money.
>
> Grazier, rural community

Cultural Development

Survey respondents were also asked to rate their perception of the impact of arts-based initiatives and projects on the cultural development of their community. Table 26 presents the overall survey responses.

Table 26. Perceptions of the Contribution of the Arts to Cultural Development.

	Very important		Important		Not important
No.	28	38	46	14	2
%	22	29.5	36	11	1.5

Source: Author's research.

Over 87 per cent of all respondents reported a very strong perception that the arts contributed significantly to the cultural development of communities. Table 27 presents perceptions of the role of the arts in cultural development by category of respondents.

Table 27. Perceptions of the Contribution of the Arts to Cultural Development by Respondent Occupation.

Local government officials (No. = 3)				
Very important		Important		Not important
66.67%	33.33%	0%	0%	0%
Local government employees (No. = 12)				
Very important		Important		Not important
25%	58.33%	16.67%	0%	0%

Artists and arts workers (No. = 74)				
Very important		Important		Not important
16.22%	25.68%	44.59%	13.51%	0%
Community-based business people (No. = 13)				
Very important		Important		Not important
30.71%	30.71%	38.46%	0%	0%
Farmers, graziers and land owners (No. = 4)				
Very important		Important		Not important
25%	50%	25%	0%	0%
Members of community organisations (No. = 22)				
Very important		Important		Not important
27.27%	22.73%	22.73%	18.18%	9.09%

Source: Author's research.

All respondent categories indicated a strong recognition of the role of the arts in cultural development, although in the case of artists/arts workers and members of community organisations there was some measure of dissent from this perception.

Table 28 presents respondents' views on the arts and cultural development by location.

Table 28. Perceptions of the Contribution of the Arts to Cultural Development by Location.

Regional centres (No. = 5)				
Very important		Important		Not important
60%	40%	0%	0%	0%
Rural centres (No. = 49)				
Very important		Important		Not important
32.65%	28.57%	28.57%	8.16%	2.04%
Remote/rural centres (No. = 74)				
Very important		Important		Not important
12.16%	29.73%	43.24%	13.51%	1.35%

Source: Author's research.

While the contribution of the arts to community cultural development was recognised as important across all locations, again there was less consistency across rural and remote/rural areas.

Nevertheless, generally the comments illustrate the strong support for the role of the arts in cultural development:

> Our festivals really help the community appreciate what we have — our history and our environment.
>
> Community artist, rural community

> Our arts network is at the centre of many of our events and people do get involved and value our local arts products — the shop set up by the arts group is very successful and tourists usually stop there.
>
> Member of community organisations, remote/rural community

> Our museum is great and reflects our culture and our history both for us in the community and for visitors.
>
> Business operator, remote community

However, one respondent took the opportunity to argue that community culture is broader in scope than the arts:

> The arts contribute to our culture but not as much as other community activities — our culture is based on sports and sporting competitions — pony club, the races and our local football competition bring people together much more than the arts.
>
> Business operator, rural community

Arts Projects, Initiatives and Enterprises

The survey required respondents to identify arts-based projects, initiatives and enterprises located in their community. Only 83 respondents (65 per cent) completed this section of the survey, but many of these respondents listed multiple projects and initiatives. Rather than listing specific details about projects and initiatives, respondents tended to report generic community activities such as community festivals and art exhibitions or list community groups and associations. Table 29 categorises survey responses and provides examples of responses by category as well as the number of mentions of projects and initiatives within each category.

Table 29. Categories and Types of Arts-Based Projects and Initiatives Present in Regional, Rural and Remote/Rural Communities.

Category of project/initiative	Number of mentions	Examples of responses
Internal projects/initiatives	113	Volunteer museums. Arts networks. Community festivals. Council funded plays and musicals. Arts and crafts groups. Community run art galleries. Cultural associations. Historical societies. Arts competitions and special exhibitions. Local choirs. Dance groups.
External projects/initiatives	146	Public art projects. Arts councils. Arts classes and workshops. Travelling exhibitions. Tourism projects.
Community clubs/ associations	162	Performing arts societies. Concert and show bands. Music groups and societies. Drama societies.
Government-sponsored activities	183	Regional Arts Development Fund (RADF) projects. Regional art galleries.
Government-sponsored infrastructure	2	Tourism facilities.
Community-based businesses/enterprises	24	Local private art galleries. Shops and outlets selling local product. Dance studios.

Source: Author's research.

Further analysis of Table 29 reveals a highly conservative and traditional view of the role of the arts in communities, which is also reflected in the additional optional comments made by respondents:

> Most of our activities only happen because of the arts council and the RADF.[1] If it wasn't for them we would have very little.
>
> Member of community organisation, remote community

1 Regional Arts Development Fund.

> Our local art gallery is very good and attracts some tourism to the town. It relies on volunteers to keep it open.
>
> Local government employee, rural community

> We have a gallery, an arts and craft centre, a Little Theatre group and a choir; we also run several workshops — silver smithing, pottery, etc. There are lots of things happening.
>
> Local artist, rural community

> We are part of the government's Heritage Trail project and it has helped put the town on the tourist map.
>
> Local business operator, rural community

Interviews and Site Visits

To add further depth and meaning to the survey results, site visits were planned and conducted in 12 regional, rural and remote communities. The 12 communities were distributed across an area comprising approximately 900,000 square kilometres.

Thirty-six formal, semi-structured, face-to-face interviews were conducted over three site visits to each of the 12 sites with local government officials and employees, local artists and arts workers, local business people, and members of local community organisations. Informal, unstructured interviews were conducted with various local people (including local retirees, publicans, teachers, shopkeepers and police officers) as opportunities presented.

Scoping the Nature and Range of Community Arts

Range and Scope

Some community-based arts projects were identified in all communities visited during the environmental scan. All interviewees indicated the availability of a range of activities within their communities with the most common community activity being arts-based workshops designed for beginning artists or hobbyists. Arts organisations, societies and clubs were also identified in every community and were reported by interviewees as significant contributors to the range and scope of local activities. Organisations identified by interviewees included arts councils, arts and crafts associations, historical societies, musical societies, Little Theatre companies, local choirs and bands. A further major activity identified during the environmental scanning process was festivals; the majority of communities visited conducted at least one major annual festival. In addition, all communities conduct other major events including annual art competitions and exhibitions.

Community Workshops

As indicated, the dominant arts-based community activity identified was art workshops, which variously include pottery, painting, print making, sculpture, lead lighting, jewellery making and silversmithing. In many cases, community groups contract external artists and practitioners to conduct these workshops. Local artists are seldom invited to fulfil these training roles and may even be reluctant to do so:

> I ran a painting course once — not my idea, I was asked by the council. It was a disaster. I'm not a teacher and the whole day was just terrible. I love art but I can't teach it.
>
> Pamela, local artist, Barcaldine

In addition to art form–based workshops, a few communities are expanding their offerings to include workshops and programs addressing the management and support of local artists and arts-based projects. Such programs include (i) building the business skills of artists, (ii) planning and creating a community cultural plan, (iii) leadership in community arts, and (iv) preparing and submitting a funding proposal. These types of programs are slowly gaining acceptance in communities but are not currently well subscribed, tending to attract only those people already committed to the development of the arts in their community.

A further interesting development was identified in two communities. Annual theatre productions have been run by local associations for many years but, in recent years, two communities have chosen to contract the skills and experience of a professional producer/director to work with community members. Community members thus have the opportunity to develop new skills and knowledge through on-the-job learning with an experienced professional:

> One young man has learnt so much from being the director's assistant at our last production that he is keen to do the job by himself next year. The Little Theatre group is not convinced because it's their major money earner for the year but I'll support him because we need to recognise the development of local talent.
>
> Marjorie, local government councillor

There was further discussion in communities about the possible transference of this learning process to other community art areas:

> We're wondering if we could bring in an artist from outside to work collaboratively with our community members to create new public art or design and build new streetscapes … not just hand it over to an outside artist but to get him to work with us so we own it in the end.
>
> Marjorie, local government councillor

Such approaches demonstrate a move away from traditional workshops to skills development based on real-world problems and the use of experts as mentors and guides.

Associations and Cultural Societies

Sites visits and interviews confirmed the presence of a wide range of arts organisations within communities. All interviewees reported that such organisations were highly valued within the community:

> Without these organisations there would be very little happening in this community. They raise money, run events and raise the profile of the arts in the community.
>
> Jack, director, development and community services, local council

Typically, these organisations are not-for-profit and are run exclusively by community volunteers committed to particular art forms and strongly convinced of their benefit to the community. Strong similarities exist between community organisations with all sample communities having historical societies, arts and crafts associations and arts councils; in addition, several communities have local bands, Little Theatre companies and community choirs. One community differed from the others visited in that it had established and maintained a significant retail outlet for the products of regional artists and crafts people. The shop has successfully operated for over a decade and is well stocked with quality local arts products including paintings, leather craft, woodwork and jewellery. The current proprietor of the shop summed up its benefits:

> We only sell local products but that's not limited to just the people in the immediate areas. Artists from the whole of western Queensland provide products to the shop. Because we have so many products and we are located right here in the main street, we tend to attract a good number of tourists. Also, we have a great range from high end, expensive stuff to locally made souvenirs so we sell a fair bit to tourists as well as locals.
>
> Lydia, proprietor of local arts retail outlet

A local artist who sells her work through the outlet outlined the benefits for the artist/producer:

> The shop has allowed me to turn a hobby into a very small business. I don't make enough to live on but it's a nice little supplement. I make jewellery using local stones so it's small and relatively inexpensive and it has that local connection so it has always sold well and is popular with tourists. I've been lucky and I now sell through other outlets mostly on the coast, but it's only been possible because I had somewhere in the local area to start selling.
>
> Liz, local artist

The most successful organisations were identified by interviewees as those working collaboratively with the community and the local council:

> The most successful organisations are those that have developed a strong relationship with council. We [the council] run a major regional gallery and some arts organisations have worked with us to maintain the gallery and in turn we provide access to gallery facilities to those organisations.
>
> Jack, director, development and community services, local government

Festivals

As shown in Table 29, the other major local activity prevalent in all communities visited is festivals, which range from seasonal events catering mainly for the local community through to major festivals attracting visitors from across the nation. Recently, a small number of region-wide festivals have been initiated. These festivals cover large geographic areas incorporating several towns and shires. Such festivals are usually coordinated by a central organising committee with representation from each of the participating towns/shires. Collaborative planning of regional festivals allows themes to be aligned to the interests and resources of all participating communities.

Interestingly, these regional festivals are not a rationalisation or consolidation of existing local events but are new festivals, adding to what some respondents perceived to be an already crowded festival program in regional and rural Queensland:

> Throughout the region we have cotton festivals, sunflower festivals, melon festivals, wildflower festivals, back to the bush festivals … We're in danger of having too many festivals; we're all competing with one another for a very small tourist market.
>
> Anthony, deputy chief executive officer, local council

Nevertheless, there are several well-established festivals in rural communities that have been successful over many years.

Infrastructure

Some of the communities visited during the environmental scan were in the process of developing significant arts infrastructure projects, typically in partnership with the Queensland State Government. The state government has a policy of supporting communities to establish significant infrastructure to stimulate tourism in western Queensland through the Heritage Trails Project, which aims to create a network of major tourist attractions stretching from town to town for over 1,000 kilometres. Most of communities involved in the project expressed excitement about the prospect of attracting increased numbers of tourists. As a result, all were planning to incorporate locally produced arts and crafts into retail outlets offered through the new infrastructure.

However, communities not directly involved in the project are suspicious of the long-term success of some of the ventures supported under the Heritage Trails Project. These communities had already developed significant arts infrastructure projects that were conceived and developed by the community without government stimulus:

> Over the last 10 years we have developed several major projects to attract people to the town — both the Jackie Howe Museum and the Wool Scour were conceived and supported by the community. We sought funding help from the government but mostly it was hard work supported by a strong community will. If we had waited a few years we could have got on the Heritage Trails bandwagon.
>
> Bob, local businessman, remote/rural community

There is a strong sense in some communities that long-term success relies on community ownership of infrastructure and that government should be supportive of ideas and strategies that are developed by communities themselves rather than imposing strategies on communities:

> It actually penalises the communities that have been active in developing new tourist attractions — we were a unique spot for tourists because we'd developed two major attractions that were well known to potential tourists and we're the only major attractions for hundreds of kilometres. Now we will have to compete with just about every town in the west.
>
> Bob, local businessman, remote/rural community

Several other interviewees agreed that communities should be involved in infrastructure projects from the beginning and that they should utilise ideas generated from within the community. They also stated that communities should not only be actively involved in the generation and analysis of ideas but that they should also manage and control the design of programs, set community priorities, contribute actively to the management of projects, and control budgets:

> We don't want to be dictated to by government — we want to take responsibility for creating our own ideas and be responsible for managing local projects and budgets. We are the ones who know most about our needs and we know how best to meet these needs.
>
> Brian, president, local arts council, remote/rural community

It seems that successful and sustainable infrastructure development might rely on a strong and powerful community voice at the centre of decision making as well as high levels of community involvement in managing projects and bringing them to successful fruition.

Support for the Arts in Communities

Support for the arts in rural and remote/rural communities is multilayered and multifaceted. Successful communities are characterised by active and committed individuals working with and through well-established community organisations supported by government at both the local and state level. The sections that follow identify the parameters of support as evidenced in the data.

Active and Committed Individuals

The arts in rural and remote communities depend primarily on local residents contributing on a volunteer basis. While all community-based individuals may make significant contributions in supporting the role of the arts in communities, some individuals make more powerful, lasting contributions. Every interviewee could nominate a single person who had made a major contribution to their community. One example of this is a woman who, with the assistance of two colleagues, planned and commenced what is best described as a local creative enterprise that uses local resources to create and sell a unique local product.

> I have a strong belief in the community — the business was not started to make a lot of money even though that's what some people think; it was started to help the community. We were dying as a community and I wanted to put us on the map and at the same time celebrate what's special about us — to recognise our history and promote our products.
>
> Melinda, local business owner, remote/rural community

While this example may be unique, numerous other examples provided by interviewees illustrate the power of the individual to make contributions with positive long-term impacts on communities, thus providing a lasting legacy for community members. Many successful community programs have relied on local arts teachers who have willingly contributed their talents and time to their adopted communities. However, rural and remote/rural teachers tend to be transient workers and their contributions are usually short term. While often the programs started or contributed to by local arts teachers fold when the teacher is transferred, there is evidence of lasting legacies in some communities:

> An arts teacher started our annual competition and exhibition several years ago. It's evolved into a major regional event. We have all made a big effort to keep it going and each successive arts teacher has contributed their time to the event — it's almost now automatic, the job comes with the position. The original teacher always tries to come back each year — when she comes she's treated like a VIP.
>
> Leanne, economic development officer, remote/rural community

The contribution of transient workers to the cultural development of local communities is not limited to arts teachers. Police, council workers, telecommunication workers and others all contribute as community volunteers.

Dedicated and Energetic Community Associations and Groups

As noted, communities visited were characterised by well-established community organisations including arts councils, historical societies, show bands, theatre groups, and musical societies. Generally these groups are active in their communities and have responsibility for planning and organising the majority of community events such as major festivals, theatre productions, art exhibitions, art workshops and programs. Some have also been responsible for significant local cultural infrastructure:

> Our historical village has been built up over many years and now is one of the biggest and best in rural Queensland. It's never received any external support or money — it's been planned, managed and funded almost entirely by our historical society. It's a real achievement.
>
> Kenny, member of local arts council, rural community

The importance of these groups to the community was recognised and highly valued by all interviewees. However, several also reported on the static and stagnant nature of many of their community organisations:

> Our groups are very active and we'd be lost without them but there is a closed shop mentality — it's like there is an unwritten rule that it's just for us. They don't have a growing membership base and they don't have a connection with other community groups — it's not that it's elitist; it's just bogged down.
>
> Kenny, member of local arts council, rural community

Other interviewees raised concerns that existing community organisations were tradition bound and that their view of the arts in community was based on concepts that were both limited and limiting:

> Each year the same people get together and make the same decisions — give the same money to the same groups. There's nothing new — no one new. It's like Groundhog Day.
>
> Helen, local artist, remote/rural community

One interviewee expressed concern about the lack of connection not only with the wider community but between arts organisations themselves.

> Most of our programs depend heavily on our organisations — each has a strong focus and commitment to their area of interest — the theatre group is really active and the spinners and weavers create a lot of interest and generate a lot of local product. But there is little networking among the groups — they all operate in their own little vacuums. If we could generate a shared focus I think we could achieve a lot.
>
> Lydia, executive officer, arts network, rural community

As indicated by the majority of interviewees, the success of community organisations usually depends on the efforts of one or two individual members who provide enthusiasm, commitment and hard work.

Government

Local, community-based arts projects are possible in many of the communities visited only as a result of consistent government support. The Regional Arts Development Fund (RADF), a state government funding program that provides annual funds to regional, rural and remote communities, was mentioned by over 90 per cent of interviewees as a major support mechanism enabling them to support local arts activities and projects:

> A lot of our activity depends on government funding, particularly through the RADF. If it wasn't for RADF we would only be able to offer a fairly limited program of arts workshops and programs.
>
> Lydia, executive officer, arts network, rural community

Funds provided through the Regional Arts Development Fund (RADF) program are matched dollar for dollar by local governments and provide a genuine stimulus for local government investment in the arts. Each community visited has an operating local RADF committee comprised of council representatives and community stakeholders. RADF committees are responsible not only for identifying local priorities and allocating and managing funds but also for reconciling project expenditure and annual reporting.

While all communities were highly supportive of the application of RADF funds, most interviewees reported that the amount of money made available through the program was inadequate to support meaningful community development through the arts. Interviewees indicated that most of the available RADF funds were currently allocated to arts-based workshops and professional development programs. One- or two-day workshops on silversmithing, jewellery making, print making, pottery and sculpture were frequently mentioned during site visits. There was little evidence during site visits that RADF funds were being used to support new approaches to the application of the arts to community development. In fact, the use of the funds was characterised by a lack of imagination and innovation, with most communities having seemingly entrenched habits and relying on traditional approaches to the arts with a somewhat blinkered focus on workshops and short programs designed primarily for hobbyists. This static approach to funding traditional activity was challenged directly by only one of the interviewees.

> We need to move to a more strategic approach to arts funding … To move away from a 'hand out' approach so that community groups will put some thought and planning into what they want to achieve and then bid for funds based on projected community outcome. The current committee approach where a small group allocates funds to well-established groups in the community just doesn't work — each year the same groups get the same money and do the same things. It kills imagination and originality and prevents new groups from emerging from within the community.
>
> Brian, president, local arts council, remote/rural community

When questioned about the evaluation of community activities and projects, the majority of interviewees indicated that projects were usually evaluated according to the number of program participants and the extent to which they enjoyed the experience. Typically, this was recorded and measured through end-of-workshop evaluation forms asking participants to rate their enjoyment of the workshop, the performance of the workshop presenter, and the potential usefulness of new skills and knowledge gained during the workshop:

> Our evaluation is usually based entirely on workshop happy sheets.
>
> Karla, community arts worker, rural community

Interviewees revealed little evidence that evaluation approaches were used to stimulate critical analysis of outcomes and approaches adopted by the community to support the arts. Nevertheless, approaches that could encourage a more reflective consideration of community arts activities may be simple and easy to achieve as indicated:

> We used to have a bit of a party after our events. We would all get together and have a few drinks and talk about what was good, what went wrong and how we might do it better. We would also get some good ideas for new things to do. Things are so busy now that we all seem to have somewhere to go so we don't get to talk so much.
>
> Maree, president, local arts council, remote/rural community

There is significant evidence in the data to argue that community members have the capability and maturity to be critically reflective but there is little evidence that opportunities to facilitate such reflection are common in communities. The adoption of approaches and provision of opportunities to stimulate and encourage critical reflection might help communities to generate new ideas and approaches to the application of the arts for community growth and development.

Perceptions of the Arts in Communities

Generally the arts were highly valued by interviewees in all the communities visited during the environmental scan, but the focus of valuing tends to differ from community to community with some concentrating more on economic impacts and others on social impacts — both negative and positive.

Economic Impacts

Over 90 per cent of all interviewees reported that the economic benefits to the community of the arts were extremely limited. Some interviewees even expressed surprise at being asked a question linking the arts to economic development:

> Well I've never really thought about it — what are other people saying?
>
> Margaret, local artist, rural community

> Our programs are not really concerned with economics — they're for art.
>
> Mary, local government employee, rural community

Overall, many interviewees reported that they had not seriously considered the economic value of the arts. Others reported that the only potential economic benefit that has been linked directly to the arts has been increased visitor and tourist numbers. However, none of the interviewees were aware of any formal activities undertaken to measure an increase in tourist or visitor numbers as a result of the arts. The majority view is well summarised thus:

> Economically the arts in rural areas just don't add up! The demand is generally low and the quality is usually mediocre. Arts activities are almost always sponsored, usually by government — they simply wouldn't be feasible without government sponsorship.
>
> Brian, president, local arts council, and local accountant, rural community

This majority view of the economic value of the arts was countered by only a few interviewees in only two of the communities. One of these communities included a long-standing local enterprise specialising in the manufacture and sale of a local product; a product based on creative design, advanced craft-based skills and imaginative marketing. The enterprise is an independent business whose product has attracted a significant increase in visitor and tourist numbers, thus increasing the flow of dollars into the town. While no formal study has been completed that documents the increase, there are significant indicators of an increase in revenue flowing into the town. Firstly, there is an increase in registered visitors to the local information centre. Secondly, tour operators, who previously ignored the town on their itineraries, now ensure that tour groups spend over an hour in the town. Thirdly, a new business, a coffee shop, has been established to cater for the spin-off demands of increased visitor numbers:

> It's put us on the map ... people used to just drive through the town, now they stop, even if it's just to look, they usually buy a drink or something to eat.
>
> Maree, president, local arts council, remote/rural community

> It's been a huge benefit to the town as a whole but we can't just rely on it for the future. We have to build new programs and new activities for locals as well as visitors.
>
> Sonya, economic development officer, remote/rural community

The second community conducted a very active program of festivals and major events including an annual Mardi Gras attracting locals and regional visitors, a biennial food and fibre festival attracting visitors from around the country, and an annual arts competition and exhibition that is widely recognised and attracts exhibitors from around the nation. There is a strong recognition of the economic value of these festivals and events:

> Each year our events attract more visitors. Our local businesses have all experienced the economic benefits of increasing numbers of visitors. So much so that we are seeing a significant increase in sponsorship by local businesses.
>
> Leanne, economic development officer, rural community

Social Benefits

The social benefits of the arts were reported as being of paramount importance by all interviewees:

> Our activities usually attract a fair number of people — people enjoy them and come back year after year. It's a real social occasion; people all muck in together and have a bit of fun.
>
> Carol, local government official, rural community

While the majority of interviewees agreed that the social value of involvement in the arts was hard to quantify, they reported that people were more likely to consider themselves to be more involved in community life after participating in group activities. Taking part in the management and operation of community events and festivals allowed people to feel useful and able to make a real contribution to the community. Finally, some interviewees stressed that participation in local community networks and organisations encouraged people to come together and work for the common good of that community. One interviewee provided the following cogent summary of the social benefits of the arts:

> It's really about working together and getting a feeling of personal fulfilment and the satisfaction about making a contribution. It's also about meeting new people and talking and listening to them and realising that everyone has a contribution to make.
>
> Maree, president, local arts council, remote/rural community

Several interviewees stressed the importance of building self-esteem and trust through open and collaborative communications with community members. Some reported that communities also need access to basic infrastructure such as meeting rooms and public spaces in which people can meet to work on projects, develop networks and strengthen connections.

While there was a strong consensus that the arts provide significant social benefits to the community, most of these benefits were reportedly related to the role of the arts in generating opportunities for social interaction. While these represent significant community benefits, including the development of a socially cohesive community, four interviewees questioned the comparative social value of the arts in community development. Their views are exemplified by Brian's comment:

> There are a lot of social benefits arising from arts-based activities in our community but, when compared with other social events, they probably pale into insignificance. Especially when we compare the arts with sporting events like our race meetings which really bring people together and have a strong community focus. Even pony club events attract a greater number of people than arts-based stuff … and football galvanises the community much more than our local theatre production or our art exhibitions.
>
> Brian, president, local arts council, rural community

Generally, all communities visited during the site visits recognised the social value of the arts and the majority of interviewees reported satisfactory participation in arts events. However, it should be noted that the majority of positive responses were related to attendance at arts-based events such as concerts and festivals and participation in workshops. There was little evidence of community-level active participation in arts-based projects that might build tangible outcomes for the community and develop human and social capital within the community:

> The arts sometimes operate in the same way sport does — it's spectator entertainment. People in this community are not involved in the arts. It's good to see but not to do.
>
> David, arts teacher, regional community, rural community

Issues Impacting on the Arts in Communities

Interviewees were asked to identify and consider other issues impacting on the arts in their community. These issues may be categorised as community engagement, funding for the arts, and demographic changes impacting on communities.

Community Engagement

Several interviewees indicated that the major issue impacting the arts in their community was members' lack of interest and engagement. In several communities the arts were reportedly seen as elitist, attracting participation by only a small section of the community. In one community a group of disengaged youths were involved in painting historical murals on the supports of the town's main bridge, creating a unique, pictorial history of the community. Council built a pathway to allow visitors and tourists to stroll through the supports and learn a little of the community's history. However, the local arts community failed to engage with or support the project with some members openly criticising the results suggesting that it was not real art.

One interviewee went even further by suggesting that the problem arose from a deep-seated negativity to the arts in the community:

> There is a major problem with negativity — not only do people not want to make an effort but they have no connection with the arts. They're just not interested and see no use in the arts.
>
> Sonya, community development officer, remote/rural community

She reported that community negativity had caused a decline in the number of community volunteers and the closure of two community organisations. She observed that the current approach of the local council to focus its efforts on increasing tourist numbers to the town may contribute to the disengagement of residents. That is, while council's approach may increase revenue to local businesses and have certain medium- and long-term impacts, there was also an immediate need for council to develop approaches more attuned to improving the liveability of the town by improving facilities for locals and engaging community members.

One interviewee reported that, while there were high levels of engagement in his community, it was limited in its reach and attracted engagement from only small sections of the community:

> We need to work harder not just to increase the number of people involved in the arts but also to increase the types of people involved — the young, the poor, the average bloke.
>
> Brian, president, arts council, rural community

Others focused on the need to change prevalent community cultures, with several suggesting that their communities were just not open to new possibilities:

> As a community we just don't know how to say 'yes' to possibilities. Our attitudes are entrenched and we are more likely to point out why things will not work rather than saying 'let's give it a try'. We need to develop a culture of experimentation — some things will work; others will fail but we need to try new things. Otherwise people will continue to do the same things and continue to think that all art should be landscapes depicting a western sunset.
>
> Ann, local artist, remote/rural community

Funding

The majority of interviewees reported that current levels of funding for the arts are inadequate. Responses were generally focused on government support for the arts:

> There's a lot of rhetoric from both state and local government about the importance of the arts to communities but that's not backed up with dollars. We're not lacking in ideas but we can't do things without money.
>
> Maree, president, arts council, remote/rural community

When questioned about other funding mechanisms such as local sponsorships and fundraising activities, several interviewees reported that local fundraising was limited to raffles and street stalls that raised very little money. Local sponsorships of the arts in communities were almost nonexistent and, where they did occur, the amounts involved were very small:

> Local businesses provide some sponsorship for major events like our festival but are usually only prepared to provide a couple of hundred dollars. But at least they are now recognising that the festival brings money into the community and their businesses benefit so they are prepared to support it. There is a long, long way to go before they begin to appreciate and support the arts in a broader way.
>
> Kerry, president, arts council, rural community

A more imaginative approach to arts funding was suggested by one interviewee who argued for a much broader-based approach to arts funding:

> I think just about everyone agrees that the arts should be a part of broader issues and the biggest issue in the bush at the moment is the environment and environmental issues are not just about grazing practices — art has a key role to play in addressing environmental issues. We should be seeking out opportunities to apply for funds available through environmental programs or just seeking to partner with environmentalists.
>
> Annette, local artist, remote/rural community

This comment raises the issue of partnerships, which, surprisingly, was not a primary focus of the environmental scanning process, as only one interviewee raised the possibility that partnerships may be a solution to many other problems/issues identified.

Demographic Changes

A commonly expressed concern related to the steady decline of rural and remote populations. From an arts perspective, this represents a real threat to maintaining the necessary talent and human resources in communities to provide leadership in the arts. However, some community leaders reported a perceived lack of opportunity in rural and remote communities for talented artists:

> We can't expect to keep people when the opportunities are much greater on the coast … but if we could generate a little more community interest in the arts we might manage to nurture local talent and even lure people back to the community, at least for a short while.
>
> Tanya, community development officer, remote/rural community

While this problem is not as prevalent in larger regional communities, these communities face problems of a slightly different nature. As roads and transport services improve, small and medium regional communities are competing with larger centres in both business and the arts:

> More and more people are travelling to [the major regional centre] for shopping, business and entertainment. As the road continues to improve, the travelling time gets less and people find it easy and convenient to travel. For shopping, the choice is greater and the prices are cheaper. For the arts, there is much more on offer — better and bigger productions, better galleries and access to arts courses through the TAFE.
>
> Anthony, councillor, regional community

Overall, interviewees reported that the major outcome of a decreasing population was the negative impact on local businesses:

> More businesses are closing every year. We maintain essential services — food, petrol, accommodation — but specialist services cannot survive. This impacts the quality of life in the community. Local artists can't get their materials locally but there are a lot of things we used to be able to buy locally that we can't anymore. As businesses close, business services leave and the closure of banks has been the most obvious of these.
>
> Lydia, community arts worker, remote/rural community

Perceptions of the Potential Role of the Arts in Addressing Unmet Community Demand

Lastly, interviewees considered potential areas of unmet community demand to which the arts may be able to make a contribution. Responses focused on the need (i) to engage community youth more effectively, (ii) to support community leadership in the arts, (iii) to support new and evolving local artists, (iv) to adopt a longer-term, more strategic approach to arts programs, and (v) to generate new ideas and new approaches to art in communities.

Youth Engagement in the Arts

The lack of engagement by young people in the arts was an expressed concern in all communities visited during the environmental scanning process. While the majority of communities indicated that local schools worked hard to engage students in art, it was seen to be difficult to transfer school-based art to community-based art:

> It's almost like the kids think its fine to get involved in art in school but it's not cool to get involved in the community arts — I think we have to somehow make it more attractive to kids but I don't know how.
>
> Melinda, president, arts council, remote/rural community

One interviewee suggested that the problem of youth engagement was a complex problem in rural and remote communities but that the solution was necessarily much broader that the arts per se:

> Youth disengagement is a complex problem and we talk about the arts and how we might get them involved but this approach reflects the whole problem with arts in the community. We are facing big problems and the arts are only a small, a very small, part of the solution. We need to address the problem of youth on many levels — we need to build facilities and programs across a whole range of areas and interests. We need programs that address what young people want and what they will engage with. Our approach to youth and the arts is too narrow and too insular — if the arts are to be part of the solution they need to be integrated into other programs.
>
> Brian, president, arts council, remote/rural community

The other possibility raised by one interviewee was the role of new technology in engaging community youth:

> One thing we do is advertise our events in the local newspaper but we forget that the kids don't read the newspapers. Not just the kids but all people are more and more getting their information from the internet. We need to develop a community presence — well at least try it, there's no guarantees that it will work but it's worth a shot.
>
> Karla, community worker, remote/rural community

The same interviewee also considered the potential role of information technology in the arts as a strategy to engage youth:

> Our arts teacher offers free art courses — two afternoons a week for anyone who would like to come. Perhaps we could encourage the technology teachers to work with her. I'm sure the school would provide community access to the community labs out of hours. It would be a way of experimenting with this new media that we hear so much about. We couldn't afford to support it as a community but with the resources already at the school, it just might help to engage kids in art.
>
> Karla, community worker, remote/rural community

Supporting Leadership and Governance in the Arts

Support and training are fundamental to helping more people become leaders in their community. Yet community arts leaders and the organisations in which they work do not receive the support and training required to play an effective role. Those people in the community fulfilling a leadership role in the arts are usually volunteers and are often not recognised as community leaders by government or other support agencies:

> There are a few people in the community who always take a leadership role. They are the few we rely on to get things done but we as a community don't give anything back. We need to nourish and support these people.
>
> David, local businessman, remote/rural community

While support for people fulfilling existing leadership roles is important, the identification and mentoring of new leadership is equally important:

> The itinerant workers are often the leaders of the community especially the arts teachers. We need to get better at recognising the leadership potential of our own people and start to support people instead of just expecting people to step up.
>
> Karla, community arts worker, remote/rural community

When questioned about the type of training that might support the development of local leaders, interviewees suggested training in negotiation, committee management, team-building, prioritising and goal-setting skills. Interviewees also suggested a range of training options in areas not typically associated with leadership — including training in developing community organisations, developing business plans, bookkeeping, fundraising, recruiting members and employees, and people skills such as dealing with conflict — suggesting that, in addition to leadership, there is a need for the development of management skills in the arts.

Identification, Development and Support for New and Emergent Artists

Just as arts leaders need to be supported, so too do communities need to identify and support emergent local artists. Several interviewees indicated that the number of local artists in their communities was declining:

> There are about 10 local artists practising in the community and most live just out of town on properties. They participate as much as they can but their contribution is fairly limited. When they retire or move from the area, there is no one to take their place.
>
> Brian, president, local arts council, remote/rural community

Another interviewee suggested that communities need to become much more active in promoting and supporting emergent local artists:

> There are many talented people in town but we need to generate interest and then support the development of these people. Our approach at the moment is a broad approach that allows everyone to participate if they want to. We probably need to continue to do this but at the same time we need to focus on real potential and develop long-term approaches to nourishing local talent.
>
> Carol, local councillor, regional community

Another interviewee developed the issue further:

> You know we have part-time positions in the council that provide assistance and guidance for farmers and business people. We should create a position to support and guide local artists. Not just in their own practice but the position could mentor local artists to take a more active role across a range of local issues — even nominate them for positions on committees and boards. That might create a bit of new thinking around the place.
>
> David, council employee, regional community

There was strong evidence across all communities that the arts and artists need to be supported. There was also evidence in some communities that issues around the identification and support of emerging artists are being added as new items on local agendas. There is, however, no evidence of any practical approaches to support these artists. The few interviewees who indicated their interest in new roles for artists in addressing broader community concerns also suggested that only an embryonic interest in the arts and artists moving towards a more integrated role could be discerned in communities at this stage.

A Long-term Strategic Focus

There is evidence from the interviews that the arts in rural and remote/rural communities suffer from approaches governed by short-term goals and strategies exacerbated by annual funding cycles that limit longer-term strategic planning. Several interviewees argued for the need to stimulate new thinking and new approaches to the integration of the arts with community goals. A small step in this direction is being undertaken by one local council that is adopting new approaches to arts funding:

> We are moving away from grants (the hand-out mentality) towards a tender-based approach. Instead of the same organisations just getting the same amount of money every year to run the same events, we are asking all community organisations to bid for funding. We hope that it will help them think about what they are doing and plan new approaches to attract funds. We also hope that it will stimulate new groups within the community. There is a lot of resistance in the community but we will continue — it will take a few years.
>
> Brian, president, arts council, remote/rural community

Several interviewees recommended a more central role for local government in planning and funding the arts in communities. There is evidence from the interviews that the communities that are most successful in supporting the arts are those with active and involved councils. Some of the most proactive councils have developed local projects aimed at integrating the arts with broader community goals. Such projects include using local artists to design new entrances to towns, commissioning concept designs to enhance streetscapes, and cultural mapping of the community. Other councils have adopted specific strategic directions for the arts in order to involve local artists and arts workers more actively in community projects. One council has developed a three-year community plan focusing exclusively on local history and the environment. By focusing community efforts so specifically, the council has been able to channel the talents and the resources of the whole community to achieve significant tangible and intangible outcomes. The community has created local attractions that have resulted in increased visitor numbers and a strong sense of history and pride in community.

New Ideas, New Policies and New Approaches

One interviewee noted that regional and remote communities are facing significant social, economic and environmental challenges that threaten their very existence:

> There are many challenges facing the community but these are big issues requiring new ways of thinking in all areas — business, agriculture, government. The arts or rather artists may have something to contribute but I think we've missed the boat with art. The problem is now so critical that it requires action now — the arts are not currently in the game.
>
> Jack, director, development and community services, rural community

This perception that the arts are on the periphery of the challenges facing communities was also indicated by the operator of a local enterprise specialising in the manufacture and sale of creative products:

> I'm not an artist. I'm not part of the arts community.
> I'm a businesswoman.
>
> Melinda, business owner, remote/rural community

There is a view in communities that current problems need new ideas and approaches and an increase in creative problem solving and innovative thinking. There is, however, little evidence that the arts are seen as making or able to make a contribution to solving current problems. One interviewee reported that a big problem for communities was that they lack a vision for the future:

> We just plod along doing the same things year in and year out. There is no view of where the community is heading or, more importantly, where we want to be heading. We are a community of just 600 people, we should be able to come together and develop a shared view of what we want our future to be.
>
> Sophia, economic development officer, remote community

The same interviewee went on to describe some approaches that might be useful to the community in developing a shared vision for the future:

> People wouldn't engage with formal processes to develop a view of future directions. One way of getting people engaged might be to work with local and external artists to develop new designs for the community — things like streetscapes and art at the entrances to the town. Some of the designs could be a bit controversial to encourage debate and discussion. The designs could be displayed publicly for comment. One outcome of such an approach would be to stimulate thinking about our future public face. We could then develop some design principles to guide future development. The other benefit would be community recognition of just what artists can contribute to the community.
>
> Sophia, economic development officer, remote community

Clearly, the data from site visits and interviews suggest that there is an important role for the arts and artists in working with communities to generate new ideas and visions for the future — a resource currently under-accessed and under-used.

8
The Case Studies

The Case Studies in Prospect

One of the key aspects of planning and implementing the survey and site visits was the identification of relevant community projects and initiatives. This would serve two main purposes: (i) to inform and illustrate key issues arising from the research; and (ii) to provide a data bank from which three projects could be selected for further and more in-depth case study analysis. The activities identified through the environmental scan fell into four broad categories: (i) activities involving the direct participation of the community in planning and conducting projects and events; (ii) activities in which community members participate indirectly in events planned and conducted by others; (iii) activities planned and supported by community-based organisations and operated primarily by the community for the community; and (iv) activities conducted by external organisations bringing new services to the community. Table 30 synthesises these to provide a framework to guide the selection of projects for detailed case study analysis.

Table 30. Types of Projects and Initiatives Identified during the Survey and Site Visits.

Category of community activity	Examples	Community outcomes			Other outcomes
		Social	Cultural	Economic	
1. Direct community participation — activities planned, controlled and influenced by the community.	Arts-based enterprises and businesses. Local festivals. Cultural tourism initiatives. Art exhibitions. Theatre productions. Cultural planning and development.	Builds community networks and improves personal ties. Improves community cohesiveness. Develops community leadership skills. Builds social capital. Encourages community collaboration. Builds community identity and pride.	New cultural products. Increases cultural capital. Improved community image (internal and external). Enhances community skills in artistic decision making and creative problem solving.	Improves human capital — new skills and abilities. Creates new revenue streams/wages for local people. Increases revenue from tourism. Develops supporting industries and enterprises.	Increases opportunities for self-expression and personal creativity. Engages marginalised people including migrants, youth, etc. Increases sense of individual worth and self-esteem. Develops new business skills.
2. Community as audience — external events or programs brought to the community either by external agencies or the community itself.	Touring exhibitions and performance troupes. Festivals (where community is participating in a regional or state-wide initiative).	Creates opportunities for social interaction. Increases opportunities for shared enjoyment. Improves exposure to the arts. Relieves stress. Provides new experiences and expands personal horizons.	Provides access to new cultural experiences.	Attracts visitors and expendable income from neighbouring towns and regions.	Increases the propensity of people to become involved in the arts. Increases access to the arts by people who have limited access.

Category of community activity	Examples	Community outcomes			Other outcomes
		Social	Cultural	Economic	
3. Community support organisations — community-based organisations operated primarily by the community for the community.	Arts service and promotion organisations. Retail outlets for local artistic products. Local art schools or collectives.	Develops community leadership skills. Stimulates community networks. Encourages collaboration.	Increases opportunity for involvement in the arts. Increases appreciation for local heritage and history. Improves community image (internal and external).	Increases revenue from sale of local artistic product.	Increases opportunities for self-expression and enjoyment. Improves individuals' sense of belonging to a community.
4. External art organisations — external organisations providing services to the community.	Art schools (programs and weekend workshops etc.). Regional and state-wide coordinating bodies/ funding agencies. Service providers. Peak bodies for the arts.	Increases access to opportunities and exposure to the arts. Develops expertise and resources not available to the community.	Provides access to new cultural insights.	Provides access to funds that may be used to generate new income streams for the community.	

Source: Author's research.

Of the four categories of activity identified in Table 30, it is argued that only two will illuminate issues being addressed in this book. Given that category one (direct community participation) projects and initiatives demonstrate a breadth of community outcomes across social, cultural and economic domains, it certainly warrants further investigation. However, category two (community as audience) provides little new information about the arts in community development and it is unlikely that projects from this category would yield useful insights. Both categories three (community support organisations) and four (external art organisations) focus on supporting the arts in community development. However, the analysis in Table 30 shows that the range of outcomes from category four is much more limited than that for category three. Hence the case studies are drawn from categories one (direct community participation) and three (community support organisations).

Framework and Reporting Structure for Case Studies

The three projects identified for detailed case study analysis are:

1. Cultural planning in a pre-innovation context — an examination of a program to stimulate arts-based community development through the development of a community cultural plan and strategy
2. Networking cultural support — an examination of the role of a state-wide support organisation with the objective of supporting arts-based community development in regional, rural and remote/rural communities
3. A cottage enterprise comes of age — an examination of the growth of a local arts-based enterprise in a remote/rural community.

All three case studies represent separate and unique approaches to arts-based community development that share the common objectives of supporting community capacity building and growth. The case study framework and reporting structure builds on these common objectives and identifies nine areas of interest to guide the case study investigations. These nine areas are identified in Table 31, which also provides questions to guide the case study investigations across the nine areas of interest.

Table 31. Case Study Framework and Reporting Structure.

Area of interest	Focus questions
Stimulus for the project/initiative	How did the project begin? Why did the project begin? Who supported the project? Who funded the project? What community needs was the project addressing? How was the community involved in the project?
Ideological platforms of the project/ initiative	On what, if any, guiding principles was the project based? How did contemporary ideological positions impact on the design of the project?
Major milestones and achievements	What are the major achievements of the project? What milestones did the project set? To what extent were these achieved?
Partnerships and networks	Who supported the project? What networks were established? What existing networks were used to support the project? What, if any, partnerships were formed? Formal or informal? How did project partnerships work? What synergies were created? What were the benefits of partnerships and networks?
Innovation and creativity	How did the project contribute to the application of creativity and innovation in communities?
Leadership	Who/what provided leadership? How was leadership exercised?
Management and evaluation	How was the project/initiative managed? How effective was the management of the project? How was the project/initiative evaluated? What were the results?
Project/initiative outcomes	What were the major outcomes of the project? Short-term outcomes? Long-term outcomes? How did the community benefit from the project?
Conclusions and implications	What are the implications of the project for the future? What can be learned from the project?

Source: Author's research.

The nine areas identified in Table 31 also provide a reporting framework for the case studies. Each of the case study reports presented in this chapter addresses the nine identified areas of interest, albeit in a structure appropriate to the individual case. The reporting structure for quotes from case study informants differs from the approach used in Chapter 7 in that names are not used to identify informants, who requested anonymity.

Case Study One: Cultural Planning in a Pre-Innovation Context

Cultural Planning: A Stimulus for Change

Blackall is a small remote/rural community located in western Queensland, approximately 960 kilometres from the state capital. It has a population of approximately 1,200 but, like many other rural/remote towns, its population has been in steady decline for the last two decades. Also like many other rural/remote communities, Blackall is confronted by unprecedented challenges as its traditional economies contract, its young people move to the cities, and cheaper imports challenge local production. These factors inevitably impact on the future viability and survival of the town itself. To address problems arising from these changes, the Blackall Shire Council sought to stimulate the creative energies of the town through the development and implementation of a cultural plan.

The genesis of the plan was the Blackall Tourism and Economic Vitalisation Strategy, which identified the arts and arts-based products as one of the platforms on which the economic potential of the region could be achieved. The strategy recognised that the shire had a wealth of arts workers, arts facilities, and arts-based products, events and festivals but also recognised that these resources were seldom harnessed in a coordinated or strategic way that could lead to measurable outcomes for the community as a whole (Blackall Shire Council, 2003, p. 4). Following the development of the vitalisation strategy, the council initiated a process to develop a new cultural plan to provide a strategic approach to building and coordinating arts and cultural activities in Blackall. The vision for the cultural plan was that it would stimulate a 'dynamic diverse direction to invigorate Blackall — its people, place and purpose' (Blackall Shire Council, 2005, p. 5). From its inception, the key focus of the plan was to achieve this vision. The plan outlined strategies to improve networking opportunities between government, arts organisations, cultural associations, local businesses and individuals. It was proposed that such networking would increase cross-fertilisation between the arts and non-arts sectors of the community. The key direction and stimulus for the cultural planning process was summarised by a Blackall Shire Council Economic Development Officer:

> Right from the beginning we were focused on what we already have, which we thought was a lot in the way of arts and crafts. But we also had a lot of other activities and things that could be enhanced through the arts. We saw the cultural plan as making the connections between things. We also thought that by making the connections, say between the arts and tourism, we could connect with the economic outcomes for the community and stimulate arts-based products (Interview 1 with Informant 1, Site Visit 1, 2004).

A Cultural Planning Working Group formed to guide the development of the plan reflected this key aim and included council officers, artists and arts workers, business owners and operators, and tourism promoters.

The cultural planning process commenced with a comprehensive mapping exercise to identify and document existing cultural facilities, associations, events and other key contributors to the cultural life of Blackall. The decision to map existing contributors to Blackall cultural life was based on the strongly held belief by the council and members of the working group that the community had unique cultural facilities and resources that would provide a strong base for further development:

> We are very proud of Blackall — we have more arts-based events and other things than just about any other community in the west. We've been doing it for years. We really wanted to build on our achievements but also make connections between the groups that haven't always worked well together. More than that, we also wanted to make new connections particularly with groups that didn't really see how the arts might help the community grow (Interview 1 with Informant 2, Site Visit 1, 2004).

The key results of the initial mapping exercise are summarised in Figure 4, which scopes local facilities, networks, associations, festivals and events in order to illustrate the breadth and depth of local arts-based initiatives in the local community.

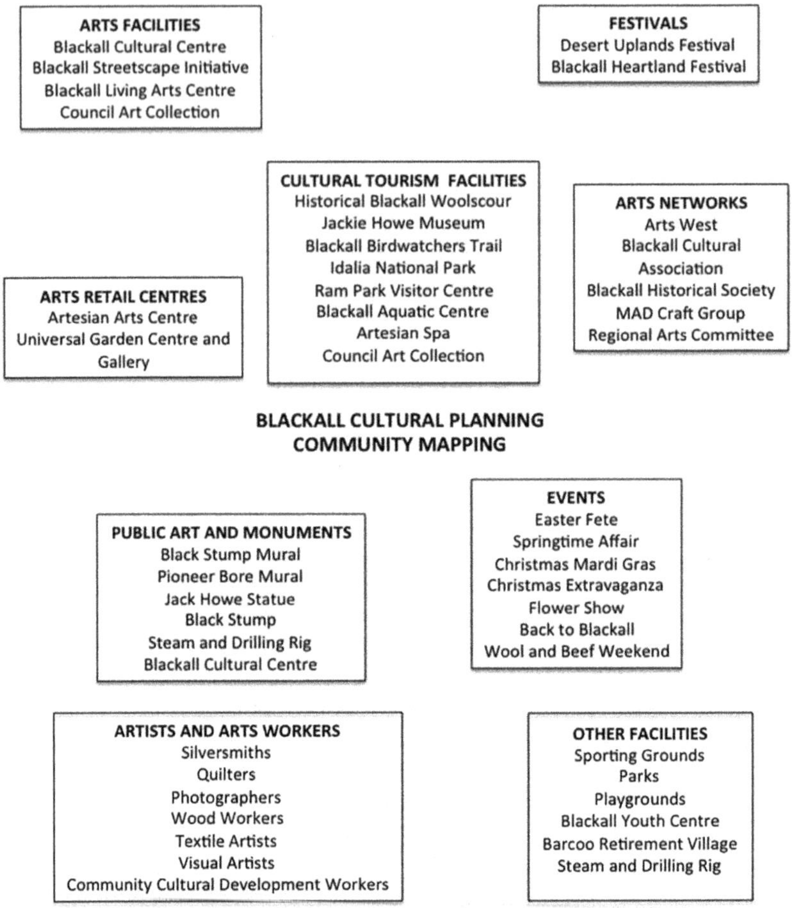

ARTS FACILITIES
Blackall Cultural Centre
Blackall Streetscape Initiative
Blackall Living Arts Centre
Council Art Collection

FESTIVALS
Desert Uplands Festival
Blackall Heartland Festival

CULTURAL TOURISM FACILITIES
Historical Blackall Woolscour
Jackie Howe Museum
Blackall Birdwatchers Trail
Idalia National Park
Ram Park Visitor Centre
Blackall Aquatic Centre
Artesian Spa
Council Art Collection

ARTS NETWORKS
Arts West
Blackall Cultural Association
Blackall Historical Society
MAD Craft Group
Regional Arts Committee

ARTS RETAIL CENTRES
Artesian Arts Centre
Universal Garden Centre and Gallery

BLACKALL CULTURAL PLANNING COMMUNITY MAPPING

EVENTS
Easter Fete
Springtime Affair
Christmas Mardi Gras
Christmas Extravaganza
Flower Show
Back to Blackall
Wool and Beef Weekend

PUBLIC ART AND MONUMENTS
Black Stump Mural
Pioneer Bore Mural
Jack Howe Statue
Black Stump
Steam and Drilling Rig
Blackall Cultural Centre

ARTISTS AND ARTS WORKERS
Silversmiths
Quilters
Photographers
Wood Workers
Textile Artists
Visual Artists
Community Cultural Development Workers

OTHER FACILITIES
Sporting Grounds
Parks
Playgrounds
Blackall Youth Centre
Barcoo Retirement Village
Steam and Drilling Rig

Figure 4. Overview of Blackall Cultural Mapping.
Source: Interviews with Blackall Shire Council Economic Development Officer.

Figure 4 represents the outcomes of an extensive mapping exercise demonstrating the scope and nature of community involvement in Blackall.

Community Development Ideologies: Tensions and Resolution

The Blackall Cultural Plan identified community cultural development (CCD) as a key guiding ideology (Blackall Shire Council, 2005b). The working group also identified CCD as a concept to ensure that the cultural planning process would enhance the lives of Blackall residents, build community spirit and pride, and foster a strong sense of local identity and belonging. However, some strain could be identified between CCD as an ideology and the key directions identified for the cultural plan. These are well reflected in the comments of one of the working group members:

> I guess we all agreed with the overall concept of CCD but we also thought that Blackall was a long way down the track with community spirit. We felt that we had a great sense of community involvement and we wanted to build on this not go back to the beginning. Culture and the arts were already part and parcel of our town — we wanted to strengthen this and we also wanted to move the arts from the periphery to the centre of planning (Interview 1 with Informant 3, Site Visit 2, 2005).

Perhaps the most critical tensions arose from the fact that the Blackall Shire Council, on behalf of the working group, contracted consultants to work with the working group and the community to develop and implement the plan. The consultants were CCD specialists and stressed the social objectives of CCD, especially social inclusion and equity. As a consequence, a major concern arose that some of the core principles of CCD given prominence by the consultants conflicted with a key identified aim of the cultural plan, which was to 'move towards the development of arts-based industries for economic outcomes' (Blackall Shire Council, 2005b, p. 6). The working group members sought to address this tension by balancing the social outcomes of CCD with the economic aims of the plan by adopting a very pragmatic definition of CCD:

> Community Cultural Development (CCD) occurs when communities come together and engage in cultural activities that enhance people's lives, socially and economically. Cultural development is about the community working together towards common interests (Blackall Shire Council, 2005b, p. 6).

Synergies, Partnerships and Connections

The Blackall Community Cultural Plan recognises the movement of the community from a traditional rural economy to one that would 'rely on diversity, tourism and cultural resources' (Blackall Shire Council, 2005b, p. 8). It identifies that arts and culture will become pivotal in creating sustainable development through value adding to existing industries such as retail, tourism, sport and recreation. The plan states that there is a need to 'explore new creative partnerships that link the arts with business and tourism' (Blackall Shire Council, 2005b, p. 8). In this context, the core platform of the plan was to stimulate opportunities for these partnerships to establish and flourish.

One practical objective of the cultural plan aimed at stimulating partnerships was 'to encourage local sporting groups to use arts and arts workers in their operational activities' (Blackall Shire Council, 2005b, p. 30). A local activity to support the achievement of this objective included promoting local artists through the display and installation of local artworks at sporting venues and clubhouses. In the years following the release of the cultural plan, two sporting organisations displayed local artworks, albeit only at the behest of those members of the Cultural Planning Working Group who were concurrently members of the sporting organisations. This is not indicative of a growing partnership between artists and sporting clubs as a result of the initiative. Far from developing working relationships, the artists whose works have been displayed in sporting clubs had no ongoing allegiance with the clubs:

> I know two of my works are there but I'm not a member and have never been inside the club. I've certainly never worked with them nor have any type of partnership with them. I'm just hoping that someone might notice and go to Artesian Arts to buy something of mine. From my perspective, it's just a marketing ploy, not a partnership (Interview 1 with Informant 6, Site Visit 3, 2006).

A related initiative was to encourage sporting groups to engage local artists to design and produce trophies. As a result of a series of metalworking and silversmithing workshops held in Blackall over the previous decade, several community artists work in metal, so the initiative was grounded in real possibilities. However, the time and costs associated with using local artists proved to be significant barriers for the clubs who could source trophies much more cheaply from external commercial providers.

A further objective of the cultural plan was to 'create a cultural network to share knowledge, innovation and expertise' (Blackall Shire Council, 2005b, p. 30). This cultural network would be designed to reflect the key strategic direction of the plan, which was to encourage and broker strategic alliances and partnerships. At the time of the last data collection visit to Blackall, the cultural network had been meeting for just over two years with active representation from the shire council, local businesses, arts retail organisations, community organisations, sporting clubs and community artists. While such representation is broad, all members of the network have been long-term supporters of the arts in Blackall with a belief that the arts offer great potential in growing the community. At that stage, however, the network had not been successful in extending its influence across businesses and organisations disengaged from the role of the arts in community growth:

> Despite our good intentions and efforts, we are still a closed shop. We support each other but we can't crack the broader business community. Most of them just don't see any value in the arts, well at least local arts. That's probably a bit unfair, they support our major events, especially our festivals, but they can't see a role for the arts in supporting their business in more strategic ways through partnerships or collaborations on particular things — maybe we just can't force it (Interview 3 with Informant 1, Site Visit 3, 2006).

This insightful comment suggests that successful partnerships probably need to evolve from a legitimate and clearly defined community or business needs that cannot be mandated or manufactured through goodwill alone. Just less than two years into the implementation of the plan, members of the working group have begun to realise that it needs revision to reflect their new understanding that they could not force the development of community and business partnerships:

> We realised that we couldn't make partnerships work unless there was some purpose to them. We could promote the potential benefits but, unless there was a clear reason, nobody was interested (Interview 3 with Informant 3, Site Visit 3, 2006).

It may be that the role of community cultural plans is limited to promoting the potential of partnerships and seeking opportunities to stimulate partnerships once a business opportunity has been identified. Aspects of the plan that aimed at ensuring open communication and information exchange go some way to creating an environment in which opportunities, if they arise, may be acted on if the plan is successful in pre-establishing, clarifying and promoting potential areas of mutual interest.

Another aspect of the cultural plan was the identification, mapping and promotion of current community capabilities on which local business could draw should the need arise. These internal promotional activities were aimed at breaking down barriers, real and perceived, between sectors of the community in order to link artists and arts workers with business and enterprises. The message of the contribution of the arts to community was well understood by local artists and arts workers and the shire council, but after two years of implementation appeared still not to be well understood by the community. The following comment by a local businessman points to an element of antipathy to the role of the arts in community building:

> Mate ... it's all well and good but it's a hobby ... something that the Mrs does in her spare time. It's never going to bring in any money for me or for the town ... maybe some spare change but that's it (Interview 1 with Informant 6, Site Visit 3, 2006).

While the Blackall Community Cultural Plan identified the key importance of partnerships within the community, the success of collaborative partnerships is likely to be some time away. Its long-term success would seem to be very dependent on the ability of the working group to work with the community in order to develop a better understanding and appreciation of the potential of the arts to improve the economic and social life of Blackall. In turn, this depends on the identification of tangible and real outcomes and models that clearly demonstrate such potential to community members.

Creativity and Innovation

Creativity is inherent in the Blackall Community Cultural Plan in that it is replete with new ideas and clever strategies. The objectives of the plan are far reaching and seek new approaches to community development based on new connections and the potential of new business opportunities. Its emphasis on the integration of the arts across all sectors of the community is challenging and far reaching in its vision and commitment. However, it is clearly in a pre-innovation phase. Innovation involves much more than simply generating new ideas; it is also about doing something with them. In Blackall, the ideas have not yet been able to be implemented so that innovative outcomes for the community currently remain a desire rather than a reality.

Indeed, the limited successes associated with the implementation of the cultural plan to date have been characterised by a lack of innovation, especially given the plan's dependence on existing programs and infrastructure as well as people already committed to the arts and community cultural development. In short, the Blackall community has been too narrow and cautious in its implementation of the plan, dealing exclusively in the known, rather than pushing the boundaries to broker and encourage diversity towards innovation.

There is also a possibility that the cultural plan has inhibited innovation in the community through too narrow a targeting of specific people and activities. It may not be enough simply to encourage the adoption of new approaches and new partnerships unless such a strategy connects broadly with all sectors of the community. Despite its laudable intentions, it may support too narrow and predictable an approach to the arts based mainly on the experiences and knowledge of the working group, the members of which have already identified as people committed to the arts. Moreover, they may be people wedded, either consciously or subconsciously, to the status quo:

> Perhaps we are just the same old group who has controlled things for many, many years. We certainly haven't gone out of our way to bring in new people with new ideas. We tend to focus on things that we know are valued by the community — we don't challenge the community. We only do the safe things (Interview 3 with Informant 3, Site Visit 3, 2006).

Major Milestones and Achievements

A major milestone in the planning stage of the development of the cultural plan was achieved when the council initiated and hosted a comprehensive training program focusing on cultural planning and community consultation. The training program was designed and delivered by an external consultant specialising in community cultural development. The training incorporated a five-day, face-to-face program followed by a six-month action learning phase in which participants conducted community consultations and undertook preliminary analyses of the outcomes of the consultations under the mentorship of the expert contractor. Participants in the training program reported that this program increased their skills and knowledge of CCD, cultural planning, and community consultations (training evaluation forms accessed during Interview 2 with Informant 1, 2004).[1] Perhaps more importantly, the action learning phase of the program allowed the participants to conduct a comprehensive consultation process involving surveys, interviews, focus groups and community meetings under the stewardship of experts. This activity provided the data on which the cultural plan was developed and also facilitated its initial analysis.

Another major milestone was the public release of the cultural plan. Community input into the plan had been based on the processes and outcomes of the community consultation and cultural planning training program and input from community members is quantified in Table 32.

Table 32. Community Consultation Responses: Cultural Planning.

Consultation	Distribution	Responses	
		No.	%
Community Survey	70	38	54
Community Meetings	1,000	161	16
Totals	1,070*	199	18

* Total population of Blackall at time of the consultation process was 1,659.
Source: Author's research.

The cultural plan was publicly released in 2005 with a community event to celebrate the artistic achievements of Blackall. The event was small and exclusive, attended by only 26 people (including 10 from the Cultural Planning Working Group and seven council employees); the event was invitation only and only 30 people were invited. It was an event characterised by a lack of fanfare, which represented a lost opportunity to engage the wider community in the implicit and explicit challenges ahead.

A third major milestone was the first annual evaluation of the cultural plan. While many aspects of evaluation are addressed later in this chapter, it is important to acknowledge that the first annual evaluation was a watershed event in the development of the cultural plan.

1 Eighty per cent of workshop participants indicated that their knowledge of CCD had 'improved' or 'significantly improved'. Ninety per cent of workshop participants indicated that their skills in planning and consultation had 'improved' or 'significantly improved'.

It exposed a major fault, namely the absence of performance indicators on which to judge the success or otherwise of the implementation of the plan. The identification of this fault forced the working group to reconsider its approaches to the implementation of the plan:

> We came to the first evaluation meeting with a fair sense of optimism and achievement. We all had stories about what had happened in the last year — our festival was a great success; our inaugural Back to Blackall weekend had attracted huge numbers of visitors; Artesian Arts was achieving well ... It was all good until we looked again at the plan and realised that these great events were only a small part of what we had sought to achieve. We had no idea how we were going in the other areas or how we would tell when we were successful (Interview 3 with Informant 1, Site Visit 3, 2006).

As a consequence, the working group decided to develop performance measures for all the strategies identified in the cultural plan. However, the group seriously underestimated the difficulty of the task and, a year after the first evaluation, a full set of performance indicators had not yet been finalised. However, the experience was overall a positive one in that the working group developed a greater understanding of the complexity of the task and the necessity of developing approaches and measures to allow the whole community to assess and understand progress and achievements. In effect, the process led the working group to a continuous improvement model and approach to the implementation of the cultural plan.

Leadership

Leadership associated with the development and implementation of the Blackall Community Cultural Plan resides within the working group. Collectively, the group has been and continues to be the driving force for the implementation and continuous improvement of the cultural plan, with both positive and negative implications. On the positive side, the group has worked effectively and efficiently to identify and address community needs through the development of the first cultural plan for Blackall, thereby putting the arts and culture firmly on the local government policy agenda. Through extensive training the group has developed key skills in community consultation and cultural planning and has become a key source of expertise in the community. Representation on the working group is broad and encompasses many sections of the community, including council officials and employees, business operators and owners, tourism promoters, arts retail organisations, community organisations, artists, and youth. On the negative side, working group representation is almost exclusively based on people who are cognisant of the potential of the arts and are thus active promoters of the arts. It is a group with insular, closed networks, a group 'preaching to the converted' (Interview 2 with Informant 4, Site Visit 2, 2005). Opportunities to transfer skills and experiences from the working group to new people from the community have been limited by the group's inability to extend its reach across all community sectors. In addition, the group lacks a single spokesperson and advocate. While leadership is a complex phenomenon, key components of leadership include authority and the power and influence to forge or refashion allegiances and networks. What is lacking in Blackall is recognisable leadership with the authority and community influence to form new alliances with people and organisations who, as yet, have little or no appreciation of the potential role of the arts in the social and economic future of Blackall. There is a voice but no face to the leadership.

Management and Continuous Improvement

Management of the cultural plan is the responsibility of the Cultural Plan Working Group reporting to the shire council through the economic development officer who works closely and collaboratively with the community support and development officer of the council. Annual evaluation of the plan's implementation is a key part of the management responsibilities. As acknowledged already, evaluation has been made more difficult because the plan did not specify performance criteria or measurable outcomes against which progress can be benchmarked. The process for annual evaluation is, at best, ad hoc and based on activities known to working group members reflecting again the closed and insular nature of the group:

> I know it's not the best approach but we are well known in the community and have our fingers in many pies so we are in a good position to know how we're going (Interview 2 with Informant 3, Site Visit 2, 2005).

At worst, the evaluation process is based on the perceptions of the planners and is not subject to more objective, comprehensive and probing evaluation processes. The economic development officer articulated this problem:

> [W]e are a group of like-minded people with an agenda; we are evaluating programs that we have a vested interest in or programs that we know are running successfully. We are not evaluating the broad objectives. We know that Artesian Arts is running profitably so we see that as an achievement but we don't know how connections with the broader business community are developing (Interview 3 with Informant 1, Site Visit 2, 2005).

An objective evaluation program with measurable and visible outcomes would assist the community to understand objectives, recognise results and celebrate outcomes. Members of the planning group appear to have subsequently focused their discussions on the development of potential success indicators and performance measures. Potential indicators developed by the planning group are presented in Table 33.

Table 33. Potential Indicators to Guide Evaluation of the Cultural Plan.

Category	Possible indicators
Infrastructure	Number and type of uses of dedicated arts facilities. The activities arising from local arts organisations. The number of other community facilities used for arts activities. The amount of council expenditure on the arts.
Participation	The number of attendees at performances, events, exhibitions and workshops, etc. The number of commissions and public artworks from council. Membership of voluntary and community arts groups.
Creative activity	Number of commissions to community artists. Number of new employment opportunities for artists.

Source: Author's research.

It should first be noted that the indicators presented in Table 33 fail to address the core objectives of the cultural plan — for example, the stated key objective is to stimulate economic and social opportunities through the arts. The indicators also fail to provide realistic measurements of outcomes specified in the plan; more precision around the indicators still needs to be developed. Yet, while the performance indicators outlined in Table 33 remain immature and require further development, at least they represent a positive step by the working group to address problems and challenges arising from the implementation of the cultural plan. This early work on indicators provides a good foundation for future annual evaluations of the plan.

A further problem with this most recent approach to evaluation is that its impact reaches only the Cultural Planning Working Group and council, neither of which involves or engages the wider community. It was suggested by a member of the working group that the skills in community consultation acquired in the initial training program could be applied to evaluation and continuous improvement:

> We learnt a lot about consulting with the community to identify their concerns. If we used these skills to evaluate the plan we could re-engage the community and get meaningful feedback. It would be simple — this is what you said you want and this is what has been done. How are we going? We could lead the process; we have the tools and experiences — surveys, interviews and focus groups (Interview 3 with Informant 3, Site Visit 3, 2006).

A continuous evaluation program based on action research and involving the whole spectrum of the community would serve many purposes for Blackall. Firstly, it would re-establish and reinforce community expectations of the cultural planning process. Secondly, it would re-engage the community in processes and allow them to celebrate success and learn from one another's experiences. Thirdly, it would promote outcomes and provide a significant marketing advantage for the council. It remains to be seen if changes to the evaluation will result in a more inclusive implementation of the plan.

Outcomes

The most significant outcome of this case study is the design and development of the cultural plan, with its significant impacts, including the placement of the arts firmly on the local government policy agenda as well as the identification and documentation of local arts-based infrastructure, arts facilities and arts organisations. The resulting community recognition of its existing achievements through the arts (including successful festivals, active arts-based organisations, arts venues and facilities) has also been a significant outcome for the community, allowing the community to focus on and celebrate past efforts previously largely unheralded by the council and community. Recognising achievements also provided a sound platform on which to build new directions for the cultural plan.

The challenge for the cultural planners of Blackall was to respect the achievements of the past, identify and build on the existing local creative capital, and stimulate innovative approaches for the future through the development of new networks and connections. As the case study data collection was able only to focus on the development and very early implementation of the plan, it is possible to comment only on evolving outcomes. The plan has contributed to a positive community image of Blackall by its inhabitants and neighbouring towns and regions:

> Just by mapping and documenting everything that is happening in Blackall, people have said … yeah that's been good, we're really doing a fair bit (Interview 3 with Informant 2, Site Visit 3, 2006).

The cultural mapping undertaken to inform the plan has showcased the breadth and depth of the role of the arts in the Blackall community and strengthened the commitment to the arts by the council and the community. The plan also demonstrated the high levels of community engagement and support for the arts in the Blackall community, as evidenced by the high level of involvement of the community in festivals and major arts events, including significant sponsorship of these events by local businesses. Festivals and major events are an important part of Blackall social and business calendars and attract significant numbers of participants and visitors.

Strategies documented in the plan have contributed to a further deepening of community engagement by encouraging local groups to increase involvement in festivals and events with particular emphasis on activities to capitalise on under-utilised community resources identified through community consultation processes. Other simple strategies to encourage community engagement through the plan include (i) the publication of events and activities on the council website, (ii) the inclusion of community events and activities on all formal council presentations to the community and external organisations, (iii) promotion of events through school programs and newsletters, and (iv) the creation and publication of arts-based professional development and training programs and workshops.

Blackall has for many years demonstrated a strong respect for its history and heritage illustrated through a very active historic society and successful preservation programs, including the restoration of the Blackall Woolscour. The cultural plan recognised these successes and sought to build on past achievements, for example, by working with the historic society to develop a series of self-guided walks for visitors. Such strategies have since proven to be very successful as Blackall boasts many historical features within easy walking distance of one another, including public memorials, murals and public art. There are also plans underway to introduce a Blackall Heritage Week incorporating re-enactments and other public events.

Another key outcome of the cultural plan focuses on local lifestyle. A positive outcome of the plan to date has been the enhancement of the Blackall streetscape and surrounding parks through the creation of dog-walking areas and cycling tracks. An artists' walk has also been developed to allow interested visitors to visit key monuments, public art installations, art retail centres and galleries.

The area of the cultural plan that has proven to be the most challenging is the focus on business and industry. In three years little has been achieved in this focus area, even though it is a primary objective of the plan. A key strategy was to value-add to industry and business through arts products, production and interpretation:

> Even though everyone understands that festivals bring tourists and additional revenue to town, business people don't see any further value. They see that the art shop sells stuff but they can't think beyond that. They're just not interested in how the arts might generate new businesses and new business opportunities (Interview 3 with Informant 1, Site Visit 3, 2006).

A key success was the inclusion in the 2006/07 council budget of a creative industry development fund, but initiatives supported through the fund have been less than successful. One initiative included the stimulation of partnerships between business and community artists to encourage them to produce a collaborative corporate gift line for council. While individual artists worked to develop a gift line, they failed to involve local businesses in the venture and the initiative consequently failed to achieve its main aim of stimulating new community partnerships.

> Local businesses still see the arts as something that has little to do with their success and have not developed an appreciation of potential benefits that might arise from more active involvement with artists and arts workers (Interview 3 with Informant 1, Site Visit 3, 2006).

While the cultural plan provides some important outcomes for the community of Blackall, they remain at a pre-innovation level. They rely on conventional practices and traditional ways of viewing the arts in community development. In short, the design and implementation of the Blackall Community Cultural Plan represents simply more of the same.

Conclusions and Implications

The development of the arts as a central component of community development and growth is a complex and challenging endeavour. At its core is recognition that the arts may add significant value to existing community products and services as well as a belief that local arts and culture is a form of capital that can yield significant returns. The Blackall Community Cultural Plan recognises this as one potential of the arts without significantly addressing it in the form of realistic strategies and support initiatives. This is a key aspect incorporated into the plan's vision, mission and key result areas, including a commitment to support artists and businesses in 'building alliances and partnerships with industries and contribute to the local economy' (Blackall Shire Council, 2005b, p. 16). However, despite the promise of this objective, it is neither fully articulated nor supported by realistic strategies or initiatives. The plan fails to capitalise on the theme of business/arts alliances and instead resorts to projects and initiatives that simply maintain the status quo, and places major emphasis on building current initiatives and programs rather than developing strategic new approaches and initiatives. In this way, the opportunity for the cultural plan to provide a catalyst for the development of new enterprises, partnerships or collaborations between artists and businesses has been missed.

In the early implementation of the cultural plan, the arts continue to have a relatively low status within the broader community, especially when compared to sport as Table 34 indicates by drawing on the outcomes of a cultural audit conducted by the Blackall Shire Council.[2]

Table 34. Number of Arts Organisations vis-à-vis Sporting Organisations.

Arts and craft organisations (No. = 3)	Sporting organisations (No. = 19)	
Blackall Cultural Association. Artesian Arts. MAD Craft Group.	All Breeders Performance Horse Club. Barcoo Amateur Race Club. Barcoo Country Cricket Club. Barcoo River Associations. Blackall Camel Races Committee. Blackall Amateur Swimming Association. Blackall Bowling Club. Blackall Cricket Association. Blackall Golf Cub.	Blackall Gun Club. Blackall Junior Rugby League. Blackall Netball Association. Blackall Pistol Club. Blackall Polocrosse Club. Blackall Pony Club. Blackall Rugby League. Blackall Tennis Club. Cone Break Pony Club. Roo Shooters.

Source: Author's research.

The Blackall Community Cultural Plan provides strategic direction for the community and a framework for everyday action. Coordinated action requires commitment and funds — the real test is still being applied in the Blackall community.

Case Study Two: Networking Cultural Support

This case study differs from the localised Blackall case study in that it focuses on an organisation providing support to communities across the state of Queensland.

2 The unpublished cultural audit material was accessed during Interview 2 with Informant 1, Site Visit 2, 2005.

The Stimulus for a Support Network

In 1981 a small group of artists and community arts workers interested in supporting community arts across Queensland met in Brisbane and formed an organisation then known as the Community Arts Network of Queensland. Their motivation stemmed from concern that communities, especially smaller rural/remote communities, needed support in developing community initiatives and guidance in accessing funds to support their programs.

During its early years, the network's only form of income was from membership fees, and it was managed and supported on a totally voluntary basis. Its initial services, which focused on the provision of information about projects and funding opportunities, were well received by arts workers and the membership base of the network grew quickly across Queensland so that, by 1984, the network was in a position to employ staff to support its operations. At that time, the Community Arts Board of the Australia Council began to provide funds to support the production of a state-wide community arts newsletter. In 1985 the network attracted small grants from both the Australia Council for the Arts and the Queensland Government (QCAN, 1985).

The network quickly expanded its services to include the provision of advice and information to community groups and arts workers not only about projects and funding but also about professional development and networking opportunities, best practice examples and guidelines, problem solving and community networking. At this time, the network also became an active lobby group for community arts by targeting national, state and local governments (Interview with past president of QCAN, 2005).

From 1985 to 1996, the network's rapid growth coincided with a growing recognition by all stakeholders of the importance of the role of local government in promoting the arts in communities:

> It was in the late '80s that everyone started to focus on working with local government. They didn't have money but they became interested in the arts and how they work to help rural communities especially (Interview with past president of QCAN, 2005).

However, the first major stimulus for change occurred in 1987 when the Community Arts Board of the Australia Council was replaced by the Community Cultural Development Unit. This represented much more than a simple name change; it heralded new directions and a new focus for the network.

The focus of the network moved from its primary objective of making art accessible to communities to a new concept that suggested the arts could be used to address key issues impacting on communities, including social issues and community economic development. A second major stimulus occurred in 1992 when the Australia Council entered into a partnership with the Australian Local Government Association to promote the importance of the arts and cultural development within integrated local area planning strategies (Interview with past coordinator of the network, 2005). The effect on artists, community arts workers and the network itself was significant, as cultural development became serious business for local governments. It was during this stage of development that the network adopted a new name, Queensland Community Arts Network (QCAN).

Partnerships and Networks

QCAN's 2007–2010 Strategic Plan identified the increase of networking opportunities in rural/remote areas as a high priority (QCAN, 1985b). It also specified the need to develop more and stronger partnerships with other agencies providing complementary services to rural/remote communities. This direction in the strategic plan represented a consolidation and reinforcement of community networking, building on strengths that have always been a core component of QCAN's operations. QCAN's effectiveness in supporting community partnerships and networks is well illustrated through an examination of a project that was designed and managed by the organisation with the stated purpose of facilitating community networks and partnerships. The project was called CultureLink.

CultureLink was established to take advantage of evolving technologies and build on their potential to link geographically diverse groups of people with common goals around community growth and development (Notes from interview with CultureLink project officer, 2006). The project used web-conferencing technologies to create a multi-community forum, thus facilitating opportunities to bring together community arts workers, local government development officers, community volunteers and others in a virtual environment in which they could share information and undertake collaborative planning:

> This is the first time we have been able to build networks across communities that are geographically diverse. We can bring people together to share projects and experiences from Burketown to Birdsville (Notes from interview with CultureLink project officer, 2006).

The web-conferencing environment facilitates effective collaboration as it is flexible and responsive to users' needs (meetings can be arranged easily and quickly to address emerging issues) and provides clear, open, high-quality voice communication, videoconferencing, and data-sharing facilities. The project plan developed by QCAN staff captures the scope of the project. In the plan, the QCAN Project Officer describes the project as an approach that 'provides new opportunities for collaboration and networking by regional, rural and remote communities and promotes the ability of these communities to exercise control over their social, cultural and economic futures' (Notes from interview with CultureLink project officer, 2006). The other interesting application of the CultureLink project was the facility to link communities with key people from across the nation. During its first year of operation, five special sessions were held linking community members to experts in community development, specialists in cultural mapping, researchers in community regeneration, and people from state and national funding bodies to advise on application processes.

While maintaining funding for the CultureLink project presents a major challenge, the value of the program has been recognised by participating communities, and the maintenance and expansion of the program, including the financial management of the program, has now become the joint responsibility of participating regional, rural and remote/rural communities. CultureLink has proven its sustainability and by accepting ownership and control over the network, communities can support their individual and collective endeavours in community development:

> We set our own agendas and get on with it. We decide what the priorities are and plan our own meetings. Each of us take turns in organising meetings and it all works out really well (Notes from interview with local government community development officer, 2006).

It will be interesting to observe its evolution as communities exercise further control over the network. It is likely that practical, community-based issues may become more central to discussions and planning.

Despite the growth of CultureLink, QCAN has failed to develop networks and partnerships beyond the arts sector. At a time when the corporate sector is increasingly acknowledging its social responsibilities and recognising that environmental and social outcomes are as important as financial outcomes, QCAN has failed to capitalise on opportunities to forge links with community-based corporations and private organisations.

Milestones and Achievements

Despite its ideological rigidity, QCAN has several significant achievements that are recognised by communities and other stakeholders. As stated in a recent strategic plan, QCAN operated a state-wide community-based service that supported and promoted community cultural development practice (QCAN, 1985b). In this context, it had two distinct but related roles in the identification and use of community assets.

Firstly, it increased community access to information, ideas, advice and expertise, thus contributing to the scope and nature of community assets. Secondly, it supported communities in the identification of their own assets and, through training and professional development, assisted communities to plan for effective application of their assets.

In this context, QCAN's major achievements relate to the provision of training and professional development aimed at improving existing community assets. For example, rural/remote communities need financial assets that are accessed mainly through the monetary resources available to them, usually through government, to implement solutions to community problems. QCAN has provided a range of well-regarded financial management training programs aimed at helping artists to access and report on funds to support arts-based activities in communities:

> The courses are great — they are practical and useful and provide tools to help me report on the use of funds — to reconcile expenditure. It's now more important than ever. We all have to be accountable (Interview with community arts worker, 2006).

The training programs also target individual artists seeking to commercialise their art practices:

> The programs really helped me learn how to price my art. I now am much more confident when dealing with shops and dealers (Interview with community artists, 2006).

In addition, QCAN's information program includes newsletters, bulletins and web updates, which provide timely information to communities on grants and funding opportunities. It also provides a training program on writing funding applications.

Communities also need physical resources, assets such as community meeting halls, theatres, galleries, parks, and museums. QCAN's role in helping communities improve physical assets is limited but, through its information program, it helps communities' awareness of opportunities offered through government. Through its advisory service, it also provides ideas and options for communities struggling to improve their physical assets. In one instance it helped a community source a community meeting hall by facilitating negotiations with local government (Interview with Chief Executive Officer of QCAN (2003–2007), 2005).

Communities also need to build on their existing human resources — the skills, knowledge and abilities of people who live and work in the community. QCAN's achievements have been twofold: helping communities through its suite of training programs and professional development events aimed at building community skills, knowledge and expertise; and, when appropriate, assisting communities to source external expertise to work with community members to develop new skills and knowledge. External experts usually work as project managers and community mentors on short-term projects:

> QCAN has helped us to identify people who will come to the community to work with us. We were interested in working on public art but we have no skills or talents so we got someone to come and work with us (Interview with local government official, remote/rural community, 2006).

Finally, communities also need to identify and build social resources — the networks within communities that shape the quality of life in community. This has been a most challenging role for QCAN, and its achievements in this regard are difficult to measure. Central to its approach to building social resources is its training program.

Each training program brings together members of the community into a social grouping that represents a fledgling network. Where training programs encompass action learning through long-term projects, these networks can be sustained for up to six months or more. While QCAN has not conducted long-term evaluations of the sustainability of these networks, anecdotal evidence indicates that they sometimes evolve into permanent groupings, thus providing a long-term asset for the community (Interview with Chief Executive Officer of QCAN (2003–2007), 2005).

Management and Continuous Improvement

QCAN has adopted an annual management cycle that produces a business plan to guide the operations of the organisation during the subsequent 12-month period. Every third year, planning activities are extended to provide for the development of the next three-year strategic plan. The development of the business plan, together with the overarching strategic plan, includes a one-day workshop for the management committee (board), the director and all staff. An external facilitator who applies a variety of planning tools usually facilitates the planning day (Notes from interview with Chief Executive Officer of QCAN (2003–2007), 2006). Other important inputs to planning include the views of external stakeholders accessed through structured face-to-face and telephone interviews, an annual internet-based survey of members, analysis of the organisation's financial position, a review of past business plans, an environmental scan of the state and Commonwealth policy environment, and familiarisation with contemporary debates and theory in contemporary art and the creative industries (Notes from interview with administration officer of QCAN, 2006).

Financial management is also critically important to QCAN, as there is an expectation that any organisation funded primarily through public funds will display a high degree of professionalism and accountability. QCAN has demonstrated high-quality approaches to financial management; however, funding uncertainty remains a persistent issue for QCAN, and static or declining government funding in recent years has contributed to ongoing and mounting organisational anxiety. While QCAN has multiple sources of funds, including membership fees, specific project grants and training fees, it is still reliant on core funding from Commonwealth and state governments. While many community organisations have moved in recent years to diversify their funding sources and reduce their reliance on government, QCAN has not actively sought to expand its funding base either by seeking commercial opportunities or by adding value to its existing product and service base. Nor has it sought sponsorship from private organisations or benefactors despite the fact that none of its programs are financially sustainable without government subsidy (Notes from interview with Chief Executive Officer of QCAN (2003–2007), 2006).

While QCAN's management processes and procedures have been formalised and structured, they have failed to recognise and adequately build upon new opportunities. The organisation's knowledge of its operating environment and the appropriateness of its products and services in a changing context would appear to have been seriously flawed:

> They [QCAN] have really missed the boat — they now spend their time checking their books and providing the same old services. Other organisations are moving with the times and providing new approaches and helping communities look at new ways of doing things but QCAN just does the same old things. I think their days are numbered (Interview with past employee of QCAN, 2006).

In such an environment, the appropriateness of performance indicators is seriously compromised. QCAN developed performance indicators relevant to its plans and objectives, but those plans and objectives have proved to be no longer relevant to the needs of its primary clients — regional, rural and remote/rural communities.

Creativity and Innovation

There have been many significant community outcomes from the support services provided by QCAN to Queensland communities, and QCAN has often adopted innovative ways of delivering support services and training to communities. However, the key issue is whether QCAN has supported communities to embed creativity and innovation in community development practices and processes. To what extent has QCAN prompted and helped community artists to reconsider their roles and to adopt new approaches relevant to the changing conditions in communities?

> QCAN has provided some great training programs and has helped us develop community skills. But it's been about maintaining current practices; it's not been about new roles and new approaches (Notes from interview with local government community development officer, 2006).

QCAN's failure to consider the potential of the arts across all areas of community development (social, cultural and economic) has seriously limited its ability to support communities to develop appropriate holistic and integrated approaches to growth and development.

Community Development Ideologies: Narrowness and Rigidity

The shift in QCAN's policy position from supporting access to community arts to focusing more actively on supporting local government attempts to address community issues was a major watershed for the network. Its interpretation and subsequent approach to the new concept of community cultural development provided the framework for its operations for subsequent decades. QCAN's approach to CCD had at its core a strong move to address equity and it wove this philosophy into its charter for support. As a consequence, its programs began to focus on (i) Indigenous arts and cultural development, (ii) people from non-English speaking backgrounds and their arts and culture, (iii) women in the arts, and (iv) art and disability (Interview with Chief Executive Officer of QCAN (2003–2007), 2005). This interpretation impacted on all QCAN operations and effectively resulted in the adoption of an affirmative action strategy for the arts to redress the disadvantage experienced by people living outside metropolitan areas. Admirable as this strategy might have been, effectively it narrowed and marginalised QCAN's scope of activity at a time when there was a real opportunity to broaden the impact of the arts across all dimensions of local government responsibilities — including social, cultural, economic and environmental (Interview with community artist, 2006). Indeed, it provided the philosophical framework within which QCAN operated from 1992 to 2008 (Interview with Chief Executive Officer of QCAN (2003–2007), 2005).

Over those two decades, QCAN held rigidly to the concepts of CCD and especially its commitment to equity and social inclusion principles:

> We believe that art and culture are core needs of all people but that there is also a need to address the barriers which restrict people's access to it. Our programs and services aim to overcome these barriers so that all members of the community can participate in cultural life (Interview with training and development officer of QCAN (2003–2007), 2005).

The activities and projects pursued by QCAN focused almost exclusively on social and cultural outcomes and CCD's role in the promotion and acceptance of diversity and inclusiveness. This focus became increasingly restrictive and limited QCAN's ability to adapt to changing requirements of governments, organisations and communities facing new challenges and grappling with new directions. QCAN, and its commitment to CCD, was becoming increasingly marginalised as it became more removed from the escalating complexity of community life:

> QCAN couldn't really see the forest for the trees — it was busy playing politics while Rome burned. We needed a flexible and agile organisation that could move with the times and add value to community life. QCAN was just running to their old agenda — they preached about community consultation but they didn't listen to us at all (Interview with a government official of a remote/rural community, 2006).

Moreover, the language and philosophy of CCD that was adopted by QCAN was neither understood nor appreciated by community stakeholders:

> We really wanted help to engage with the community but all we got from QCAN was ideological gobble-gook (Interview with community arts worker, 2005).

As a result, QCAN was all too often operating at the periphery of community life on narrowly defined projects and services:

> I was a member for 12 years but it became more and more irrelevant. The library service was good but the other stuff that was supposed to help us help communities was just useless (Interview with community artist, 2005).

One case study informant suggested a way forward for QCAN:

> They need to get their hands dirty — they need to engage with communities and support the integration of the arts in all aspects of community development. They need to engage not just with local governments but also with community organisations and private sector agencies. They need to promote the potential of the arts across all community services — economic as well as social and cultural (Interview with community arts consultant, 2006).

This challenge outlines a potential new way of operating for QCAN. However, during the data collection phase of the case study, there was no indication that the management of QCAN was open to discussions about new ways of operating or new directions.

Leadership

There are three aspects of leadership relevant to QCAN. Firstly, QCAN is an organisation providing advocacy for communities to government and government agencies, specifically by supporting the role of the arts in community growth and development. In this context, QCAN has been expected to provide leadership in cultural policy development as well as interpreting and explaining the impact of new policy developments on communities and their programs. Secondly, as a state-wide service organisation, QCAN's objective is to stimulate and mentor community leadership through its programs and services. While these first two leadership roles are externally focused, the third and final role focuses internally on organisational leadership and deals with organisational restructuring and redirection, organisational effectiveness and efficiency, development of new services, staffing, and organisational facilities.

Leadership of contemporary arts organisations is challenging as leaders have to remain on top of an evolving policy context as well as being able to represent the needs of their constituents. Advocacy for communities and community arts workers has been central to QCAN's philosophy and operation for two decades. Consequently, QCAN has been active in its involvement in national collaborative efforts to increase the visibility of the sector and secure funds to support the work of the sector. The leadership of QCAN has led national delegations to key decision makers to lobby for the sector's needs and attempt to secure funding to support it. Over recent years especially, it has actively participated in national discussions/forums on the future of the sector — especially during a recent review of the sector by the Australian Council for the Arts, which was seeking to develop new ways of working with communities through the arts.

However, leadership and advocacy require a deep appreciation of the changing policy context and operating environment and QCAN's demonstrated philosophical rigidity towards analysis of the changing nature of the environment has rendered its leadership in the sector ineffectual. At a time when the sector is struggling to come to terms with emerging concepts such as 'creative communities' and 'knowledge-based economies', QCAN has maintained an equity-based approach to community development at the expense of broader, more encompassing concepts emphasising creativity and innovation as drivers of community economic growth and social cohesion:

> It's [QCAN] really kept its head in the sand — things have moved on but QCAN is still living in the '70s. It just doesn't get it (Interview with community arts consultant, 2006).

Furthermore, its continued emphasis on community cultural development as a primary tool for social change has resulted in limiting the impact of its programs at the community level. Its role in stimulating and mentoring of community leadership has thus been marginalised due to QCAN's decreasing understanding of the complexities of issues facing communities.

At the organisational level, QCAN has certainly demonstrated effective and efficient leadership in the management and accountability of its programs. However, in times of decreasing budgets, QCAN's strong management focus on accountability and efficiencies rather than new strategies on the pathway to greater financial independence has proved disastrous for the organisation over the long term.

Outcomes

Throughout its history, QCAN has maintained a sizeable membership comprising community organisations, arts organisations, local government, local government agencies, and individual artists and arts workers. The membership also includes non-artists, cultural planners, teachers, and community development workers. QCAN conducts annual surveys of its members to collect data on the outcomes of those products and services. Membership surveys have consistently rated the information services as the single most highly valued service provided by QCAN. These services provide information to members including updates on grant availability and funding opportunities, upcoming professional development and training events, and summaries of significant reports (with web links to full copies of the reports):

> The bulletins and web services are great. I've just won a grant that I would not have known about without QCAN (Comments provided by members in the annual survey of QCAN services, 2006).

> It's important to keep up to date with changes in policies and the web site provides a great summary of developments (Comments provided by members in the annual survey of QCAN services, 2006).

After the information service, the next most highly rated support service provided by QCAN to communities was training and professional development. The accredited training and professional development services that were most valued by survey respondents were those programs focusing on community consultation, cultural planning and the maintenance and protection of culture. The most popular non-accredited training was focused on the development of practical skills for arts workers ('Grant Writing for the Arts', 'Understanding the Public Art Commissioning Process', 'Commercialisation of Your Independent Practice') and skills for community workers and other stakeholders ('Being a Creative Community', 'Community Arts at Work', 'Introduction to Community Cultural Development') (Data from annual survey of QCAN services, 2006). Outcomes of training services include the development of new community knowledge and skills.

In a recent membership survey conducted by QCAN, respondents were asked to nominate possible new training courses that would be of use to them. Respondents suggested a range of practical and generic courses targeting skills that could be applied at the community level including project management, strategic planning, networking, business skills, communication skills, financial management, developing a business plan, and marketing and promotion (Comments provided by members in the annual survey of QCAN services, 2006). This indicated an ongoing demand for training courses by communities and an appreciation by communities of the training services provided by QCAN. QCAN incorporated this feedback into its planning for future training programs.

Conclusions and Implications

QCAN is highly visible within the arts and cultural sectors of Queensland, providing a link between artists, communities and local and state governments that has been sustained by quality products and services, and supported by effective and efficient governance and management structures. Over its years of operation, QCAN has responded to many challenges and threats, and has responded to most by developing new products and services and improving its business operations to increase its efficiency. It is managed through effective quality systems, has a highly competent and engaged management committee and competent and committed staff. However, despite its business effectiveness, QCAN has failed to take advantage of changing policy positions arising primarily from the new centrality of creativity and innovation in economic growth. Consequently, it has also failed to recognise and take advantage of opportunities arising from these new directions.

In environments where there is a heightened awareness of creativity as a driver of the economy, there is also a growing demand for lateral thinking and innovation. Consequently, there is increasing pressure on arts and cultural organisations to develop new ways of engaging with communities and the economy. When QCAN failed to respond to the challenges presented by national policy movements away from community arts and CCD towards a broader, more encompassing concept of creative communities, it demonstrated a failure to understand adequately and react appropriately to contemporary changes related to the creative economy and creative communities.

Case Study Three: Cottage Enterprise Comes of Age

Case study three presents a small arts-based enterprise flourishing in a small remote/rural community.

The Stimulus

Tambo Teddies is a small, cottage-based enterprise creating boutique teddy bears made from products sourced from the local environment around Tambo, a remote/rural township in western Queensland. The town consists of a main street with a small number of public buildings (including council offices, library and a learning centre), two hotels, two service stations, a disused picture theatre, and a general store selling drapery, vegetables and groceries. From the main street stem several roads scattered with the modest houses of Tambo residents. On any day, the main street provides temporary parking for a few road trains carrying cattle and wool to market, shelter for several of the town's residents, and sanctuary for more than a few of the town's dogs. The current population of Tambo is approximately 350, although it has been steadily declining over the last two decades (the population in 1991 was 690).

The stimulus for the new enterprise occurred unexpectedly in 1992 when three local women were invited to attend a state government–sponsored workshop to examine options for the future of remote/rural towns in western Queensland. The workshop was one of several conducted across Queensland by the Queensland Department of Primary Industries to stimulate job creation in small rural communities. Approximately 20 local Tambo people attended the workshop, most being council employees, local graziers and businessmen. Two of the three women present at the workshop reported that discussions focused on community access to government subsidised infrastructure development projects, including dams and roads, assistance for existing primary industries (wool and cattle), and the development of new primary industries based around timber getting and sawmilling (Interview 1 with Informants 1 and 2, 2004). The tone and direction of the workshop was summarised particularly cogently by one of the women in attendance:

> We were the only women there and we mostly ignored by the men at the meeting … and, when we split for small group discussions, we found ourselves sitting by ourselves on the veranda of the hall while the 'big business' was being discussed inside by the men (Interview 1 with Informant 1, 2004).

In this environment, the three women focused their discussion on what they considered to be the key questions raised by the workshop. What can be done to stimulate jobs in the town? What new enterprises might be possible? How can existing skills and resources be better used? (Interview 1 with Informants 1 and 2, 2004).[3] Their discussion was summarised by one of the participating women:

> I remember that we all made ourselves a cup of tea and sat on the veranda and chatted about what we thought the town really needed. We wanted something that would involve the people in town who had some time on their hands and we wanted to make sure it was something that reflected the region. Our first idea was for a gift shop that would sell local products but we remembered that we didn't really have any local products [laughter] … so we wondered if we could develop some. We thought about our local produce and we got stuck, not surprisingly, on wool. It was a time when wool prices were very low and the region was in the middle of a drought and we felt sure that we could come up with some way of using wool to create a saleable product and at the same time promote wool and the industry as a whole. I can remember that we talked a bit about the qualities of wool and what we might use it for that was a bit new and interesting — then the brainstorm — teddy bears (Interview 1 with Informant 1, 2004).

The three local women established Tambo Teddies in 1993 to manufacture teddy bears from pure merino wool and other local products.

However, when the small groups reported back to the workshop, the other workshop delegates did not receive the idea enthusiastically: 'There was a polite response but the men were not really taken with the idea' (Interview 1 with Informant 2, 2004). A few days after the workshop, the idea became a major point for discussion among many of the townspeople who decided almost unanimously that the idea would not work. One of the women described this as 'good-natured ridicule', but another explained that, like many small remote/rural towns, there was very real community scepticism in Tambo reflecting a community concern, perhaps fear, of change — concern that impacts negatively on the generation of new ideas and the creation of new

3 Questions listed from interview notes were based on memory of workshop participants. While some original workshop documentation was able to be sourced, specific questions to be addressed by workshop delegates were not available in the sourced documentation.

ventures. Despite this less than enthusiastic community response, the three women decided that they could and would do it and thus commenced a journey that they now characterise as one of sheer hard work and frustration:

> Looking back, we were quite naïve. We thought that we could just make some woollen teddies — no problems. We had no design expertise other than sewing and knitting. We had no appreciation of the difficulties of sourcing materials — yes we learned quickly that there were other things needed for teddies besides wool, such as eyes! We didn't understand that we needed special equipment for cutting and sewing woollen hides. We didn't understand just how hard it was going to be (Interview 2 with Informant 1, 2005).

After many months of designing and planning and a few false starts, the first Tambo Teddies were ready for sale in February 1993 (Interview 1 with Informant 2, 2004). They were presented to the public at the Charleville Sheep Show and over 20 Tambo Teddies were sold (Tambo Teddies, 1994). Since that time the enterprise has steadily grown and now employs three full-time and approximately 40 part-time staff (representing over 11 per cent of the total population of Tambo and making it the largest employer in town) (Interview 3 with Informant 1, 2006). The teddies have also become a major tourist stop in western Queensland, attracting the attention of tourism operators who now make scheduled stops in Tambo, a destination that had previously been ignored in their itineraries (Interview 1 with Tambo Shire economic development officer, 2006). The enterprise has also stimulated the establishment of other businesses seeking to take advantage of the increased tourist flow. In particular, a coffee shop has now opened in the building adjacent to Tambo Teddies (Interview 1 with coffee shop owner, 2006). Tambo Teddies are also now sold throughout the world through an online purchasing facility embedded into the enterprise's website: www.tamboteddies.com.au (Tambo Teddies business records viewed during Interview 3 with Informant 1, 2006).

Community Development Ideologies: Ignorance and Bliss

The three initiators of Tambo Teddies had very clear business objectives for their enterprise, which were summarised in the initial business plan for the enterprise in 1994: 'to develop a small business that builds the profile of the local community, uses resources from the local community, and provides a new revenue stream for the community' (Tambo Teddies, 1994). Given that these objectives explicitly connect the development of the business with stimulating community growth and development, it is worthy of note that the three developers of the concept had no exposure to any of the community development ideologies (see Chapter 3) that have provided development platforms for the other cases studies and community vignettes examined by this research:

> We had never heard of those things. If you go to community meetings today everything is about community development theories. It's almost like we are now expected to follow a recipe and then everything will be all right. I've never really understood the value of the theories. We saw ourselves as three ordinary people with ordinary backgrounds who wanted to develop a new business based on sound business principles and practices — that's all (Interview 1 with Informant 1, 2004).

Blissful ignorance of community development theories and ideologies seems to have given the women freedom to focus all their energies on sensible business development and the quality of their product. This strong business focus was not always understood or appreciated by people working in community arts, as is demonstrated by the following comment from a community arts worker in another community who was asked about the potential of creative enterprises such as Tambo Teddies:

> They're running a business and yes it's been successful but they have no real understanding of the role of arts in the community. We are trying to involve this community in arts to develop a better and richer community feeling — we're not just trying to make a profit (Interview with arts worker from a neighbouring community, 2006).

Over almost 20 years of business operations, Tambo Teddies has attained and maintained a national and international reputation for quality while retaining a distinct local identity. It is best described as a cottage enterprise or a boutique rural business specialising in an original product. It is a business with roots firmly in the arts and crafts market and consequently with links to the concept of community art, despite the fact that these links have never been of concern or interest to the business operators: 'Right from the start we were concerned with business not art. We saw ourselves as businesswomen not artists' (Interview 2 with Informant 2, 2005). There was also a sense among the three women that the arts and crafts community of Tambo was insular and marginalised and, while not necessarily anti-business, that involvement with them would not enhance business development:

> We didn't want to get involved with the arts and crafts people in town as we saw this as a real threat to the business. There was a lot of backbiting in that crowd and they were really just focused on accessing arts funding to run workshops and other activities. Of course, that stuff's important but we were just not interested in accessing government money. We wanted a business that worked (Interview 2 with Informant 1, 2005).

Despite the strong emphasis on business development and the determined approach to keep Tambo Teddies separated from the arts and crafts sector, the business enterprise has many characteristics in common with community art. The teddies are hand crafted, individually numbered and named after sheep and cattle properties in the Tambo region, linking the product to the community. Customers can further individualise their teddies by choosing to dress them as true-blue Aussies in moleskin pants, check shirt, plaited belt, 'bear-as-a-bone' coat, hat and swag. Each year the enterprise also releases a limited edition teddy designed around a special theme. A recent edition focused on the history of Tambo and honouring the early settlers. The teddies are high-quality, high-priced articles retailing from approximately $100 for a basic model to $300 for a limited edition bear.

Tambo Teddies is now a mature, stable small business/cottage enterprise with a reputation for high-quality products. In recent years there has been active consideration by the owner/operator of potential expansion opportunities including franchising of the concept, but these have been rejected for two main reasons. Firstly, the owner and key staff have a strong commitment to supporting and promoting Tambo and, even though increased revenue may have economic benefits for the region, there is a strongly held belief that expansion would dilute the special connection of the bears to the region and reduce the impact of the product in the market. Secondly, the owner wishes to maintain the lifestyle she has achieved through her hard work and is focused on consolidating the product's appeal while enjoying life and work in the local community.

Major Milestones and Achievements

The first major milestone for the enterprise occurred just three months after the establishment of the business in 1995 when the partners purchased their first industrial fur overlocker to sew the teddies. The machine was second-hand and cost $1,500, and each partner contributed just over $500 to purchase the machine and a few sheepskins, cotton and accessories to manufacture the teddies (Tambo Teddies business records accessed during Interview 2 with Informant 1, 2005).

> When we started we had no idea that we would need specialised machines — we thought that we would just use our home machines. This small outlay convinced us that we were really starting a business — it was our own money! It was scary but really exciting (Interview 1 with Informant 1, 2004).

In the next four years additional equipment and resources were purchased as meagre profits were made — seven industrial fur overlockers were purchased to meet growing demand. The demand also created new local employment opportunities as the enterprise began employing local woman as part-time sewers (Tambo Teddies business records accessed during Interview 2 with Informant 1, 2005).

The second major milestone also occurred in 1995 when the three partners set up a Company Limited by Guarantee (Tambo Teddies Pty Ltd) and each of the three partners became directors.

> We were really in business. Looking back it's amazing — none of us had any real experience with business but we were committed and willing to work hard so that was really what got us over the line (Interview 2 with Informant 2, 2005).

The new company was cash poor but determined to manage financial risks by keeping investment levels low. The business was expanded only when it was financially viable (Interview 2 with Informant 2, 2005). Another aspect of the business that the women saw as a significant achievement is the fact that they received very little in government grants to establish the business. In 1994, $600 was granted by the Queensland Small Business Corporation towards the cost of developing Tambo Teddies' first business plan (Tambo Teddies business records accessed during Interview 2 with Informant 1, 2005):

> We always thought that we needed to stand on our own feet and not rely on government support. All of us thought that accessing public money was a recipe for disaster and would make us less able to sustain and operate a viable business. We have only ever, in all our years, received a small grant of $600 (Interview 2 with Informant 1, 2005).

An unexpected milestone for the company occurred in its eighth year of operation when a national current affairs show televised a story on the company and its products.[4] The story was broadcast nationally and generated major national interest in the product:

> We were not prepared for the demand the story generated. We were run off our feet. The telephone just rang off the hook with orders. We had to increase our part-time staff by 10 (including a person just to answer the phone) and we still couldn't meet the demand. It was great as it came at a time when the market was slowing a bit and our confidence was low — it really picked us up and was a boon to the business (Interview 2 with Informant 1, 2005).

As well as generating a new market for the teddies, this milestone also encouraged the directors to think about expanding and resulted in the establishment of the Tambo Teddies website to cater for growing demand both nationally and internationally. The website allows potential customers to learn about the history of the teddies and Tambo, view the various products, and place orders for the teddies. It is estimated that the website now generates about 25 per cent of all orders (Tambo Teddies business records accessed during Interview 2 with Informant 1, 2005). Also at about this time, the company directors were invited by the Toowoomba Regional Development Board[5] to accompany an official contingent on a trade trip to Japan, a trip that generated significant international demand for the teddies (Interview 3 with Informant 1, 2006).

Not all milestones have been positive for the key stakeholders in the company. A major milestone occurred five years after the establishment of the company when one of the directors wanted to end her association with Tambo Teddies. For the first time the company had to be valued so that the two remaining directors could buy the departing director's share of the company. The valuation process was hotly debated between the directors and it became evident that a satisfactory solution could

4 A videotape of the televised story was accessed during Interview 2 with Informant 1, 2005.

5 Toowoomba is the main regional centre for Tambo and south-western Queensland.

not be achieved without external intervention (Interview 2 with Informant 2, 2005). An independent business assessor was brought in to value the company and an agreement was eventually reached and an agreed payment made to the departing director.

Four years after this event, one of the two remaining directors also made a decision to leave Tambo, a decision that generated bitter discussion about the future of the company. The departing director wanted to establish a branch of the teddies in her new town, essentially proposing a franchise of Tambo Teddies. The remaining director felt very strongly that such an action would jeopardise the uniqueness of the product and have a negative impact on the Tambo community (Interview 2 with Informant 1, 2005). After much debate, a solution was reached that maintained a single company operation based in Tambo. The solution was based on a single payment from the remaining director to the departing director based on the existing value of the company and a percentage of estimated potential growth.

Synergies and Partnerships

One of the very first problems faced by the three women at the time of the establishment of the company was sourcing a suitable venue from which to launch the proposed new business. They approached the Tambo Shire Council who offered the fledgling business the use of the local Post Office Museum. They were given two rooms at the back of the museum with the proviso that the women would also accept responsibility for operating the museum. The benefits for the council were that the museum would significantly increase its operating hours and would be staffed by full-time operators (Interview with council official during Site Visit 2, 2005); until this time, volunteers and council employees had staffed the museum on a part-time basis. In return, the council would provide the two vacant rooms rent-free and would pay for electricity and other utilities. This arrangement began a productive partnership between council and the fledgling enterprise, which was to last several years. The nature of the partnership is wryly described by a current council official:

> We would like to claim that we had foresight and vision to support what has become a very successful business and a real community asset but it was more a case of having two spare rooms that were not being

> used and the proposed arrangement suited us as we could keep the museum open all the time. We really didn't think the teddies would be so successful (Interview with council official during Site Visit 2, 2005).

Regardless of the motivation for the partnership, the results have been significant. While not necessarily recognised by the partners at the time, the partnership demonstrates the role of the shire council as an incubator for new business (Notes from interview with economic development officer, 2006). Although the approach did not include business development assistance, it did allow Tambo Teddies to commence business in an environment where costs could be kept low thus allowing the limited funds to be directed to product research and development (Notes from Interview 2 with Informant 1, 2005).

The partnership with the local council has changed and evolved over the years. After four years of occupying council premises, Tambo Teddies moved out of the museum into a vacant shop in the main street. The directors felt that the business needed a more visible profile to attract passing tourists and visitors (Notes from Interview 2 with Informant 1, 2005). The move proved to be very successful and, as noted, Tambo Teddies has become a significant stop on the tourist trail through western Queensland. The growing potential of an increasing tourist market had now been recognised and appreciated by the council who designed and erected pedestrian crossing signs in the main street reading 'Teddies Cross Here' (Interview with council official during Site Visit 2, 2005).This action firmly entrenched Tambo as the home of the teddies and cemented the ongoing relationship between the local business and government. It also illustrates clearly the impact of creative work in enhancing the attractiveness of a region to visitors and tourists thus contributing to the economic viability of the region (Interview 3 with Informant 1, 2006).

All other local partnerships with the community have been firmly on a business footing, the business never having relied on volunteer services for any of its operations:

> Except for our free rent for the first few years, we have paid for everything. Our relationships with other community businesses or organisations have always been on a purely business basis. We contract the services we need, whether it is renovations or hide cutting (Interview 3 with Informant 1, 2006).

Innovation and Creativity

Tambo Teddies is a business that has grown and evolved as a result of determination and hard work, but this should not overshadow the fact that inspiration, creativity and innovation have been the hallmarks of the business's growth and development. Its success is, in part, due to the fact that it has built on local knowledge, skills and resources applied in ways that have created innovative opportunities for the community. While creativity and innovation are downplayed by the business owners who continually state that they as just ordinary business owner/operators (Interviews 1, 2 and 3 with Informants 1 and 2, 2004, 2005 and 2006), an analysis of the development of the business demonstrates the continual application of creative decision making, problem solving and innovative thinking. Table 35 provides examples of how the business has used these skills across a range of aesthetic and business issues.

Table 35. Creativity and Innovation in Business Development — Tambo Teddies.

Processes and skills	Application	Evidence
Aesthetic problem solving	The business had to develop new patterns for the design of the teddy bears. New designs had to take account of challenges using woollen hides. Appreciation of the interconnection between materials and resources and the final product. Resources had to be sourced to meet design principles. Appreciation of the opportunities arising from community distinctiveness.	Interview 1, Informant 1 (2004) Interview 1, Informant 2 (2004) Interview 1, Informant 1 (2004) Interview 1, Informant 2 (2004) Interview 1, Informant 1 (2004) Interview 1, Informant 2 (2004) Interview 2, Informant 1 (2005) Interview 2, Informant 1 (2005) Interview 1, Informant 1 (2004) Interview 1, Informant 2 (2004) Interview 2, Informant 1 (2005) Interview 3, Informant 1 (2006)
Technical problem solving	Specialist equipment had to be sourced and purchased. Staff had to be located and trained within the community.	Interview 1, Informant 1 (2004) Interview 1, Informant 2 (2004) Interview 1, Informant 2 (2004) Interview 2, Informant 1 (2005)

Processes and skills	Application	Evidence
Synthesis of business and artistic ideas into creative outcomes and products	Development and negotiation of partnerships with local government while maintaining creative and business integrity. Integration of community history and culture with artistic ideas to develop a new local product. Integration of business with community needs through training and employment.	Interview with local councillor (2005) Interview with economic development officer (2005) Interview 2, Informant 1 (2005) Interview 2, Informant 2 (2005) Interview 1, Informant 1 (2004) Interview 1, Informant 2 (2004) Interview 1, Informant 2 (2004) Interview 2, Informant 1 (2005)

Source: Author's interviews.

Leadership

The success of Tambo Teddies has been dependent on the continuous leadership of one energetic person who has consistently demonstrated vision, originality and commitment. The current director of the enterprise has provided continuous leadership for almost 20 years. While she does not view herself as a leader, she has nevertheless demonstrated persistence, stamina and tenacity and has faced significant challenges to the business:

> I've been with the business for its whole life. It's not always been easy but it's been a great life for me — I've loved it. I've moved from being a teacher aide at the school to running my own business. It's been hard but I've survived. I survived fights and backbiting but I achieved some great things for the town and its people. I don't see myself as a community leader or any the type of leader — just a hardworking business woman (Notes on Interview 3 with Informant 1, 2006).

Notably, there have been times of business disruption due to differences in the vision and direction of the business partners. There have also been other challenges arising from the design and development of the product, including difficulties in relation to sourcing materials, resources and skills:

> We made a lot of mistakes at the beginning especially — the selection of the wrong hides made sewing almost impossible. Sewing on the industrial machines was very different from what we were used to and we had to spend a fair bit of time training our recruits. At one point, it seemed that we would never get ahead (Interview 2 with Informant 1, 2005).

Leadership was a topic that interviewees involved in this case study were comfortable discussing but the current director of Tambo Teddies was self-deprecating when asked to comment on leadership issues:

> I'm just a businesswoman and like everyone else, I'm just trying to make a living. I know that there have been benefits to the community along the way but other people should also take the credit. I just run a business (Notes on Interview 3 with Informant 1, 2006).

However, the self-deprecation evident in all key players should not be mistaken for a lack of confidence. The people responsible for the success of Tambo Teddies are confident, dynamic and forthright women who have been determined to succeed. They are generally recognised by the community as successful business people and community leaders, whether they like it or not:

> They have put Tambo on the map. We are recognised as the home of the teddy. What has been remarkable is that they have done it by themselves. Other communities in our region have tourist attractions but they have all been funded and developed by the government. This is the only one for thousands of miles that has been established as a successful business from nothing. It's a credit to them (Interview with Tambo Shire council official, 2005).

Local business owners have also recognised the leadership qualities of the current director:

> I've been here all my life and I have to admit that I thought it was a stupid idea that would never lead anywhere. I've had to eat my words and it's because of [her] determination and drive. She ignored all the talk behind her back and got on with the job. My takings are up 20 per cent on what they were three years ago and it's all because of those teddies (Interview with local business owner during Site Visit 2, 2005).

Community leadership and recognition are not always positive, and Tambo Teddies' leadership has suffered in some quarters, and still does, from regional and local jealousies and suspicions:

> There's no doubt that she has been incredibly successful but it's for her own pocket. She's making thousands of dollars a week and I'd like to know how much goes back into the community (Interview with local community member during Site Visit 2, 2005).

The key players in the development of Tambo Teddies have demonstrated that community leadership can stem from any area; a fundamental requirement is a desire and a willingness to follow through with creative ideas and focus on solid outcomes.

Management and Evaluation

The management of Tambo Teddies has been based on sound business principles since its inception. Growth over almost 20 years of operation has been generally slow and steady. The evaluation of the company has been an ongoing and continuous aspect of business management, and the company has informally but regularly set business objectives. That is, while the process has never been formally addressed through the development of a formal annual strategic or business plan, goal setting has been a strong feature of development:

> While we did some business planning at the beginning of the business, we didn't really find the process worthwhile. We usually just set some aims for ourselves — things like selling the first 100 teddies and then just set about trying to do it. Sometimes it took us a bit longer than we thought but that was OK. Every time we had a bit of a profit we would buy something we needed to improve the business (Interview 2 with Informant 1, 2005).

This uncomplicated approach to evaluation and improvement was possible because of the small nature of the enterprise and the simplicity of its operation. While it may not be a model that could or should be applied more broadly, it has been demonstrably successful in the case of Tambo Teddies.

Outcomes

Tambo Teddies has yielded many significant outcomes for the community of Tambo through the establishment of a viable and sustainable business with flow-ons to the whole community. One significant achievement has been the development and community recognition of new community skills. Entrepreneurship, business skills and project management skills are now perceived by the community to be useful in building community capacity (Interview with economic development officer, 2005). A more tangible outcome is the existence of an original and marketable product strongly linked to community consciousness and one that has brought significant economic and social returns to the community (Interview with shire councillor, 2005). It has generated tourism for the town resulting in increased visitor numbers to the area and increased revenue flow for existing businesses (Interviews with local business owners, 2005 and 2006). It has also resulted in the development of a secondary spin-off business, an adjacent coffee shop and snack bar to cater for the augmented tourist trade.

Other major outcomes have included the development of increased employment opportunities within the community that has occurred in two ways. Firstly, the enterprise itself has become a major employer for the community. Secondly, local people have been employed to support the spin-off businesses (coffee shop and snack bar). While all the direct employment benefits have been in part-time or casual employment, this has had a significant impact in a town with a population of fewer than 400 people.

The initiative has also generated a positive community image, both internally and externally. Within the community, residents feel that the enterprise has created an image for the community that makes it unique in western Queensland:

> We weren't really known for anything before the teddies. Well, the best thing was the roadhouse that used to have a good name with the truckies for the food. Now it's pretty well known as the home of the teddies by most travellers, especially the grey nomads. Even if people don't know it exists, they have plenty of signs both in town and on the way in to alert them to the fact. It seems that teddies have some appeal to most people — it's something different that they haven't seen before. It's not just another historical museum or monument (Interview with local business owner, 2005).

Some of the residents of Tambo are proud of the fact that it has been an initiative that has been developed without outside assistance. This pride is well presented by the following comment from a Tambo resident:

> You know there's a lot of tourist stuff in the west. Charleville has that star-watching thing, the cosmos thing; Blackall has the Woolscour; Barcaldine has the Workers Museum; Longreach has the Stockman's Hall of Fame; and Winton has the Matilda Centre — they've all been funded by the government but we did it without their help, without anybody's help (Interview with local long-term resident, 2006).

Conclusions and Implications

While there have been many factors influencing the success of Tambo Teddies, one stands above others and that is the leadership shown by the company director over a period of over 20 years. Her initiative, drive, enthusiasm and commitment to business development and community growth have provided the foundation for the success and longevity of the enterprise. Her combination of business acumen, inspiration and community resources has allowed the enterprise to develop and grow into a sustainable business generating significant social and economic outcomes for the community. The other significant finding from this case study has been the existence of a significant disconnect between the success of this cottage enterprise and the contemporary theories and ideologies guiding community growth and development. In the case of Tambo Teddies, the ideologies were unknown to the developers of the enterprise, who knew their community and set their own objectives for community development, following their instincts in the development of approaches to stimulate economic development, generate community pride and involvement, and encourage community partnerships. The case study raises provocative questions about the role of community development theories in providing foundations for approaches to community growth including: To what extent are contemporary community development theories relevant to the development of creative enterprises? To what extent do they provide an adequate balance between economic, social and cultural outcomes? How do they encourage local leadership and innovation? Might they perhaps be too narrow and too focused to encourage genuine community creativity and innovation?

Perspectives from the Case Studies: Commonalities and Differences

Table 36 provides a snapshot of the key findings of the three case studies. The major findings are presented for each area of interest identified in the case study framework and reporting structure.

Table 36. Summary of Key Findings of Case Studies.

	Cultural planning in a pre-innovation context	Networking cultural support	Creative enterprise comes of age
Project name	Blackall Shire Council and community	Queensland Community Arts Network (QCAN)	Tambo Teddies
Stimulus	Local government desire to extend the scope of cultural activity in the community by developing and implementing a community cultural plan.	Identified need by a group of artists for a state-wide support network for community arts.	Provided by external agency through Futures Search Workshop (state government).
Ideology	Strongly connected with the ideology of community cultural development (CCD) but driven by practicality rather than ideology.	Strongly guided by community cultural development (CCD) as an ideology. CCD provides a strong framework for all QCAN activities.	Not ideologically based — focus on the development of a sustainable business.
Partnerships and networks	Partnerships limited to local environment — linkages achieved mainly with local agencies and organisations. External organisations and private consultants used to support the project.	No formal partnerships other than those with funding organisations. Networks exist with communities throughout Queensland.	Partnership with local government. Community networks neither involved nor supportive.
Creativity and innovation	Little evidence of creative and innovative approaches to the planning process. (The implementation of the cultural plan may encourage more innovative approaches and stimulate community creativity.)	Some evidence of creativity in project design but little support for the adoption of creative and innovative approaches at the community level.	High levels of creativity and innovation critical to the success of the enterprise.
Major milestones and achievements	Development of a cultural plan. Implementation strategies and projects to support the cultural plan.	Successful information services to Queensland communities. Creation and maintenance of community networks. Registration as an accredited training organisation and the provision of training services to Queensland communities.	A creative product. Sustainable local businesses. Increased tourism. Spin-off businesses. Development of secondary and specialised products.

	Cultural planning in a pre-innovation context	Networking cultural support	Creative enterprise comes of age
Project name	Blackall Shire Council and community	Queensland Community Arts Network (QCAN)	Tambo Teddies
Leadership	No identifiable and singular leader. Leadership by committee.	No singular leader. While individual members of staff have demonstrated leadership in various projects, the organisation suffered from a lack of vision and direction in its overall approach to supporting communities.	Success has been dependent on the continuous leadership of one energetic person demonstrating vision, originality, and commitment.
Management and continuous improvement	Sound management practices. Poorly designed and implemented review processes/poorly designed performance measures.	Sound management practices. Poor evaluation and review practices (little evidence of continuous improvement approaches).	Sound management practices. Continuous improvement embedded as business improvement.
Outcomes	Recognition of the creative capital existing in community. Improved coordination of cultural and arts-based approaches including special events and festivals.	The development of comprehensive information services to support community artists and arts workers. Sustainable communities of practice across communities to build knowledge and share expertise across communities. Formal and informal training programs for artists and community arts workers.	A creative enterprise manufacturing an original and marketable product strongly linked to community consciousness. Increased employment opportunities within the community. Increased tourism. Positive community image (internal and external).
Conclusions and Implications	A cultural plan will at best only provide a framework for further work. To move communities towards more creative and innovative approaches, models and benefits will need to be demonstrated to community members.	While QCAN mechanisms for networking and information sharing are important, they do not contribute to the stimulation of new ideas and new approaches.	The creation of arts-based enterprises in remote/rural communities is possible and leads to significant social and economic benefits to the community.

Source: Author's research.

While an analysis of the findings in Table 36 summarises and highlights the significant outcomes of community programs, projects and initiatives, it also exposes key issues and challenges influencing the potential of the arts in community development. Paramount among these is the need for the arts and artists to stimulate and support more creative and innovate approaches to community development. Table 36 also suggests that arts-based ideologies, while providing a philosophical platform for many projects, may also be inhibiting the development of practical, integrated and collaborative approaches to community growth. Other issues and challenges shown in Table 36 include the importance of successful community networks and partnerships in stimulating collaboration and cooperation across community and the centrality of passionate, dedicated, strong and community-based leadership in successful community development and growth.

These findings provide a framework on which guidelines and models to guide future arts-based community development may be developed. Principles on which such guidelines and models might be developed include:

1. Community members should focus more broadly on creativity and innovation rather than the traditional primary focus on arts and culture — a focus on creativity and innovation will allow community issues and opportunities to be considered in an inclusive, integrated manner that has the potential to encompass all community interests and skills
2. Community development programs and initiatives should build on existing community skills, resources and ideas
3. Arts-based community development should engage all relevant community stakeholders using networks and partnerships where appropriate
4. Community networks and partnerships should, where possible, cross social, cultural and economic domains to exploit potential new linkages between previously disparate community groups
5. New ideas and new approaches should be generated from within communities and not imposed by external agencies and organisations
6. Successful guidelines and models derived from these principles may need to incorporate the development of new strategies and tools that encourage creative thinking and steer communities into new ways of planning and doing.

9

Conviction, Connection, Creativity and Courage: A New Model for Creative Community Development

The Impact of the Arts on the Growth and Development of Rural and Remote/Rural Communities

The last two decades of academic literature and a range of popular publications have documented the importance of the role of the arts in community development (Eger, 2003; Goldbard & Adams, 2006; Matarasso, 2001; Phillips, 2004; Psilos & Rapp, 2001; Reeves, 2002; Williams, 1995). While this claim may be undisputed, the primary focus of much of this documentation has been urban and regional development and regeneration. When contextualised in urban environments, the arts are linked to the enrichment of the quality of life for urban citizens and the enhancement of economic vitality.

One of the most visible ways in which the arts have impacted on urban communities is through the reclamation of obsolete or under-utilised buildings typically located in abandoned industrial or warehousing sites. Initially, artists looking for affordable urban spaces claim these buildings for residential and studio uses. These fledgling artistic enclaves soon attract others to the new vibrancy and enhanced cultural life and provide an important economic stimulus for developing neighbourhoods. Gallery owners, high-end retailers, cafes and restaurants follow and, over time, land values and rents rise to reflect the new desirability of the neighbourhood — although this means that the artists who stimulated the economic recovery initially can no longer afford to stay in the area and begin to search for new, more affordable spaces, and so the cycle begins anew.

The benefits of this cyclic process have been well documented (Evans, 2005; Gertler, 2004; Landry et al., 1996) and illustrate the positive and productive role of the arts and artists in urban regeneration. Figure 5 models how the arts are increasingly providing a catalysing force for social, cultural and economic growth in urban communities. It also points to the inevitably cyclical nature of arts-based growth and development in urban communities.

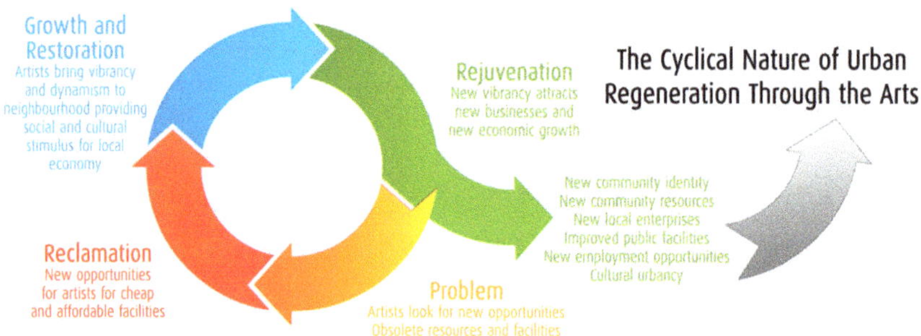

Figure 5. Cyclical Change and Growth in Urban Communities.
Source: Author's research.

While artists may ultimately be forced to abandon reclaimed neighbourhoods as prices and rents increase, their initial catalysing force gives rise to a lasting cultural, social and economic community legacy. Enduring community outcomes include (i) a new neighbourhood identity based on creative vitality, cultural vibrancy and social energy, (ii) new community resources and facilities in the form of performance venues, galleries, and parks and gardens, (iii) new businesses and enterprises in the form of retail outlets, cafes, restaurants and commercial galleries, and (iv) new employment opportunities arising from the growth of new businesses and enterprises. The community benefits arising from urban regeneration provide a platform for continuous cyclical growth and development integrating social, cultural and economic outcomes.

While urban regeneration provides an explicit and dramatic example of the impact of the arts on communities, there are many other developments demonstrating a range of positive arts impacts on urban environments. For example, several studies have focused on the direct economic impacts of the arts on urban environments, especially benefits arising from exhibitions and performances that generate significant tourism and associated revenue opportunities (Gertler, 2004; Healy, 2002).

Other studies have focused more specifically on the synergies between major arts-based community activities and new business development opportunities in communities (Phillips, 2004; Walker, Jackson & Rosenstein, 2003). One example of this activity is arts business incubators that assist artists and artisans to develop business skills and entrepreneurial approaches to business development (Phillips, 2004). Researchers have also examined the role of the arts in building social, cultural and civic capital in urban neighbourhoods through programs aimed at lessening social isolation, improving recreational opportunities and building social networks (Bulick et al., 2003; Hampshire & Matthijsse, 2010; Jeannotte, 2003; Williams, 1995). Economists have increasingly examined the economic impact of the arts in enhancing the amenity and liveability of cities and towns, thereby attracting new economy workers (Eger, 2003; Grodach, 2011; Markusen et al., 2008; Montgomery, 1990). The scope and impacts of these and other arts-based activities undertaken in urban communities are presented in Table 37, which draws on an analysis of the contemporary literature to identify and scope the major areas of arts-based development extant in urban communities categorised under six broad headings: major arts infrastructure, major arts-based resources, urban-based arts organisations, major arts events, arts education facilities, and urban regeneration activities.

Table 37 illustrates clearly the impacts of major arts-based resources, institutions and opportunities extant in urban communities. It also demonstrates that the outcomes of arts-based activities in urban communities encompass the social, cultural and economic spheres of life.

Table 37. Impact of the Arts in Urban Communities.

	Examples	Impacts		
		Social	Cultural	Economic
Major arts infrastructure	Large performance venues. Libraries. Galleries.	Community resources. Improved liveability. Improved amenity.	Improved cultural access to resources. Access to high-end resources.	Employment. Economic returns on infrastructure investment. Tourism.
Major arts-based resources	Opera companies. Theatre companies. Ballet companies. Orchestras. Choirs.	Improved liveability. Greater number of social options and opportunities. Networking opportunities. Improved amenity.	Talent recognition and development. Access to cultural resources. Increased cultural opportunities.	Employment. Tourism. Opportunities for arts-based businesses and support agencies.
Urban-based arts organisations	Arts councils. Professional associations. Unions. Guilds.	Social cohesion and networking. Sense of community. Professional networking.	Talent recognition and development. Cultural collaboration and networking.	Access to employment opportunities. Access to grant and funding information.
Major arts events	Blockbuster art exhibitions. Major theatre productions. Festivals.	Improved liveability. Greater number of social opportunities. Sense of community. Improved amenity.	Access to cultural resources. Increased cultural opportunities.	New business opportunities. Tourism. Opportunities for arts-based businesses and support agencies. Economic returns on infrastructure investment.

	Examples	Impacts		
		Social	Cultural	Economic
Arts education facilities	Conservatoria. Art schools/colleges. Drama schools. Film and television schools.	Professional networking. Improved liveability.	Talent recognition and development. Access to cultural resources. Access to knowledge and skills.	Employment opportunities.
Restoration and regeneration activities	Revitalisation of disused building and precincts. Business opportunities.	Improved liveability. Improved amenity. Enhanced sense of community.	New cultural resources. New cultural enterprises.	New businesses. New opportunities. New revenues.

Source: Author's research.

While it can be argued that the themes of regeneration, social cohesion, economic vitality and cultural vigour so strongly associated with various applications of the arts in urban communities may also have broad relevance to rural and remote/rural communities, the platforms and opportunities for development are, in fact, vastly different. There is, for example, no rural or remote equivalent to the process of urban regeneration, nor have there been comprehensive studies of the existing or potential synergies between the arts and rural economic development. While the impact of the arts in rural and remote/rural communities has not featured significantly in the contemporary literature on community development, there have been important pockets of unique, arts-based activity that have been identified by and documented in the current research. One such example is the Tambo Teddies case study, which demonstrated the application of conviction, creativity and courage to the development of an innovative, remote/rural enterprise built on the unique insights and skills of the local community.

This book has analysed such activity to probe how the arts have been harnessed by rural and remote/rural communities to meet their distinctive and unique challenges. Figure 6 draws on these findings to identify and map the major areas of arts-based activity extant in rural and remote/rural communities. These activities have been categorised under seven broad headings: regional and local festivals and celebrations, local art organisations and working groups, local schools and education organisations, local art exhibitions and performing arts productions, touring exhibitions and productions, local galleries and arts retail outlets, and community arts projects. A mapping strategy has been adopted as appropriate to illustrate the identified rural and remote/rural activity because such examples are more disparate and outcomes and impacts are less integrated than in urban communities; consequently, the logic of a tabular format is less appropriate. Figure 6 also provides examples of activities undertaken in each of the seven categories and summarises and highlights the major impacts of these on community growth and development.

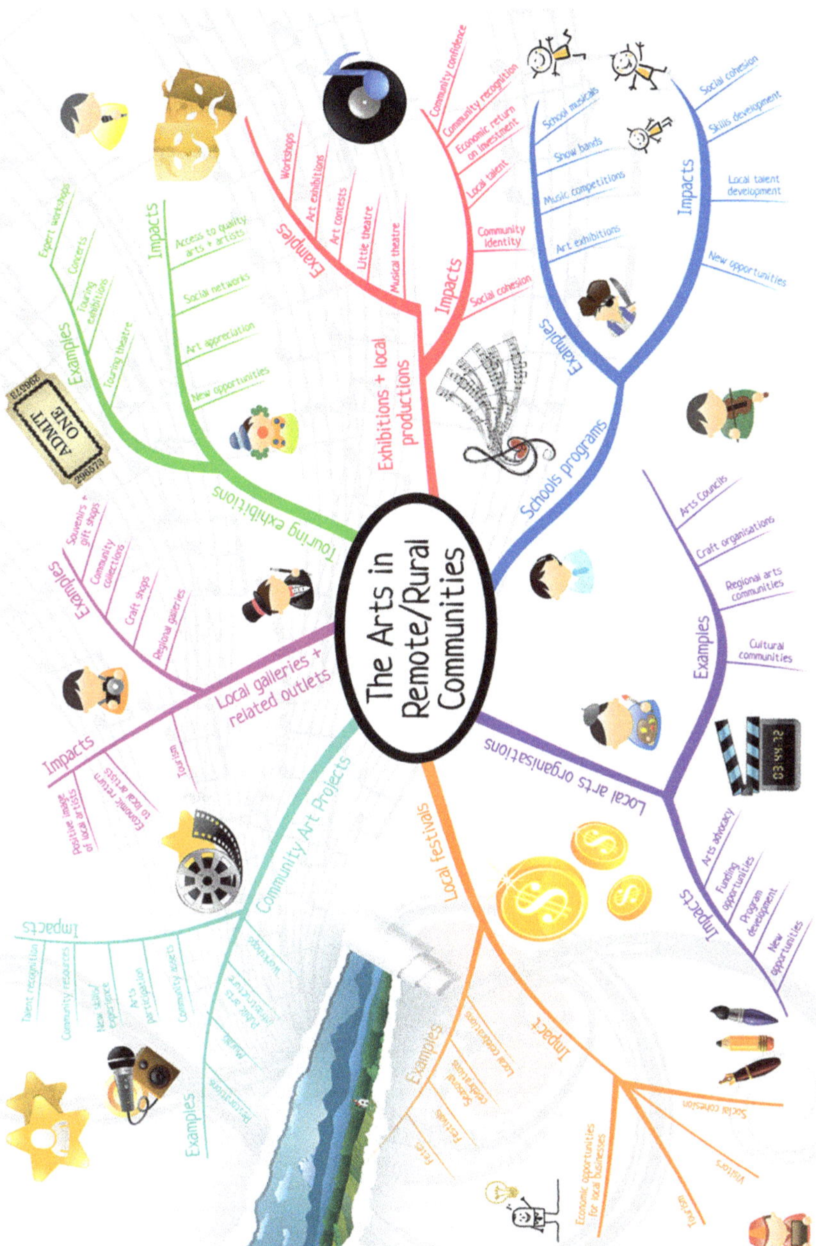

Figure 6. Mapping Arts-based Programs and Initiatives in Rural and Remote/Rural Communities.

Source: Author's research.

Significant issues arise from a comparison of the presentation of urban arts-based activities as presented in Table 37 and the mapping of rural and remote/rural activities as presented in Figure 6. Firstly, the mapping illustrates that the arts-based activities characteristic of rural and remote/rural communities differ significantly from those in urban environments, which have provided the basis for much of contemporary research in arts-based community development. Secondly, there is little evidence from this mapping that rural and remote/rural communities are focusing as strongly on arts-based economic outcomes, as are urban communities, such outcomes in rural and remote/rural communities being generally limited to fundraising plus some spin-offs for local businesses from increased visitor numbers at festivals and community events. Thirdly, the activities identified in rural and remote/rural communities are typically short-term, event-based endeavours exemplified by festivals, art contests and exhibitions, community art projects, and art workshops. While it could be argued that these events offer unique and authentic experiences that reflect local traditions and are relevant to the particular needs of rural and remote/rural communities, they are also in the main proscribed, insular and lacking longevity in both design and implementation. Characteristically, urban-based projects and activities demonstrate outcomes that focus on long-term regeneration and growth while rural and remote/rural projects are generally narrowly focused on short-term outcomes.

Critical Differences Between Urban and Rural and Remote/Rural Communities

A comparative examination of Table 37 and Figure 6 demonstrates that urban environments, especially major cities with their concentrations of people, skills and infrastructure, differ significantly from rural and remote/rural communities in their potential for application of the arts, especially in the areas of economic and cultural development. Economically, urban centres are not only the fiscal powerhouses of the arts but also act as incubators for the development of businesses and industries that supported or are related to the arts. This is clearly demonstrated by statistics that show 65 per cent of all arts-based jobs are located in major cities (Borghino, 2000). Culturally, urban communities with their major galleries, museums, theatres and other cultural facilities are key sites of cultural meaning and identity and thus provide the foundations on which the arts and the major cultural products and services associated with the arts are developed (Wood, 2001). These major cultural nodes act as attractors for visitors and tourists, further stimulating new revenue opportunities for urban communities to cater for tourists' demands for accommodation, food and entertainment. It is unrealistic to expect that rural and remote/rural communities with their small populations and limited arts-based resources and infrastructure could replicate the economic and cultural successes of urban communities.

Despite these critical differences, rural and remote/rural communities are perhaps overly influenced by urban plans and developments as, in the absence of alternative and more appropriate strategies, the temptation to compare, align themselves with and even emulate urban environments remains strong. Put simply, rural and remote/rural communities are increasingly seeing the benefits of the application of the arts in cities and, as a consequence, are asking: 'How can we get a piece of the action?' Such observations often influence rural and remote/rural community-planning decisions and result in development approaches that attempt, sometimes unthinkingly, to replicate urban-based activities. Some of these approaches have been mapped in Figure 7 and include touring exhibitions, regional galleries, community infrastructure development, the building of arts facilities and the creation of arts support services. These align to urban approaches (Table 37) such as major galleries, theatres, other public arts infrastructure, large arts companies, arts organisations and professional associations for the arts and artists. However, the differences in scale between the two types of communities are vast and the potential benefits to rural and remote/rural communities of these approaches, particularly in economic terms, remain very limited compared with the corresponding returns in urban environments.

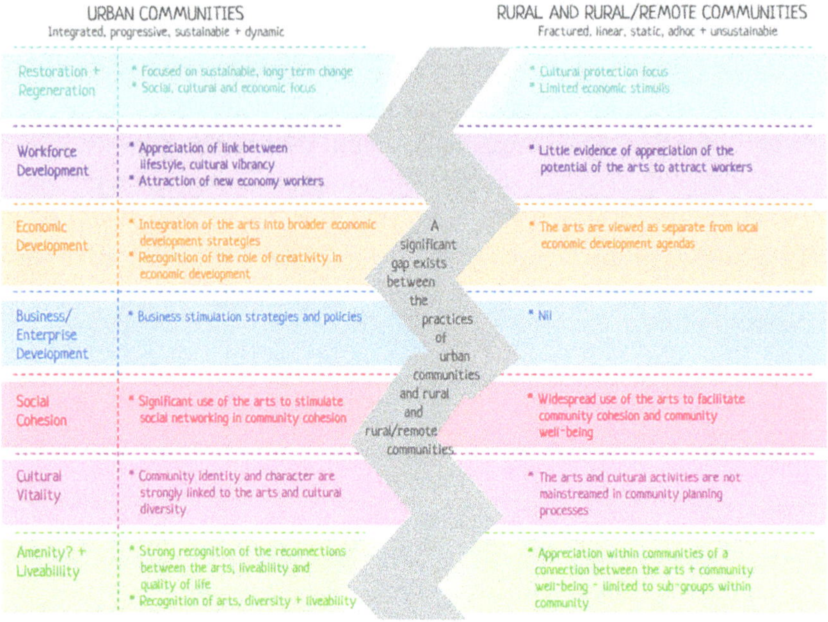

Figure 7. Comparison of the Development Processes used in Urban Communities and Remote/Rural Communities to Stimulate and Support Arts-Based Development.

Source: Author's research.

More importantly, these simple differences in the scope and size of approaches are symptomatic of deeper and more significant divides. Drawing on the findings of the current research to identify and document the major impact areas for the application of the arts in communities, a useful comparison may be made between the processes adopted by urban communities and those adopted by rural and remote/rural communities. Seven major impact areas can be identified from the contemporary literature: (i) community restoration and regeneration, (ii) workforce development, (iii) economic development, (iv) business/enterprise development, (v) social cohesion, (vi) cultural vitality, and (vii) amenity and liveability. Figure 7 uses these seven impact areas to compare approaches between urban and remote/rural communities.

Figure 7 illustrates that urban communities are increasingly aligning their arts programs and initiatives with contemporary ideas about the nature of the arts and their potential contribution to economic, social and cultural development. As a consequence, urban programs are just as likely to address economic concerns (e.g. workforce development and business development) as they are social and cultural concerns (e.g. community engagement, the maintenance of community values and the preservation of cultural heritage). Alternatively, Figure 7 demonstrates that similar processes adopted by remote/rural communities are, by comparison with those of urban communities, narrow and insular. Despite their best intentions, rural and remote/rural processes are usually limited to specific, single-discipline peak activities such as the preservation of an historical site, the conduct of a single event such as an art competition, or the creation and construction of a public monument, as distinct from more all-encompassing grass root developments. Rural and remote/rural processes are also usually aimed solely at social outcomes, increasing community networking and maintaining social cohesion. Figure 7 demonstrates that there is little or no appreciation in rural and remote/rural communities of the potential to use the arts to support economic aims. Arts-based activity in rural and remote/rural communities clearly sits apart from major community planning agendas, including plans to increase tourism, attract workers, attract new businesses, build community infrastructure, and improve the liveability of communities.

Figure 8 extends consideration of the similarities and differences between urban and rural and remote/rural communities by focusing on the outcomes of arts-based, community-building projects and initiatives.

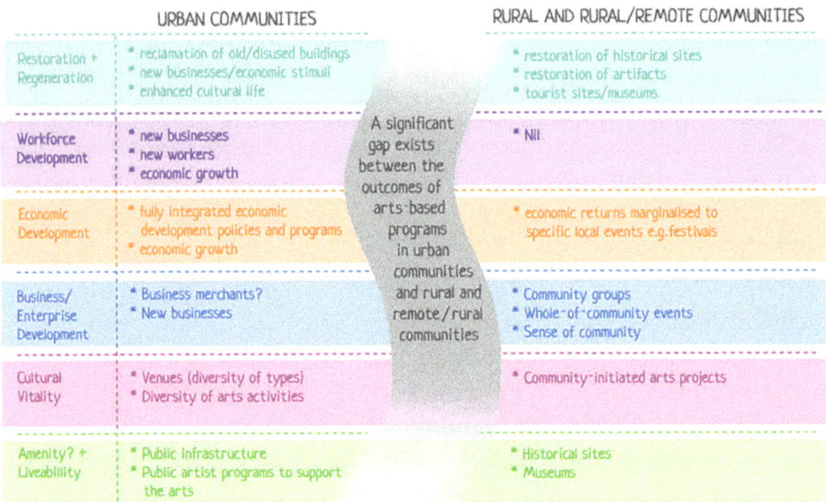

Figure 8. Comparison of the Outcomes of Arts-Based Community Development Strategies and Programs in Urban and Remote/Rural Communities.

Source: Author's research.

As arts-based programs in urban communities are often integrated into whole-of-community planning processes, they usually impact across economic, social and cultural spheres of influence. Figure 8 captures the multidimensional aspect of outcomes by listing economic indicators (new businesses, new workers, new revenue streams) as well as social spin-offs (networks, partnerships) and cultural outcomes (diverse venues and activities). By contrast, Figure 8 illustrates that outcomes in remote/rural communities are narrowly focused on small-scale projects that have little impact on local economies and provide few long-term benefits to communities other than opportunities for social outcomes related to the maintenance of social cohesion and community well-being.

Despite these significant differences in approaches and outcomes, remote/rural communities remain keen to explore the arts as generators of community growth. This research, however, demonstrates clearly that the challenge for remote/rural communities is to resist the temptation to replicate urban approaches and, instead, to recognise and build on the existing skills and talents of their residents by creating opportunities and new approaches through the arts based on their geographical distinctiveness or lifestyle uniqueness.

Can Urban Processes be Usefully Applied in Remote/Rural Contexts?

Claims currently being made for the contribution of the arts to communities, as has been seen thus far, are diffuse, although contemporary claims for the arts in community development extend beyond their contribution to the regeneration of urban buildings and neighbourhoods. They are more multidimensional than mathematical formula, illustrating returns on investment from festivals and other arts-based events, and more varied in their impacts on communities in terms of the social, cultural, environmental and economic aspects of community development. Contemporary claims attest that the arts provide communities with the tools to address a very wide range of civic concerns in creative and cost-effective ways (Birch, 2002). The evidence to support such broad claims is provided through research that has demonstrated the arts' role in student learning (Banks, 2010; Fiske, 1999), building a strong workforce with the skills for the future (Psilos, 2002), offering positive opportunities for disengaged youth (Davis, 2008), developing new enterprises and industries (Cunningham, 2004), promoting tourism (Phillips, 2004), engendering civic pride (Reeves, 2002), and developing community identity and social cohesion (Williams, 2000). To what extent can these and associated claims be substantiated when applied to urban communities or remote/rural communities? Table 38 presents the major claims being made for the arts in supporting community growth and compares how these claims impact on communities in urban and remote/rural environments.

Consideration of Table 38 suggests that, despite major differences in approaches and outcomes between urban and remote/rural communities, there may be opportunities for remote/rural communities to learn from urban processes and adapt them selectively to suit their specific challenges and strengths.

Table 38. Exploration of the Potential of Urban Practices for Use by Remote/Rural Communities.

Arts impact area	Hypothesised benefits to communities	Current practices in urban communities	Applicability of urban strategies to remote/rural communities
Education	Student skill and talent is recognised and developed, providing a pool of future arts workers. Students who study the arts demonstrate stronger overall academic performance (Bryce et al., 2004; Fiske, 1999). Arts programs improve self-confidence, build communication and problem-solving skills and prepare young people to be creative thinkers for the modern workforce (Banks, 2010; Davis, 2010; Fiske, 1999).	Specialised art programs are offered by dedicated teachers in urban schools, colleges and universities, providing many opportunities for students to develop talent and build skills. Urban students have significant access to major cultural institutions to support arts-based learning (museums, art galleries, theatres, etc.). Significant research programs are undertaken to investigate the impact of the arts in urban schools, especially the positive impact of learning through the arts on school achievement in all disciplines.	Applying urban-based education strategies to a remote/rural context presents significant challenges. In particular: • Remote/rural schools cannot afford the costs associated with specialised arts programs; • Specialist arts teachers are not present in remote/rural schools; • Specialist programs offered by arts colleges and universities are not easily accessible to remote/rural students; • The resources of major galleries and other art institutions are not easily accessible by remote/rural schools.

Arts impact area	Hypothesised benefits to communities	Current practices in urban communities	Applicability of urban strategies to remote/rural communities
Tourism	The arts attract tourism to communities (Phillips, 2004). Cultural tourism plays a critical role in community revitalisation (Landry & Wood, 2003; Phillips, 2004). Cultural tourism has been identified as a key strategy for jobs and economic growth (Landry & Wood, 2003; Psilos & Rapp, 2001).	Major museums, art galleries, historical buildings and other cultural icons provide key tourist attractions in major cities and towns. Urban cultural institutions (museums, galleries, etc.) host major international exhibitions and major theatre productions attracting national and international tourists stimulating economic growth. Urban cultural institutions (galleries, museums, etc.) provide specialist educational programs and opportunities often based on the work of major artists and art movements attracting special interest groups. Major cultural events (theatre productions, festivals, etc.) are major tourism drivers in urban communities.	While remote/rural communities lack major cultural infrastructure, arts-based approaches to the development of local tourism are feasible. Although the breadth and scope of activity differs significantly, urban practices have the potential to provide useful insights to guide remote/rural communities. In particular: • Remote/rural communities may learn from urban approaches that focus on identified strengths and build tourism programs around them. The challenge is to identify unique rural strengths and special aspects of the rural environment or lifestyle; • Urban approaches may also be applied to existing tourism programs that focus primarily on geographical features and lifestyle (e.g. farm stays, national parks, etc.); • Local festivals and cultural events that capture the uniqueness of rural life or celebrate the distinctiveness of rural history or geography.

Arts impact area	Hypothesised benefits to communities	Current practices in urban communities	Applicability of urban strategies to remote/rural communities
Economic Development	The arts are being increasingly recognised as a key contributor to economic development (Brault, 2005; Cunningham, 2006). The arts contribute to urban revitalisation and community renewal strategies by attracting visitors, businesses and new residents, thus encouraging consumer spending (Evans, 2005; Gertler, 2004). The arts contribute to the appeal of an area, encouraging corporate relocation and new jobs (Florida, 2002; Yigitcanlar et al., 2007).	The link between the arts and economic development is well established and widely acknowledged by policymakers and community developers. Urban governments, community organisations and business associations are increasingly recognising and acting on the potential contribution of the arts to economic development strategies. This recognition is the basis for integrated planning approaches now commonplace in urban communities. Urban locations have recognised that vibrant cultural communities attract workers and businesses to regions and are actively pursuing and promoting the benefits through the arts. Cultural vitality has become a key marketing component of councils seeking the relocation of major businesses and enterprises. The arts are increasingly generating jobs in urban environments through employment opportunities associated with major exhibitions, theatre productions and the spin-off businesses associated with major arts infrastructure and resources. Urban-based arts businesses and organisations are demonstrating financial sustainability.	Although shire councils in remote/rural communities are increasingly appreciating the potential of the arts in economic development, this recognition is not yet translating into tangible strategies and programs. While the concepts have been demonstrated in urban communities: Remote/rural communities have not been able to apply urban lessons successfully; Differences in breadth and scope between urban and remote/rural communities mean that urban approaches cannot be simply transferred to remote/rural communities. New, creative approaches based on unique rural talents, skills and resources must be designed and developed: Communities need mechanisms for the identification of local skills, resources, talents and opportunities; Communities need to create economic opportunities from unique local skills and resources rather than to duplicate urban approaches uncritically. Rather than focusing on small-scale, one-off activities like public arts (especially murals and sculptures), communities need to integrate the arts into community development plans that address development challenges in an integrated way. Communities also need to be realistic about the potential of the arts in the creation of new businesses and employment growth. The limitations of smaller populations will lessen the impact of outcomes.

Arts impact area	Hypothesised benefits to communities	Current practices in urban communities	Applicability of urban strategies to remote/rural communities
New businesses and enterprises	The link between the arts and the development of new businesses is increasingly being recognised by researchers, artists and business people (Cunningham, 2006; Eger, 2003; Freeman, 2007). The arts develop skills that are highly valued in business including risk taking, problem solving, decision making, creative thinking and visualising (Florida, 2002; Phillips, 2004).	The skills of artists are increasingly being applied in urban businesses associated with the creative industries including publishing, marketing, advertising, film and television, and other industries. The concept of artists and business people working together on new business development opportunities is still resisted in urban communities. Various urban-based business products are increasingly being enhanced by the arts and artists especially in technology-based businesses. The concept of the arts contributing to leadership, management and strategy development in businesses and enterprises is embryonic in urban communities and there are few examples of the concept in practice.	Due to the embryonic nature of development in this arts impact area, remote/rural communities have the unique opportunity to provide leadership, not only in their own communities but also to urban communities by: • Developing innovative, practical models in business incubation and development; • Creating supportive environments to encourage the growth and sustainability of new arts-based businesses that could inform urban communities. While the link between business and the arts is still not well recognised in remote/rural communities (which are dominated by traditional small businesses), these smaller communities with their strong, confined social networks, family-owned enterprises and active community associations may: • Have greater scope and flexibility to create and support business incubators; • Develop innovative approaches to business development.

Arts impact area	Hypothesised benefits to communities	Current practices in urban communities	Applicability of urban strategies to remote/rural communities
Development of social capital	The arts have long been linked to social outcomes; outcomes that are fundamental to community formation and maintenance (Brault, 2005; Reeves, 2002; Williams, 1995). Research has demonstrated that the arts are key contributors to the development of social capital through the promotion of community identity; the development and maintenance of community pride and confidence; and development of social networks and community cohesion (Green & Sonn, 2008; Williams, 1995).	The connection between the arts and social capital building has long been appreciated by urban communities. Activity in building social capital is usually confined to discrete urban neighbourhoods and local networks that have used the arts to build cohesive community networks and partnerships.	Remote/rural communities are well versed in the role of the arts in social capital building. Urban strategies may provide some insights into future programs but remote/rural programs are already based on: • An appreciation of the strong interconnectedness between the arts and social capital building; • A well-established platform of success in social capital building through community art projects, little theatre companies, craft cooperatives and other programs and initiatives; • Arts-based projects that have strengthened social networks, built community pride and reduced social isolation in remote/rural communities.

Arts impact area	Hypothesised benefits to communities	Current practices in urban communities	Applicability of urban strategies to remote/rural communities
Re-engagement of youth at risk	For young people at risk, involvement in the arts can provide positive outlets, build new skills, build self-esteem and improve opportunities for further growth and development (Davis, 2008; Grams & Warr, 2003).	Urban arts-based programs provide proven and effective interventions for youth at risk. Programs in urban correctional facilities are providing positive results in young offenders	Despite acute recognition of the increasing problem of youth at risk in remote/rural communities (as evidenced by increasing rates of youth depression and suicide), the application of arts-based programs as interventions is fairly limited because: • There have been few examples of successful programs in remote/rural communities; • Expertise necessary to run successful programs is scarce in remote/rural environments.

Source: Author's research.

Opportunities for Mutual Exchange and Increased Interdependence

One of the most important aspects of the findings presented in Table 38 is that it is possible for remote/rural communities to adapt and apply some of the broad principles and processes that have been adopted in urban communities. However, these must be applied in ways that build on the realistic identification of their own local strengths, resources and talents. Attempting to replicate projects designed for different contexts, environments and peoples will ultimately end in failure for remote/rural communities. Principles, philosophies and ideas can be beneficially and mutually shared across urban and remote/rural communities, contributing to debate, discussion, planning and the development of contextualised practices based on access to local talent and resources, and addressing local challenges and problems. The sharing of models, processes and practices may also be beneficial to communities once they have developed clarity around their objectives and desired outcomes. While some of the successful remote/rural community building projects identified through this research have utilised ideas and processes from other community projects, all have had their origin in the idiosyncratic mix of individual skills, creativity and talent residing in communities.

Opportunities for remote/rural communities to learn from approaches and programs used in urban communities are substantial, particularly so in areas of tourism and economic development. However, remote/rural communities need to recognise that, while the arts may provide economic flow-on effects from increased tourism and urban regeneration, investment tends to gather where major populations reside. Small communities need to appreciate that adopting specific practices and programs used in bigger population centres are unlikely to be realistic or viable. Communities also need to accept that, while local arts-based events contribute significantly to the building of social capital and thus the development of the fabric and character of remote/rural communities, economic success directly emanating from the arts and arts programs is likely to be achieved solely through the development of small-scale local businesses.

Small-scale projects and businesses in rural and remote communities can be very influential and successful beyond the boundaries of the local community, as has been effectively illustrated in the case of Tambo Teddies. This and other successful local businesses in remote/rural communities identified through this research are increasingly tapping into consumers' burgeoning interest in local products, partly as a reaction against the dulling uniformity accompanying the rise of the global economy and global culture. Local businesses and enterprises can have important roles in assisting rural and remote communities to become sites of influence and opportunity through the initial identification of what is unique and distinctive, and the subsequent development of products and services that build on this local uniqueness and distinctiveness. To capitalise on the potential of new and emerging opportunities, rural and remote communities need to adopt creative and innovative approaches to stimulate and encourage the design, development and manufacture of local, arts-based products. Courageous communities that recognise that creativity and innovation sit at the core of all product development will be in a better position to consider a new role for the arts and artists in a range of community projects and business opportunities. In this way, remote/rural communities can provide leadership in the development of new and innovative enterprises that may provide the benchmark for arts-based business development in urban communities.

However, recognition of local resources and talents in building innovative approaches to community development is only the first step towards a solution. To take advantage of new opportunities, remote/rural communities will need to view themselves as collaborators rather than as competitors with urban environments. While collaboration through the arts, particularly in the development of arts-based community products and services, may be new and challenging to remote/rural communities, it is eminently possible for them to build on their history of successful interdependence with urban communities in other areas. Through this interdependence, remote/rural communities have developed an appreciation of a complex web of mutual relationships and networks that allows communities to leverage from one another's strengths. This provides a foundation for the development of new relationships based on the evolution of new arts-based businesses and enterprises that will also need a multifaceted web of relationships and interactions that extend between and beyond various sectors and different disciplines.

The research presented in this book has argued that models for arts-based community development in urban environments are now well established and understood. It has also argued that our knowledge and understanding of the potential of the arts in remote/rural communities remains limited and constrained. It has identified that, both nationally and internationally, there is a growing interest by government, academic and business institutions in the role of the arts and, more broadly, the creative industries in development. This interest has, in turn, focused attention on the contribution of the arts in regional development. By their nature, regions are large and diverse and contain elements of the urban, suburban, rural and remote. Regional development approaches primarily build on the interdependence of these elements. Such processes may give rise to new forms of urban/rural interactions that stimulate new markets, networks and opportunities for arts-based enterprises.

Remote/rural communities are geographically part of regions and have the potential to fashion for themselves a key role in arts-based regional development programs. The leadership role of remote/rural communities has, however, failed to attract serious consideration in the arts-based community development literature. Nevertheless, successful small business models that are abundant in remote/rural communities have the potential to form networked clusters of enterprises and become the foci of approaches to regional development. They provide a new lens through which the contribution of the arts in remote/rural communities can be examined more forensically. Given the context of regional development, if micro, small and medium-sized enterprises operating locally in remote/rural communities are able to interact directly with established distribution and marketing organisations, then arts-based enterprises in rural and remote communities will be well placed to take advantage of new business opportunities. More importantly, these expansive models of regional development provide new prospects based on a rapidly broadening view of creativity. New opportunities for remote/rural communities are likely to arise as all industry sectors become interested in the value of creativity to business and economic development.

Rethinking the Roles and Responsibilities of the Arts in Community Development

In urban and remote/rural communities, the arts claim to contribute in a multitude of ways to community growth and development across social, cultural and economic spheres of influence. Nevertheless, there is still much to learn about the practicalities of arts programs and initiatives and how achievements can be measured against the claims made for the arts, particularly in remote/rural locations. There is also a dearth of information about how the arts integrate with and support other community development processes and strategies, and vice versa. In order to probe the connections between the arts and other local community development processes, this research identified a variety of non-arts-based community programs and actions that contribute to community growth and development. The outcomes of such non-arts programs were examined to determine how they impact in those development areas that are claimed as the province of the arts, including areas relevant to social, cultural and economic domains. Socially, these impact areas embrace the development of community identity, the maintenance of social cohesion, and the creation of community facilities and resources. Culturally, they include the development of cultural infrastructure, cultural programs, and community facilities and resources. Economic impact areas encompass the development of community assets to stimulate tourism, economic development plans and programs, as well as the stimulus and support of new business opportunities.

Figure 9 identifies and maps major areas of activity currently undertaken in remote/rural communities to support community development. Areas identified include community sport, local government programs, community service organisations, community clubs, museums and historical sites, and religious organisations. Figure 9 also provides examples of activities undertaken in each of the identified areas and points to their major impacts on communities.

Table 39 builds on Figure 9 and points to the many associations, clubs, schools, government agencies and community associations working across a range of community areas that are achieving outcomes comparable with those claimed by the arts.

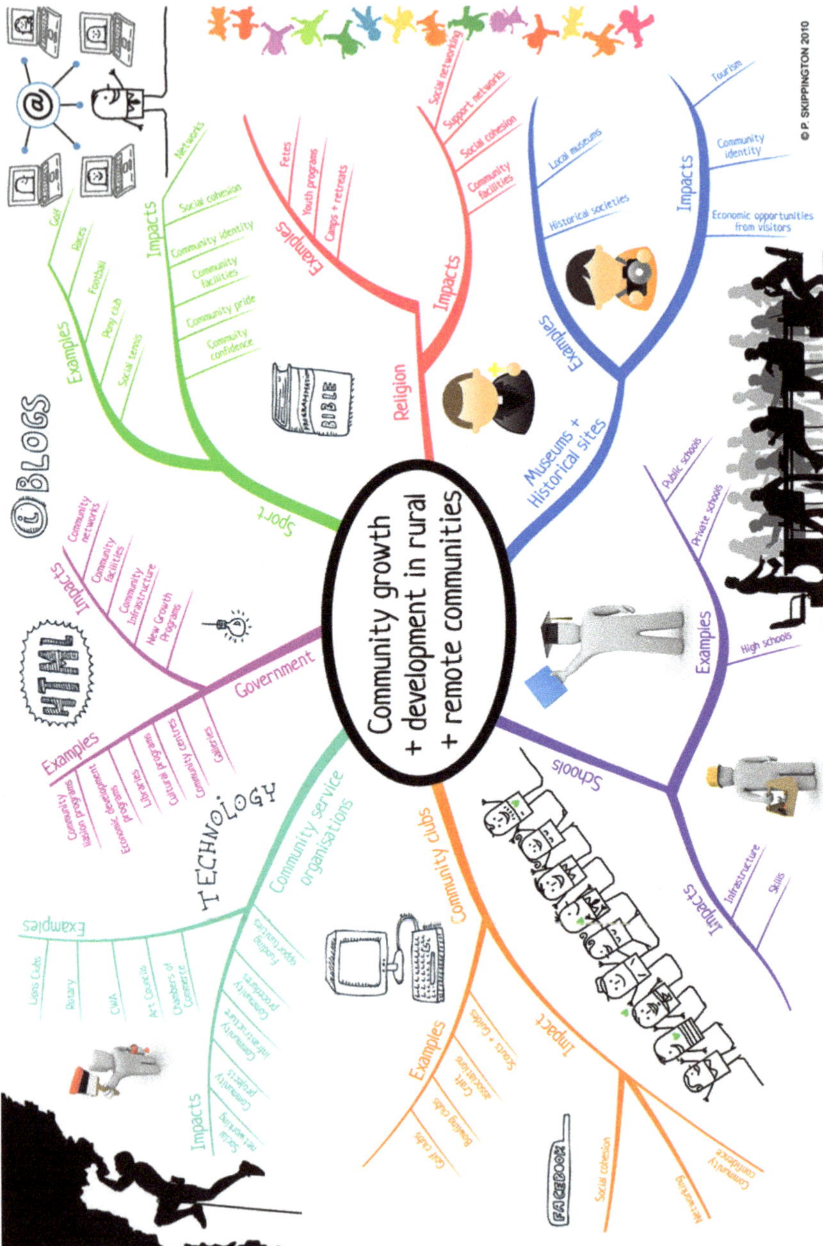

Figure 9. Mapping of Generic Community Development Programs and Initiatives in Rural and Remote Communities.

Source: Author's research.

While all clubs and organisations are making significant contributions, sporting clubs may warrant further exploration. As a dominant feature of remote/rural communities, sporting clubs create significant opportunities for social networking and the maintenance of social cohesion. They also develop important community facilities that can be used for a range of purposes, for example, clubhouses provide additional community venues for community meetings, performances and community celebrations. Competitions held by sporting clubs stimulate a strong sense of community pride and assist in the creation of community identity and cohesion. Sport in remote/rural communities often relies on inter-community competition of which regional travel is a key component. Communities hosting such sporting events usually benefit economically from increased visitor numbers in much the same way as claimed for arts-based events such as performances or exhibitions. While sport is just one area of community activity presented in Figure 9, it exemplifies how a range of community activities can achieve outcomes similar to those claimed for the arts.

Each of the community organisations and institutions identified in Figure 9 and Table 39 has a commitment to improving community cohesion independent of any connection with the arts and community artists. Many are equally committed to the achievement of economic objectives, including the demonstration of sound fiscal policies and the development of financial and business skills by relevant community members. While there is little current evidence in remote/rural communities of direct stimulus to business by community organisations and institutions, there is potential for chambers of commerce and local business associations to become much more active in this area. The analysis of the contribution of various organisations and institutions in Table 39 demonstrates: (i) contemporary claims for the role of the arts in remote/rural communities have seemingly ignored the significant contribution of other areas of activity to the achievement of the same aims; (ii) the arts themselves have failed to create a differentiated role within community development; and (iii) to date, the arts have failed to form integral partnerships with other areas of community activity. This dislocation of the arts from other areas of community activity would seem to be an inalienable fact. Hence, Table 40 presents a sample of community micro-level activities within four areas of community development: economic development, social cohesion, cultural growth and development, and protection and preservation.

Table 39. The Arts and Community Outcomes.

Community development outcomes identified through environmental scanning and community mapping activities (Developed from Figures 6 and 7)	Arts activities, programs and organisations that contribute to the achievement of identified community outcomes (Developed from Figure 6)	Other community activities, programs and organisations that contribute to the achievement of identified community outcomes (Developed from Figure 7)
Social outcomes. Improved social cohesion. Community networks. Increased sense of community identity. Community confidence. Community pride and recognition.	School programs (musicals, show bands, art exhibitions, etc.). Community events (Little Theatre, art contests and exhibitions, etc.).	Church camps, retreats and excursions. Youth programs run by church groups. Sporting programs and events. Scouts and Guides troops.
Economic outcomes. Skill development/human capital building. Economic returns on community investment. Grants/community development funding. New community assets and resources. New opportunities for local businesses. Tourism/increasing revenue form visitors.	Festivals and community celebrations.	Community historical societies. Church camps, retreats and excursions. Youth programs run by church groups. Sporting programs and events.
Cultural outcomes. Development and nurturing of local talent. Access to specialist people and resources.	Community art projects. Community art training programs run by external experts. Local arts councils and community groups.	Development of cultural infrastructure by local governments and community organisations.

Source: Author's research.

Table 40. Micro-Level Activity in Remote/Rural Communities.

Economic development	Social cohesion
Business development. Business incubation. Infrastructure development and maintenance. Job creation. Tourism development and promotion.	Special events. Parks and reserves. Public safety. Sport and recreation. Theatres, halls and community centres.
Cultural growth and development	**Protection and preservation**
Arts programs and projects. Art galleries. Museums. Libraries. Community arts festivals.	Protection and preservation of historically, culturally or environmentally unique sites. Promotion of environmental uniqueness. Waste management.

Source: Author's research.

While Table 40 is not exhaustive, it nevertheless highlights the nature of key community building activity. The key questions are thus: What is the role of the arts and artists in achieving outcomes across these areas? How might the arts work with other community interest groups to achieve coordinated and integrated outcomes?

As we begin to consider the implications of these questions, it is necessary also to take into account broad claims made over the last decade that the arts, through their contribution to individual creativity and innovation, have become central to community economic development and social growth. While such claims now come from many quarters and derive from many theories, their genesis is based on contemporary opinion about knowledge-based economies and the associated recognition of individual creativity as a key contributor to growth and development. This research has found that, for the many rural and remote communities, the solution lies not just in improved infrastructure, facilities and amenities but in recognising and cultivating creative capital already extant within the community. Creativity and talent reside in all communities but can remain dormant if not actively identified or stimulated. What is needed now is a new direction and approach to stimulating creativity and talent across all aspects of community life. This research proposes new roles and responsibilities for the arts in remote/rural communities.

These will be critical but not necessarily indispensable to community development — in essence, the arts will become recognised as a part of a larger canvas.

Interconnections Between Innovative Enterprises and Creative People

If the future prosperity and well-being of remote/rural communities is to depend increasingly on the creativity and adaptability of people living and working in those communities, then further consideration of the role of the arts in stimulating and supporting that creativity is essential. However, approaches orientated towards developing the creativity of local residents through the arts is contrary to much current practice in remote/rural communities. For example, this research has identified that many remote/rural communities import artistic expertise and creative skill sets rather than identifying and building on what exists or developing new skills in current residents. Other community programs and initiatives that purport to support community growth and development through a strong focus on the skills of local people are limited in their impact by the narrowness and insularity of their philosophical platforms. For example, some arts-based programs operating in remote/rural communities have adopted equity and social justice principles as their core but have failed to expand these principles to encompass a broader view of community development. Likewise, the tunnel-visioned doggedness of many community arts programs in focusing on small-scale, narrowly conceived community projects seriously limits their impact on broader community problems and issues and forever relegates them to the periphery of community life.

Remote/rural communities, as well as the organisations that purport to support them in development programs, must open their minds to new vistas of activity in order to develop comprehensive and integrated visions on which to articulate and build plans for their futures. Communities must develop a deep understanding and appreciation of the breadth of terms such as creativity and innovation, and apply these new understandings to community planning and development. Such plans must ensure they adopt community-wide perspectives that integrate work across many fields of endeavour. In this context,

Figure 10 proposes a new conceptual framework designed to generate creative remote/rural communities with the dual objectives of building innovative businesses and enterprises founded on the creativity, imagination and vision of local residents.

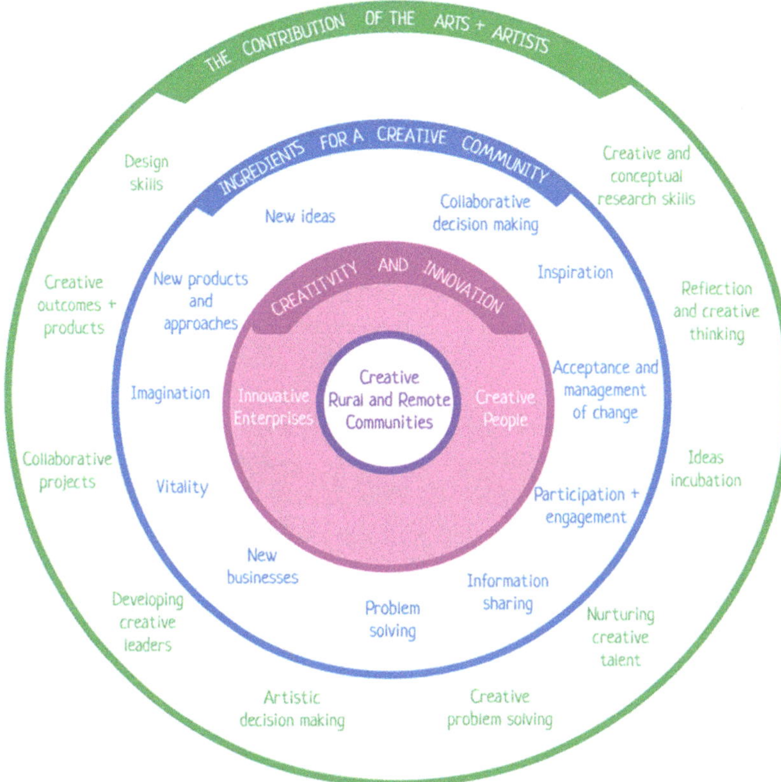

Figure 10. A Conceptual Framework for the Development of Creative Remote/Rural Communities.

Source: Author's research.

Figure 10 identifies the core ingredients necessary for communities to nurture creative people who are capable and willing to contribute to the development of innovative enterprises. These people will need tangible skills as well as more intangible qualities and attributes relating to behaviour and thought. Tangible skills include skills in collaborative decision making and negotiation, tools and approaches to stimulate the creation and development of new businesses, expertise in the design and development of new products and services, proficiency in creative problem solving, and new mechanisms for information sharing. Less tangible attributes required to support the development of a creative community encompass openness to new ideas and a willingness to pursue new directions, a recognition of the importance of imagination and inspiration as core ingredients of community creativity and productivity, community acceptance of change as a growth process and an associated willingness to manage change productively, and an openness and willingness towards active engagement in community planning and participation in community projects.

Figure 10 also hypothesises a potential role for the arts in supporting the development of a creative community. While the arts and artists have an important role to play, artists and arts workers must now work proactively to become less insular and narrowly focused on specific art forms and projects. While artists will always have particular interests and contribute to individual art forms and projects, they must also learn to think more broadly and apply their knowledge and skills across all areas of community activity including leadership. The unique understanding and appreciation that artists have developed in relation to how imagination, creativity and innovation work in art must be expanded and applied across the full spectrum of community development impact areas. Artistic capabilities that are valuable in creative community development include decision making, creative problem solving, design skills, reflection and evaluation. It was recognition of these capabilities and attributes that prompted Rolls Royce to send its engineering trainees to spend a week at the Tate Liverpool, problem solving with artists as an integral part of their training. The company wanted to create a new model for learning that integrated the acquisition of technical skills with the development of personal, critical and creative thinking skills through direct engagement with the work of artists (Davis, 2008). Artists also have the potential to contribute to creative community leadership, the management of collaborative projects, the generation and incubation of new ideas and approaches, and the nurturing of creative talent.

The achievement of the vision of creative remote/rural communities presented in Figure 10 with its primary focus on creative people and innovative enterprises for remote/rural communities requires new approaches and ways of thinking. While the challenges arising therein will impact on all community residents and influence the operation of all community organisations and institutions, Figure 11 identifies four categories of community stakeholders with key roles and responsibilities in supporting community development: community organisations/institutions, government, community enterprises, and artists and arts organisations.

Community organisations/institutions in remote/rural communities work across a range of community areas from community welfare to business development. This category includes sporting clubs, service clubs, special interest groups, welfare groups and local chambers of commerce. While the government category includes all levels of government, Figure 11 recognises that local government must necessarily have a primary role in stimulating and supporting the development of creative communities. The business landscape of remote/rural communities is dominated by micro businesses and this category of stakeholder provides the platform for the development of new approaches to business development. Community artists and arts organisations provide the fourth and final category of key stakeholders.

Each of the four stakeholder groups identified in Figure 11 has specific roles and responsibilities in supporting remote/rural communities to embrace creativity and innovation. Many of these roles and responsibilities are challenging and demand different ways of thinking and doing in the knowledge that the rewards will include new economic opportunities, stronger social connections within and between communities, and a stronger and more inclusive sense of community identity. Stakeholder groups should work individually and collaboratively to organise ways to reinvent themselves for the burgeoning opportunities arising from the new emphasis on creativity and innovation, to prepare for active ownership of community initiatives, and to initiate education strategies to meet the challenges arising from new directions.

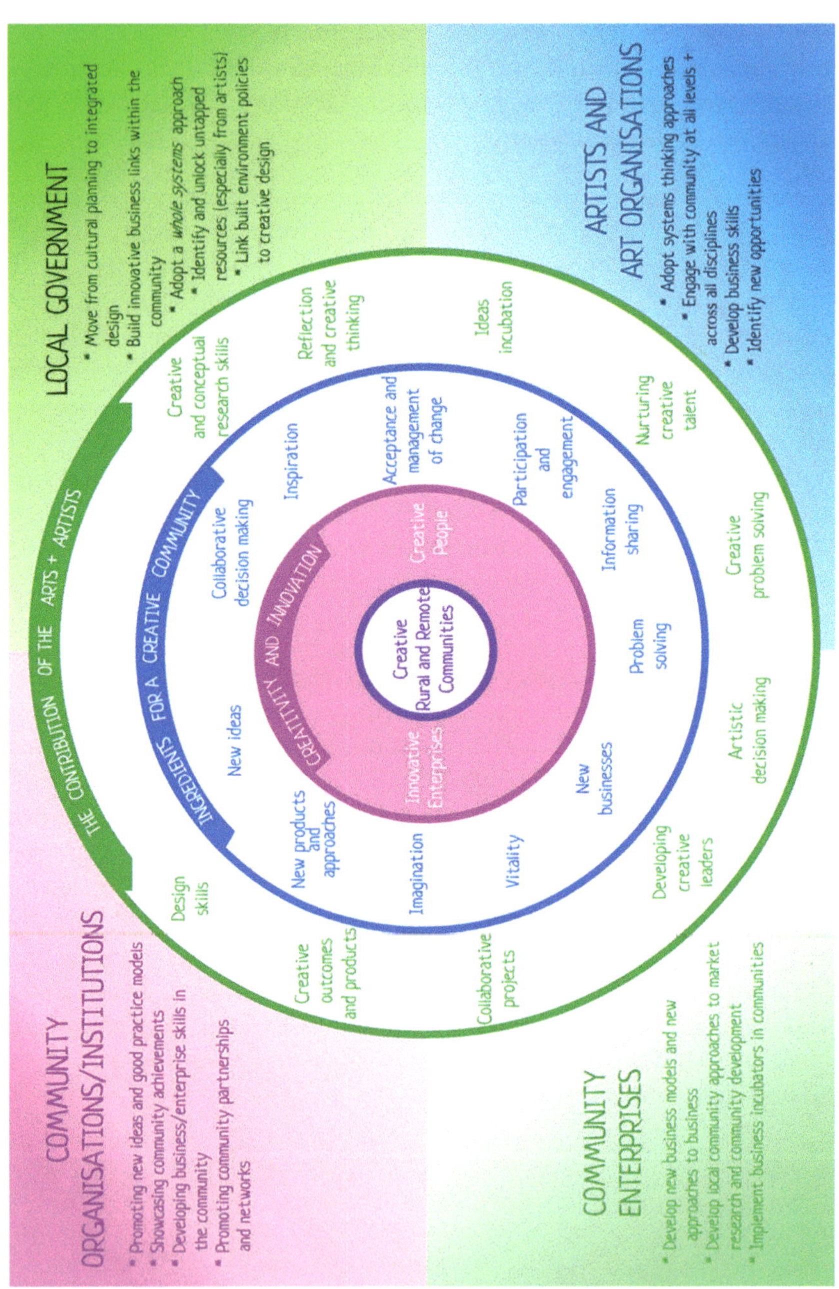

Figure 11. Strategies for Key Stakeholders in Supporting the Development of Creative Communities.

Source: Author's research.

Community organisations/institutions have multiple roles and functions designed to meet specific community demands. At one end of the spectrum are taxpayer-funded public instrumentalities concerned with public safety, economic development and community health and welfare. At the other end of the spectrum are community-based organisations that are typically not-for-profit and voluntary emerging from specific community interests and projects. Such organisations/ institutions have for decades been fundamental to life in remote/rural communities. Organisations such as the Country Women's Association (CWA) have addressed community concerns and built community networks that have contributed significantly to the creation of a sense of meaning and purpose to community life. Other community organisations have provided essential welfare services to communities sometimes struggling with social and health issues. Still others have raised funds to build community infrastructure, including sporting facilities, amenities in community parks and gardens, and equipment to assist health services. While these services must continue, new directions that encourage creativity and innovation in communities challenge community organisations to broaden their roles to include active support of the development of social and human capital.

For example, service organisations could become more active in identifying and promoting new business models and business opportunities drawn from within their own communities as well as from other communities. They might promote new and original approaches by facilitating critical debate and discussion about their potential relevance and contribution to the community. Service organisations could also facilitate the development of appropriate business skills to ensure community residents are equipped to take advantage of new opportunities as they arise. This might best be achieved through action learning and mentoring approaches that allow residents with different skills, backgrounds and experiences to come together to develop new skills and adopt original collaborative approaches to business development. Other community organisations may best contribute by promoting and showcasing new directions in community achievements and the fresh ideas and approaches through which these were generated. They should also recognise the contribution of individuals and accept that successful community initiatives have their origins in individual skill, creativity and talent.

For several decades, governments at all levels have been active in the development of policies and programs to support community growth and development. They have embraced the community-building mantra in an effort to encourage communities to exercise more control over their own futures. But despite the rhetoric, the methods and techniques adopted by governments have continued to be based on the provision of one-off funding grants or programs that focus on single issues rather than adopting whole-of-community approaches geared towards sustainability and longevity. Many existing government programs and initiatives fail to encourage active community involvement or empower community members with the skills and enthusiasm to initiate and manage change. Creative solutions to community challenges that build on new ideas and opportunities need to be conceived and implemented locally. The key role is for local governments who, working in association with other levels of government, will need to develop and encourage imaginative, dynamic and innovative approaches to community development.

A key strategy for local government is to adopt a whole systems approach to planning and development. This will involve identifying relevant individuals and community groups with whom to work collaboratively, including groups with little prior involvement in formal community planning. Governments need to embrace the diversity that exists in communities and work to ensure all community voices are heard and can contribute constructively to community planning. Most importantly, community plans must be comprehensive and integrated, ensuring that their cultural, social and economic elements are interdependent. Outcomes will impact across all community interest groups while simultaneously contributing to comprehensive outcomes for community growth. Other areas where local governments could become more active include building links within communities that connect businesses not only with one another but also with people and organisations whose contribution to business development has been previously overlooked, including artists and arts-based community organisations. In such ways local government can work to unlock hitherto under-utilised community talents, skills and resources.

Perhaps the biggest challenge for communities in moving towards creativity and innovation comes from the stakeholder group that potentially has the most to gain — community businesses and enterprises. Small businesses, especially those in remote/rural communities, are usually built on traditional business models operating in conventional, time-honoured ways. This is exemplified by the businesses that have been the core of community life — the general store, the local hotel, the stock and grain merchants, the pastoral agents, the local mechanic, etc. The challenge for community businesses in the twenty-first century is to look outside traditional business approaches and create new models to take advantage of emergent opportunities to generate wealth within communities. Such models should be designed and developed to tap into evolving markets and changing consumer expectations. They should also take advantage of previously untapped community resources to build innovative and sustainable community businesses.

Artists and art organisations operating in remote/rural communities are critical to the stimulation of imaginative and creative approaches to community growth and development. They are at the heart of endeavours to recognise the vital role of creativity and innovation in enhancing economic development and capitalising upon the linkages between art, community and commerce. While artists recognise that creativity is core to their work, they must now appreciate that creativity must also sit at the core of every community task and business. They must also begin to understand that their unique skills, imagination and originality can stimulate and fuel creativity in communities across many diverse dimensions and disciplines. The challenge for community artists is to acknowledge this broader role and to relinquish the trivial themes and small-scale projects that ensure that their influence remains on the periphery of community life. Artists and art organisations can provide the innovative tools and approaches to encourage the community reflection, debate and discussion vital to the development of fresh community directions. To achieve this, the arts and artists must interact purposefully and meaningfully with other community groups and functions in a collaborative investigation of integrated options for new visions, novel ways of acting, and innovative projects and initiatives.

While a focus on the development of holistic, innovative and creative communities will incorporate many of the positive features of current community thinking and action, it can also provide a bulwark against the insularity of some current approaches in order to develop visions, directions and programs that are both integrated and interdisciplinary.

A primary focus on creativity and innovation supported by the arts promises to (i) facilitate access to new ideas, information, people and organisations, (ii) provide opportunities for the development of innovative modes of economic development, social cohesion, personal expression and cultural development, (iii) respond to the needs of business and industry in communities, (iv) create and develop fresh and positive images of rural and remote communities, and (v) develop new ways of looking at and seeing problems.

A New Model

Realising the potential of the models and approaches outlined in this chapter signifies enormous but not insurmountable challenges for remote/rural communities. Navigating new environments and developing practical ways of proceeding is often confronting for communities steeped in tradition and mired in conventional approaches to development. The key to success is to start with fresh eyes, to critically survey the environment, and to identify and build on existing community strengths. Figure 12 presents the creative community development pyramid (CCDP) designed to assist communities firstly to identify and consolidate existing strengths and, secondly, to use those strengths as a platform for the adoption of community-wide, integrative practices to achieve sustainable new outcomes for remote/rural communities.

At the base of the creative community development pyramid (the purple layer in Figure 12) are the community building blocks that provide the foundations for future growth and development. Many of these building blocks are strengths that communities have already developed; others represent areas where communities may need to develop new strengths. Moving up the pyramid are higher level practices (the blue layer in Figure 12) that operate by linking and combining community strengths from the purple layer and applying them in fresh, integrated ways to achieve innovative outcomes. The top layer of the pyramid (the green layer in Figure 12) represents the achievement of community outcomes that contribute to the establishment and maintenance of sustainable and creative communities.

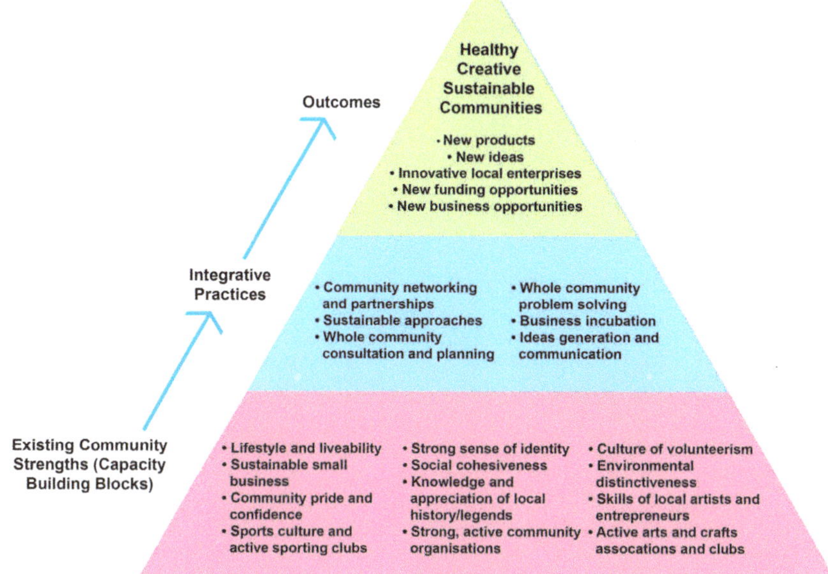

Figure 12. Creative Community Development Pyramid (CCDP).
Source: Author's research.

The pyramid is designed to be a broad guide to communities and is deliberately non-prescriptive. For example, the existing community strengths listed in purple at the base of the pyramid are indicative only and should not be considered an all-encompassing list. Several remote/rural communities will have developed many of the foundational strengths listed in the pyramid while others may have developed specific strengths not currently listed in the pyramid. Likewise, the integrative practices listed in Figure 12 are suggestions rather than prescriptions as it is anticipated that communities will develop approaches based on particular needs and strengths. Consequently, the creative community development pyramid is designed to evolve and develop in complexity as individual communities gain experience in applying it to their idiosyncratic development needs and contexts. The next chapter outlines four potential scenarios in which the pyramid may be applied.

10

The Arts as Creative Community Powerhouse

The four potential scenarios presented in this chapter provide examples of how the creative community development pyramid (CCDP) might be applied in practical applications to create new opportunities and build new community capital.

Taking Advantage of New Tourism Opportunities

A unique opportunity has presented itself to the remote/rural community of Barrington. The discovery of a major dinosaur fossil site 50 kilometres outside Barrington offers the community a major tourism opportunity. The Barrington local government and long-term residents have observed that other towns within the region have failed to capitalise on similar opportunities over the years, and are determined to ensure that the fossil discovery brings major long-term benefits to the town. The community realises that to encourage tourists to visit and experience the town, as well as the nearby fossil site, they must add value to the tourist experience by developing unique and desirable products and services.

The recently released CCDP offers the community a practical new planning tool. Using the CCDP, the Barrington local government initiates a planning process with a critical analysis of current community strengths and weaknesses using the purple base of the pyramid (see Figure 13).

Several community strengths are identified including (i) the vigour of local businesses and their willingness to work with government and community groups to address community problems and opportunities, (ii) the strength of community pride and confidence, (iii) a strong sense of community identity, (iv) a deep knowledge of community history (including local myths and legends), and (v) an active and talented arts community.

Using the blue middle area of the CCDP, the local government then examines the potential appropriateness and usefulness of available integrative planning processes. To recognise and build on the identified community strengths they firstly host an open, whole-of-community meeting to brainstorm ideas on how the community might benefit from the new tourism opportunity. In order to ensure representation from identified core strength areas, the Barrington local government specifically invites local business people, community elders, local historians and artists. The meeting identifies several ideas and two of these ideas are selected by the community for further investigation: (i) a simulated, interactive journey through time incorporating ancient myths and legends associated with the fossil remains and a more recent history of the community, and (ii) the creation of a series of unique local souvenirs commemorating the dinosaur fossils and celebrating the uniqueness of the Barrington region. By referencing the blue level of the CCDP (see Figure 13), government facilitates the creation of two small planning groups inclusive of at least one representative of each area of identified community strength, and sponsors and funds each group to conduct a feasibility study and, if appropriate, to develop a business plan for each of the identified ideas.

Both groups use community skills and resources to test the feasibility of the ideas and develop business plans drawing on the combined expertise of local government, local business people, community historians, community artists and others. As a consequence, the resultant plans are not only financially viable, creative and sustainable but also have high levels of community support and commitment.

The implementation of the plans achieves significant outcomes over the next five- to 10-year period. Within 12 months of the completion of the planning process, a simulated, interactive CD combining local myths and legends with information about the Barrington community has been produced and sold through several community outlets. Initial sales of the CD are sound indicating that the initial financial investment would be returned to government within 18 months. The CD also wins several prestigious national awards, resulting in community artists being recognised and offered commissions for further work.

Perhaps more importantly, the content and graphic representations on the CD stimulate interest from state governments and commercial agencies who recognise the potential of the idea and invest in the broader application of the work. These and other agencies fund the development of a $6 million experiential museum that builds on the original concepts, histories and artwork developed for the CD. The museum becomes a major tourist attraction and within 10 years is generating annual revenue of $4 million. It also becomes a major employer for the town and generates several spin-off businesses including cafes and gift shops.

The second idea also proved successful for the Barrington community, with designs for seven original souvenirs being developed by local artists. Four of the designs are selected for manufacture (based on the input and financial projections of local business people), two being manufactured locally after the identification of specific local skills and resources. Local manufacture generates additional employment opportunities for local youth. Early healthy sales of the souvenirs are further boosted by the opening of the experiential museum (arising from the implementation of the other community idea — the simulation journey through time).

Figure 13 illustrates how the Barrington community used the CCDP to guide them in linking identified key community strengths of environmental distinctiveness, knowledge of local history, small business acumen and an active arts community to develop new approaches based on sound, sustainable business practices that create a unique and innovative tourism program.

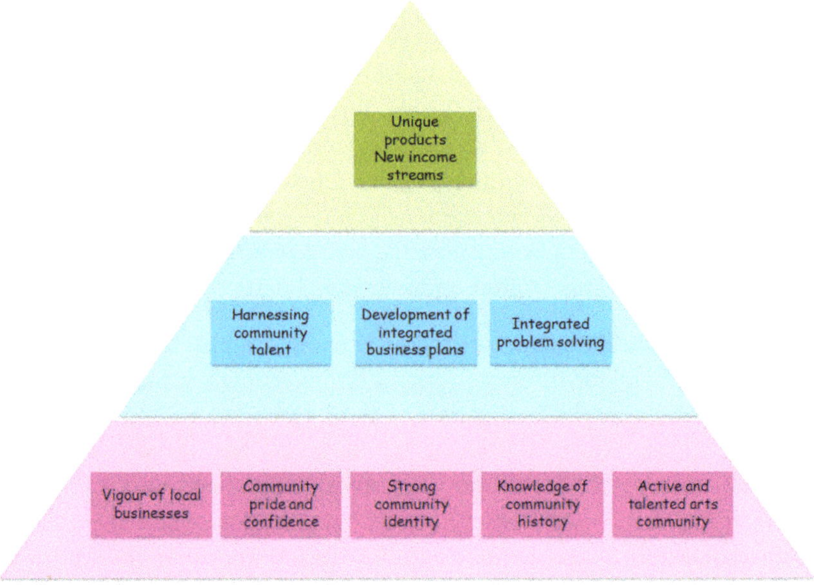

Figure 13. Barrington's CCDP Approach.
Source: Author's research.

Overcoming Youth Unemployment

Wangoola is a small remote/rural community with a major youth unemployment problem that has progressively worsened over the last five years. The Wangoola Arts Council, the chamber of commerce and the cricket club have been lobbying local government to support action to develop new programs and projects to address problems associated with youth unemployment for several years but without success. These three community groups have now become aware of the new community-planning tool, the creative community development pyramid. They have learnt of the successes achieved by neighbouring communities in applying the pyramid to develop solutions and new approaches to community challenges. Using the bottom purple level of the pyramid (see Figure 14) and working initially only within their own organisations, they develop a picture of the core community strengths on which to build new approaches to combat youth unemployment.

These include a strong business community with sound skills, an active arts community and an energetic sporting community. The organisations also used the bottom purple layer of the pyramid to identify and document several community weaknesses that were contributing to the unemployment problem. These included a lack of community pride, especially among young people, a lack of community identity and a resulting lack of shared community direction and social cohesiveness, and a sense that the community had little to offer young people in terms of liveability and lifestyle.

While the three organisations felt that their work at the purple level of the pyramid was worthwhile, as it provided a platform for the development of proposed future action, they still faced three key challenges. Firstly, they realised that the simple identification and documentation of community strengths and weaknesses would fail to convince local government of the need for action. Secondly, without local government support and assistance, work could not progress to the second blue layer of the pyramid, which would allow for the development of strategies and business plans. Thirdly, they needed to consolidate community support for new directions. The organisations decided to strengthen their initial identification of community strengths and weaknesses by conducting a community survey. It was felt that that survey would (i) strengthen their negotiating position with local government, (ii) provide a mechanism to gain community interest in the issues, and (iii) offer an opportunity to canvass future action with community stakeholders.

Members of the three organisations worked collaboratively to design and conduct a survey that included a questionnaire, interviews with selected stakeholders, and a targeted youth forum. By extending, consolidating and validating the results of initial identification of community strengths, the survey processes provided a strong case for community action that could now be presented to local government. Government agreed to support and fund a community-wide planning process to canvass ideas and develop strategies to address problems associated with youth unemployment. This resulted in the formation of a community planning group comprising key members of the original three organisations, two local government representatives, youth representatives and representatives of other community groups. The planning group focused on planning practices drawn from the blue level of the CCDP (see Figure 14), especially (i) whole of community problems solving, (ii) ideas generation, and (iii) community networking.

Several solutions and ideas were generated and a small number of these identified for immediate application gained the financial support of local government. One idea with an immediate community outcome was the development of an environmental walkway. Located 15 kilometres outside the town of Wangoola is the western border of the Gumpybung National Park, a very remote site accessed only by a rarely used track. State government funds were sourced to develop a campsite and environmental walkway to provide an introduction to the rare flora and fauna of the site for locals and potential tourists. Local government agreed to upgrade the road to the park. At this stage, six young community members (under 25 years of age) were identified to plan and manage the project. They were provided with selected mentors drawn from both within and outside the community to cover areas of support such as project planning, project management, financial management, staff management, environmental management, arts and graphics, and community history. Despite this high level of advice and support, decision making rested with the six young people, as did responsibility for all project outcomes.

Short-term project outcomes included employment opportunities for community residents under 25 years of age, new skills for young people in the community, an increased sense of community pride and identity, a strong sense of confidence in community youth, and recognition of the distinctiveness of the community. Arising from and related to these social outcomes were a number of additional community activities including the annual Gumpybung Festival, the Wangoola-sponsored regional Gumpybung Cricket Festival, and the Gumpybung Arts Festival focusing on local flora, fauna and history. Longer-term outcomes included (i) increased tourist numbers, (ii) new economic opportunities meaning increased revenue flows in the community, and (iii) new local businesses catering for increased demand from tourists. An interesting and unexpected further long-term outcome arose from the initiative of two of the original young people selected to manage the environmental walkway. These two individuals, using their newly developed skills in business and management, enhanced confidence, fresh attitudes and attributes, and community networks, built a community enterprise based on adventure trekking. Within five years, holiday makers attracted by wilderness areas previously inaccessible to the public were using the businesses services to plan and conduct their adventure holidays. The business's profit at the end of the sixth year reached $450,000 and won the state government's award for the most innovative new business. In the same year, the partner of one of the business owners started a bed and breakfast accommodation service to further capitalise on increasing visitor numbers. Figure 14 summarises the ways Wangoola used the CCDP to achieve their community outcomes.

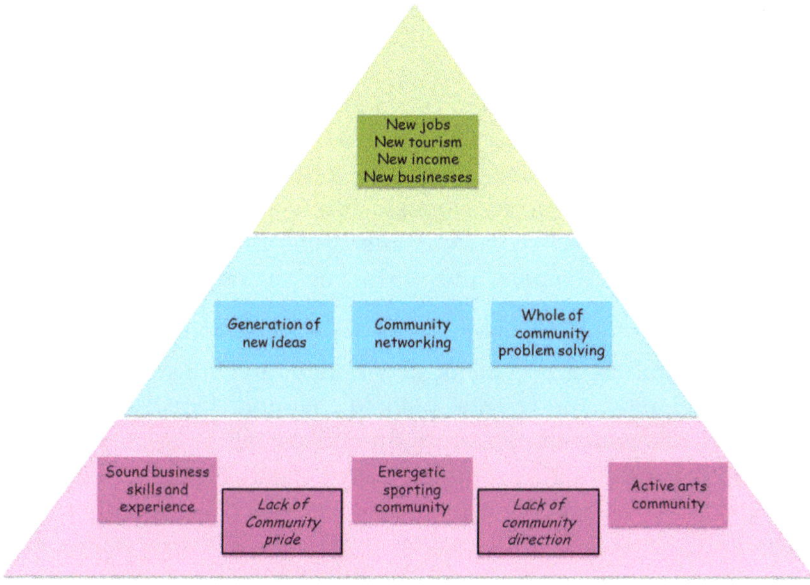

Figure 14. Wangoola's CCDP Approach.
Source: Author's research.

Coping with Population Increases

Jabbaroo is a small town located approximately 900 kilometres by road from the state capital. At the recent national census its population was recorded as 940, reflecting a slow decline in population growth over the past 20 years. During recent years, Jabbaroo has been the temporary home to an array of visiting geologists, archaeologists, surveyors and mining engineers from the major global mining company, Rio Grande.

The residents enjoyed hosting the scientists and engineers who mixed well with the townspeople and provided interesting insights into pre-mining investigations and operations.

Recently, however, Rio Grande has discovered vast reserves of iron ore in the land surrounding the community and, after four years of surveying and planning, mining operations located 50 kilometres north of Jabbaroo are now about to commence. The residents and local government of Jabbaroo have mixed feelings about large-scale mining activities. While they recognise the significant economic benefits that will flow from mining operations (including improved transport infrastructure, increased local revenue flows, new business opportunities, and new employment opportunities), they are nevertheless concerned about the potential problems arising from mining (including escalation of the costs of living associated with increased demands for local goods and services, the lack of available and affordable housing and accommodation, loss of land for traditional economic pursuits such as grazing and agriculture, potential dilution of community cohesiveness, and the loss of community identity).

Jabbaroo community concerns have become heightened by a Rio Grande declaration of two major new policy directions for its mining operations. Firstly, Rio Grande plan to abandon their fly in–fly out policy that allowed mining staff to fly into the mine to work a 14-day shift and then fly out for a commensurate period of leave. The existing policy is to be replaced by a program focusing on the recruitment of couples and families to work and live in the local Jabbaroo community. Secondly, the company will recruit skilled immigrants to overcome relevant national skill shortages. As a result, the Jabbaroo community faces major social, cultural and economic challenges arising from a potentially massive population explosion. Specific social and cultural challenges are also likely to arise for the predominantly conventional, Anglo-Saxon community in attempts to incorporate new social and cultural perspectives as it embraces a much more multicultural community.

These issues are understood and respected by the mining company and Rio Grande has a strong commitment to working cooperatively with the community. However, due to the wealth, power, prestige and experience of the company, several community leaders are concerned that Rio Grande will exert excessive influence and control over the community development agenda and limit community involvement and decision making. Community leaders have been made aware of the new community planning tool, the creative community development pyramid and appraise its applicability to their situation.

Convinced of its potential, they present the tool to Rio Grande officials arguing that it provides a framework for discussion, negotiation and planning. Following agreement, the company and the community work collaboratively to identify core community strengths from the purple base level of the pyramid (see Figure 15). Community strengths identified include a robust community spirit and sense of identity, a solid connection with local history, heritage and the environment, and strong community networks, associations and institutions (including sporting clubs, service organisations and arts organisations).

Rio Grande and the community of Jabbaroo also use the purple section of the pyramid to identify and discuss potential threats to and opportunities for the community from the escalating mining operations. By balancing the strengths against the threats and opportunities, the company and the community are able to work through issues and plan developments based on the practices identified at the blue level of the CCDP (see Figure 15), especially in relation to (i) developing partnerships, (ii) collaborative problem solving, (iii) ideas generation, and (iv) community networking. With Rio Grande providing significant financial support, several projects commence immediately. These include:

1. Land for new housing selected to ensure housing is distributed across community boundaries and not established as mining enclaves
2. Architectural plans for new housing for mining families are reviewed to allow designs to be modified to reflect the traditional historical features of existing community housing
3. Building on identified community skills, strengths and interests, Rio Grande commits to (a) the development of a community equestrian centre focusing on programs and facilities for experienced riders but also incorporating beginner lessons for new members of the community, (b) building a state-of-the-art entertainment, sporting and recreation complex to attract touring exhibitions and shows, and encourage local productions and events, (c) building a lake to ensure a bountiful water supply and provide new water-based recreational facilities, and (d) the design

of a heritage trail to protect, promote and communicate the history of Jabbaroo

4. Funding to research the forgotten or unrecognised contribution of immigrants to the growth and development of the Jabbaroo community with the view to establishing a unique cultural centre/museum. This is seen as a positive way of recognising and promoting the potential contribution of mining-related, new immigrant settlers to the future of Jabbaroo
5. A community development fund is established to stimulate and revitalise existing networks and community organisations. The fund will be managed by a group of local residents drawn from areas of community strengths (identified through the CCDP).

Short-term outcomes of the Jabbaroo/Rio Grande partnership include increased community optimism about the opportunities arising from mining in the area, a sense of community empowerment and control over change, new employment opportunities for community residents, new skills for young people in the community, and a renewed sense of community involvement through the stimulus provided to community networks and organisations (see Figure 15).

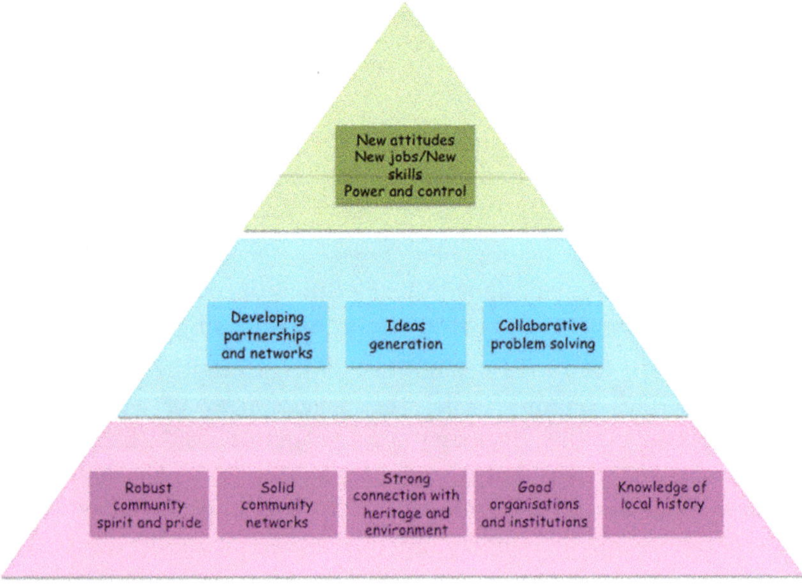

Figure 15. Jabbaroo's CCDP Approach.

Source: Author's research.

It is anticipated that longer-term outcomes will include (i) a larger and more diverse population stimulating new community ventures, (ii) new economic opportunities and resultant increased revenue flows in the community, and (iii) new local businesses catering for increased demands.

Making the Most of New Infrastructure

Several months ago the small, remote/rural community of Waratah was advised that it would be one of the first Australian towns to have access to greatly improved communication services through the broadband infrastructure being deployed through the Federal Government's National Broadband Network (NBN).

This means that all the homes and businesses in Waratah community will have access to high-speed broadband. A small group of friends comprising the local computer repair man, a teacher, a telecommunications worker and a local artist meet over dinner and discuss what the new services might allow them to do, professionally and personally. Excitement grows during the dinner as they bounce ideas off one another including:

1. Greatly improved employment opportunities through telecommuting
2. New business opportunities (not just for technology workers but for everyone)
3. Access to new markets
4. Access to experts and specialist information
5. New educational opportunities through tele-learning
6. New media opportunities.

Towards the end of the evening, reality clouds their excitement as they realise that their potential dreams cannot be achieved without hard work, careful planning and community involvement. The friends decide to form a Waratah Broadband Advancement Working Group. Over the next few weeks, the group of four expanded to 20 passionate and committed people. However, apart from good intentions and ideas, they had little experience or skill in transforming ideas into reality.

The teacher in the group had recently come across a new community planning tool, the creative community development pyramid, and recommends that the group consider its usefulness in their endeavours.

Using the purple level of the tool the Waratah Broadband Advancement Working Group identify the strengths and weaknesses of the community awareness and readiness for broadband services (see Figure 16). Identified community strengths included a well-established and vibrant group of artists, a strong culture of volunteerism, community involvement and participation, and a history of innovation in technology (Waratah was one of the first communities to establish an internet cafe in the early 1990s). Above all, the group identified what they believed was a pioneering spirit that set the community apart from neighbouring communities — as evidenced by a small local core of innovation businesses (a retail outlet for local products, a remote adventure tourist agency and a spa using the waters of the Great Artesian Basin), a forward-thinking local council that has established library internet services, and involved government agencies (especially the schools, who were actively involved in a range of community initiatives). However, the group also used the bottom, purple level of the pyramid to identify a key community weakness — the unwillingness by older members of the community to adopt new technologies. Coupled with this was the recognition that the potential of broadband services would need to be successfully demonstrated to the community in order to understand and appreciate its potential. The discussion arising from working on the purple level of the pyramid consolidated the group's proposed directions and objectives. They were determined that the community of Waratah would not simply be a passive receiver of the broadband services and associated information; they would use the opportunity to become proactive providers of services.

Using the outcomes of their discussions, the group prepared a report for council outlining the opportunities for the community and reporting on the existing community strengths that could be harnessed to take advantage of the opportunities presented by the broadband rollout. They also sought a small grant to conduct a feasibility study (funding to address the blue level of the pyramid). The feasibility study sought community input into planning for opportunities arising from the broadband rollout. Several community meetings and workshops were held generating many ideas. These ideas were gradually winnowed and consolidated to produce a manageable number of key strategies. Sub-groups of the Waratah Broadband Advancement Working Group were formed to develop business plans for each of the strategies. These sub-groups identified and used planning and development practices drawn from the blue level of the pyramid, which included (i) community-wide idea generation activities, (ii) whole-of-community problem solving, and (iii) community business networking and partnership development. Using these community-building processes, several projects and initiatives were designed and implemented:

1. A community infrastructure program to increase community access points to internet services
2. A local government initiative to provide new interactive services for the community including bill paying, community surveying, community meetings/forums through videoconferencing, and the establishment of a electronic community soapbox/speakers' corner
3. A Waratah Combined Businesses E-shop — a partnership of local businesses collectively selling local produce and products, including locally produced art and crafts
4. The Waratah New Media Experiment — a program to create and showcase new media arts by the local community.

These projects resulted in the development of new community skills, partnerships and opportunities for the community to work together to take advantage of new national infrastructure development (see Figure 16).

The four projects outlined above provided a preliminary foundation for the Waratah community to build a presence as a user and provider of broadband services. During the subsequent decade, Waratah consolidated itself as an innovative provider of broadband services.

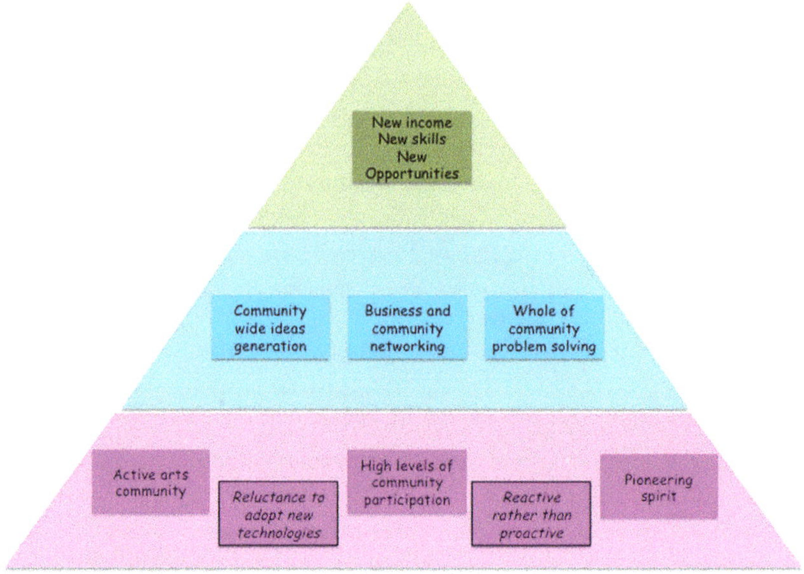

Figure 16. Waratah's CCDP Approach.
Source: Author's research.

Building on the Strengths of the Model

The community development model outlined in this chapter provides a mechanism to encourage community collaboration across diverse community interest groups and stakeholders. It provides a simple and flexible framework that can be adopted and used by individuals (business people, artists, government employees, etc.), community groups (sporting clubs, arts councils, chambers of commerce, etc.) and governments. It recognises that creative talent and skills reside in all individuals and community groups, and focuses on identifying and harnessing those talents and skills and using them to develop collaborative community solutions. In this way, the model overrides community-building approaches based solely on convention, tradition or the power and influence of specific community groups.

The model is designed to be a broad guide through which communities can make decisions and take action in a meaningful and structured way. The scenarios provided in the previous section demonstrate how the model might be used by different communities.

However, if communities are to make the most effective use of the model, it seems appropriate for further work to be undertaken to add depth to the model. Such work might include the identification and development of new tools, mentoring programs and other aids to help communities undertake specific tasks to support the implementation of the pyramid. Such tools, guides and aides might include checklists to aid the identification of community talents and skills, tools to assist in community surveying, guides in how to conduct community focus groups or public meetings and business incubation guidelines.

Reflections, Directions and Implications

The research outcomes presented in this book contribute significantly to the current range and scope of community-building approaches and strategies available to remote/rural communities by providing a previously largely unexamined focus on the role and potential of the arts in broad-based community development. Specifically, the creation of the creative community development pyramid makes an important contribution to new knowledge in the field of community development. The CCDP provides a mechanism through which community stakeholders can work collaboratively to develop holistic, innovative and creative solutions to community problems. It also facilitates communities in the process of recognising and building on existing community resources and, importantly, allows them to incorporate many of the positive features of current community thought and action. The CCDP allows communities to develop visions, directions and programs that are both integrated and interdisciplinary. The primary focus on creativity and innovation supported by the CCDP has the potential to (i) facilitate community access to new ideas, information, people and organisations, (ii) provide opportunities for the development of new modes of economic development, social cohesion, personal expression and cultural development, (iii) respond to the needs of business and industry in communities, (iv) create and develop new and positive images of rural and remote communities, and (v) develop new ways of looking at and seeing problems.

The proposition that skills and processes such as creative decision making, problem solving, critical analysis, presenting alternative viewpoints, collaboration and networking, which are inherent in the artistic practice, have high potential relevance in assisting rural and remote communities to address the challenges and opportunities arising from social, cultural, technological and economic transformation is well supported by the research. The study's aim to develop new arts-based models, strategies and approaches to provide a framework for the development of practical strategies to be used by remote/rural communities has been met through the creation of the CCDP. The CCDP provides a planning tool through which communities are enabled to work collaboratively in the achievement of integrated responses to community development. It encourages communities to identify, recognise and use the idiosyncratic talents and resources existing in the community, including local artists, government officials, members of community organisations, business owners and other key stakeholders.

While the CCDP represents the culmination of the current research, its development and creation have been possible only through the achievement of the first three research aims. That is, the CCDP draws on the research findings that have identified and documented (i) the contemporary challenges facing remote/rural communities, (ii) current ways of using the arts to support community development in remote/rural communities, and (iii) contemporary strategies that recognise the centrality of creativity and innovation to the survival of remote/rural communities.

Given that this research focuses on remote/rural communities, its findings can only, at this stage, be demonstrated as relevant to communities with populations of fewer than 4,000 people located farther than 400 kilometres from a major population centre. That acknowledged, it is clear that, for remote/rural communities, the CCDP offers an important starting point to stimulate novel ways of thinking about and facilitating the design and implementation of new approaches to community development in remote/rural communities. Crucially, it provides a framework on which further work may be undertaken. The scenarios provided in this chapter exemplify the ways in which the CCDP might be used by communities in practice. While modifications may be needed as communities begin to apply the tool to real problems and challenges, it is also anticipated that the application of the CCDP will create new opportunities for further development of complementary and supplementary tools and methods to support community decision making and problem solving. For example, communities adopting business incubation as a community strategy may create further models, guidelines and tools to assist key community members to implement strategies to stimulate and support new business development.

Implications for Further Research

The research has direct implications for further research in three major areas:

1. The evolving role of the arts and artists in community development including social, cultural, economic and environmental development
2. The continuing application of new approaches to community development through the trialling and further refinement of the CCDP
3. The implications of the growing recognition by communities, government and business of the centrality of creativity and innovation to growth and development.

The Evolving Role of Arts and Artists

Firstly, in challenging the conventional lauding of the arts as maverick, the research advocates for arts-based community development approaches based on more inclusive strategies that encompass the talents and experience of all community stakeholders. In particular, it challenges artists and arts workers to be less insular and to apply their knowledge and skills broadly across a range of community concerns. Specific further research projects arising from these findings might include:

- An exploration of the leadership potential of artists: As communities seek to address the increasingly urgent need to adapt to changing economic and social circumstances, they will need creative and innovative leadership. Such a project might initially determine the contemporary leadership qualities required by communities to respond to contemporary changes and challenges. Using these qualities as benchmarks, the current knowledge, skills and capabilities of local artists would be identified and mapped against the required capabilities. Ultimately, the project would determine the extent to which artists are equipped to take community leadership roles and, if necessary, investigate mechanisms for the professional development of artists in leadership.

- The potential for innovative partnering: As communities increasingly appreciate the necessity to build on existing community resources and talents they need to investigate the development and maintenance of collaborative networks and partnerships. In this context, it is important to examine existing community networks and partnerships to determine their structures, function and operations. This information would provide the basis for (i) a critical analysis of the benefits and deficits of current networks, (ii) a broadly based investigation of other approaches to networks and partnerships, including franchise arrangements, regional hubs and business networks, to determine their appropriateness in community settings, and (iii) the development of new models of more inclusive and integrated collaborative networks and partnerships.
- The potential for joint problem solving: The National Review of Visual Education begins by citing the decision by Rolls Royce to send its trainee engineers to the Tate Gallery to work alongside artists in visual problem solving (Davis, 2008). Other examples of diverse problem solving with artists are also cited. Yet no in-depth research has been conducted into the relative and distinctive contributions of the partners in such ventures. There is a strong case for research that examines the operation of such problem-solving partnerships in order to devise principles from which to set these up purposively rather than serendipitously.
- Listening in community consultation: Henderson & Mayo (1998) mentioned in part the critical role of listening in community development, arguing that stakeholders need training in how to listen to and work with communities. Given that artists have traditionally operated on the fringe in communities, active and careful listening is likely to be a key tool in achieving both mutual respect and integration. Research to explore the roles and functions of listening in community consultation has the potential to provide further strategies and tools to help develop comprehensive and integrated approaches to community development.

Trialling and Refining the CCDP

Another area of further research arises from the implementation of the CCDP developed by the current research. Subsequent research projects could usefully focus on the critical evaluation of the CCDP in operation in remote/rural communities. These could include:

- An examination of the CCDP in practice in specific remote/rural settings to enhance and refine the model. Benefits of such an examination would include (i) the provision of information on which to commence continuous improvement of the CCPD, (ii) increase the data on which remote/rural communities build capacity, (iii) build experience and skill within communities, and (iv) contribute to the further enhancement of the model.
- A further project could take elements of the CCDP and analyse the processes that take place within communities as they work through the process. For example, research may test the hypothesis that a key practice from the middle planning layer of the pyramid (integrative practices) is ideas generation by examining and documenting the processes used by a range of communities. The project could then use the resultant data to develop specific models and tools to help other communities working through specific elements of the CCDP.
- While the CCDP was developed specifically for use in remote/rural communities, its usefulness in other environments warrants further examination. A potentially useful project could test the application of the CCDP in other communities including larger rural communities, regional communities and maybe even outer urban communities.

Creativity and Innovation in Community Development

Finally, the current research's primary focus on creativity and innovation provides new challenges for researchers examining community development. By focusing on the concepts of creativity and innovation rather than specific community contexts such as community arts or community health, future researchers may be challenged to examine opportunities for the development of integrated modes of economic development, social cohesion, personal expression and cultural development. They may also be challenged to move away from what seems to be a research fixation on the examination and evaluation of government policies and programs towards research that explores the potential role of businesses and industries in community development. There are also opportunities for research to conduct and document best practice case studies arising from development approaches creating and developing fresh and positive images of remote/rural communities.

Implications for Education

The research also has implications for education, particularly arts education. If the arts are to adopt a more integrated role in the nation's economic, social and cultural life, particularly as creativity and innovation are recognised as crucial to growth and development, then arts education at all levels needs to be reassessed, redirected and realigned towards the centre rather than the educational periphery. Teaching approaches, especially at school level, will need to adopt more integrated, interdisciplinary approaches, building links between the arts and other disciplines. National arts curricula will need to focus on the development not just of artists but of critical and creative thinking for all students. The acquisition of creative problem-solving skills will enable all students to gain the additional confidence and the flexible, adaptive tools to understand and appreciate the complexities and challenges of their role in everyday twenty-first century life. Through appropriate national curricula, students will discover that artists work individually, in and across groups, and that the arts inform divergent creative and mainstream industries and contribute to the development of vibrant and inclusive communities.

At colleges and universities, arts education approaches will, of course, need to continue to consolidate specialist skills development but will also need to develop new programs and learning strategies that seek to encourage broader connections between artists and critical social and economic agendas. Programs might also adopt action learning strategies, encouraging and facilitating arts students to undertake learning projects in partnership with government, businesses and/or other organisations. At one end of the spectrum such projects might facilitate arts students working with architecture firms to incorporate art solutions/products into new buildings. More radically, at the other end of the spectrum, arts students might work with local governments and property developers to design new neighbourhoods, ensuring art and liveability are compatible with economic returns and sustainable outcomes. In higher education, art colleges and universities may consider adopting mentoring programs that match students not only with other artists but with business people, government officials or community leaders.

Implications for Policy

The outcomes of the research also have implications for government policy development. State governments interested in stimulating community development through creativity and innovation will need to review policies and funding programs to ensure that communities have increased flexibility and enhanced ownership. Current policies and funding regimes operate in ways that encourage the segmentation of community work — for example, community health programs are controlled and funded separately from education and community welfare programs while current funding for arts programs is segregated from all other community activities. State governments need to ensure policies for community development are formulated with a view to breaking down barriers and encouraging integrated, seamless approaches to whole-of-community development. While global government approaches have become popular in recent years, the policy focus has, to date, been on the achievement of cost-efficiencies and the reduction of duplication. While these objectives are important, it is timely that the policy focus be broadened to address the potential benefits of integrated approaches to communities and the people who live and work in them.

It is also recommended that local government policies be reviewed in light of the outcomes of this research. As local governments provide a direct interface with their community they are in a unique position to facilitate change through practical approaches to community growth. Local governments need to become less focused on tradition and conventional approaches to community growth; they need actively to seek more innovative and imaginative ways to stimulate positive change in their communities. They also need to ensure that their policies facilitate and encourage integrated approaches to the design and implementation of community programs and projects.

Equally, local governments need to ensure that their planning processes are inclusive, not just to ensure thorough and proper consultation but to identify existing community talents and resources that can contribute to planning and implementation processes. In this context, the CCDP developed by the research provides a framework for the development of new policies and practices and is an appropriate tool for immediate use by local governments in the review and analysis of current policies.

Implications for Artists, Arts Workers and Arts Organisations

Finally, the research has strong implications for artists, arts workers and arts organisations. The outcomes of the research encourage artists to become much less insular and inward looking, and to actively seek opportunities for engagement with broader community issues and concerns.

Likewise, arts organisations need to work with artists to assist them in developing not just new skills but also new attitudes. If artists are to accept the challenge of the research to engage more broadly in community life, they will need to emerge from their silos, hone and redirect existing skills, and acquire a range of new skills. While they will always benefit from professional development in their specific art forms, they will also need skill development in communication, consultation and negotiation. Those who wish to work in new areas and with innovative concepts may need skill development in project management, financial management and human resource management. Importantly, all will need to develop attitudes focused on seeing the arts as a part — perhaps in many instances and projects a key part — of a wider community agenda of change and development. In each instance and opportunity, the challenge for artists is to determine how the arts might contribute to key community concerns and to plan concertedly with other community members to ensure such contributions are brought to fruition. Failure to engage in such issues may mean that artists and their contribution to community life become even more marginalised.

Artists have, possibly more than any other group, enjoyed the freedom associated with the unpredictable, the unconventional, the maverick that lurks within us all. The Janus face of the maverick offers societal freedom — the licence to cock a snoot at the confines of society's norms — but often the vice-like restriction of penury is the other face of that life. The revaluing of creativity now offers artists an opportunity to explore different dimensions of freedom in partnership with individuals and groups previously seen as strange bedfellows for the arts. It offers opportunities to embark on a trajectory of challenge by collaborating on solutions beyond the known and enjoying the professional, creative, social, cultural and economic rewards implicit in such activities.

Bibliography

Adams, D. (2009) *A Social Inclusion Strategy for Tasmania,* Hobart: Department of the Premier and Cabinet, Tasmanian Government.

Adams, K. (2005) *The Sources of Creativity and Innovation,* Washington: National Centre on Education and the Economy.

Ainsworth, R. & Ritchie, J. (2002) *North West and Far West Regions,* Sydney: Regional Arts New South Wales.

Archer, R. (2009) 'Industry that Pays, and Art that Doesn't', *Griffith Review,* 23. griffithreview.com/edition-23-essentially-creative/industry-that-pays-and-art-that-doesnt. Accessed on 7 February 2010.

Argent, N. & Walmsley, J. (2008) 'Rural Youth Migration Trends in Australia: An Overview of Recent Trends and Two Inland Case Studies', *Geographical Research,* 46, 2: 139–152.

Arts Queensland (2007) *Queensland Arts Industry Sector Development Plan 2007–2009,* Brisbane: Queensland Government.

Arts Queensland (2007a) *Queensland Heritage Trails Network,* Brisbane: Queensland Government.

Aspen Institute (1996) *Measuring Community Capacity Building,* Washington: The Aspen Institute.

Athanasopoulos, G. & Hahid, F. (2003) 'Statistical Inference and Changes in Income Inequality in Australia', *Economic Record,* 79, 247: 412–424.

Atkinson, R. & Easthope, H. (2009) 'The Consequences of the Creative Class: The Pursuit of Creativity Strategies in Australia's Cities', *International Journal of Urban and Regional Research,* 33, 1: 64–79.

Australia Council for the Arts (2006) *Funding Guidelines 2006,* Sydney: Australia Council for the Arts.

Australian Bureau of Statistics (2008) *Australian Historical Population Statistics 2000,* Canberra: Australian Bureau of Statistics.

Baker, W.E. (2000) *Achieving Success Through Social Capital: Tapping Hidden Resources in Your Personal and Business Networks,* San Francisco: Jossey-Bass Inc.

Banks, G. (2010) 'Advancing Australia's "Human Capital Agenda"', The Fourth Ian Little Lecture, Melbourne, 13 April 2010, Productivity Commission, Melbourne. www.pc.gov.au/news-media/speeches/advancing-human-capital. Accessed on 25 June 2011.

Barr, C.J. (1998) *The Sampling Strategy for Countryside Survey 2000,* Edinburgh: Scottish Department of the Environment Transport and the Regions.

Bayliss, D. (2007) 'The Rise of the Creative City: Culture and Creativity in Copenhagen', *European Planning Studies,* 15, 7: 889–903.

Beer, A., Delfabbro, P., Natalier, K., Oakley, S. & Verity, F. (2003) *Developing Models of Good Practice in Meeting the Needs of Homeless Young People in Rural Areas,* The Australian Housing and Urban Research Institute. www.ahuri.edu.au/__data/assets/pdf_file/0025/2797/AHURI_Positioning_Paper_No62_Developing_models_of_good_practice_in_meeting_the_needs_of_homeless_young_people_in_rural.pdf?utm_source=website&utm_medium=report.PDF&utm_campaign. Accessed on 22 June 2016.

Beer, M. & Nohria, N. (2000) *Breaking the Code of Change,* Harvard: Harvard Business School Press.

Belliveau, M., O'Reilly, C. & Wade, J. (1996) 'Social Capital at the Top: The Effects of Social Similarity and Status on CEO Compensation', *Academy of Management Journal,* 39, 3: 1538–1568.

Birch, T.L. (2002) 'The Arts in Public Policy: An Advocacy Agenda', Washington: National Assembly of State Arts Agencies (NASAA). www.nasaa-arts.org/Advocacy/Advocacy-Tools/advocate_policy.pdf. Accessed on 28 May 2008.

Blackall Shire Council (2003) 'Blackall Economic Vitalisation Strategy', unpublished paper.

Blackall Shire Council (2005) *A Cultural Plan for Blackall 2005–2010,* Blackall: Blackall Shire Council.

Blackall Shire Council (2005a) *Blackall Community Cultural Plan 2005–2010,* Blackall: Blackall Shire Council.

Blakely, E.J. & Leigh, N.G. (2010) *Planning Local Economic Development: Theory and Practice* (4th ed.), London: Sage.

Bohm-Parr, J. (2011) 'Glass Studio Sustainability: A Southern Perspective', unpublished paper presented at the Making Futures Conference, 15–16 September, Plymouth, United Kingdom.

Borghino, J. (2000) *The Arts Economy: Overview,* Sydney: The Australia Council for the Arts.

Bott, J. (2006) 'The Role of Government Agencies on Regeneration', paper presented at World Summit on the Arts and Culture, Newcastle, United Kingdom. australiacouncil.gov.au/news/media-centre/speeches/jennifer-bott-speaks-at-the-world-summit-on-arts-and-culture-newcastle-uk-2/. Accessed on 22 June 2016.

Bott, J. (2006a) 'The Australia Council: A CEO's Reflections', paper presented at Pacific Edge Regional Arts Australia National Conference. australiacouncil.gov.au/news/media-centre/speeches/the-australia-council-a-ceos-reflections/. Accessed on 22 June 2016.

Bourdieu, P. (1986) 'The Forms of Capital' in Richardson, J. (ed.) *Handbook of Theory and Research for the Sociology of Education,* New York: Greenwood, 241–258.

Bourdieu, P. & Wacquant, L.J.D. (1992) *An Invitation to Reflexive Sociology,* Chicago: University of Chicago Press.

Bourke, L. (2003) 'Toward Understanding Youth Suicide in an Australian Rural Community', *Social Science and Medicine,* 57, 12: 2355–2365.

Brault, S. (2005) 'The Arts and Culture as the New Engines of Economic and Social Development', *Policy Options,* 26, 3: 56–60.

Brehn, J. & Rahn, W. (1997) 'Individual-Level Evidence for the Causes and Consequences of Social Capital', *American Journal of Political Science,* 41, 3: 999–1024.

Bridges, W. (2007) *Managing Transitions: Making the Most of Change* (2nd ed.), New York: Perseus Books.

Broughton, C. & Chambers, J. (2001) 'Reconsidering the Revolution?: Australian Public Sector Administration in 2000', *Australian Journal of Public Administration,* 60, 1: 81–88.

Brown, P., Hesketh, A. & Williams, S. (2002) *Employability in a Knowledge-Driven Economy,* Working Paper 26, School of Social Sciences, Cardiff: Cardiff University. www.cardiff.ac.uk/socsi/resources/wrkgpaper26.pdf. Accessed on 22 June 2016.

Bryce, J., Mendelovits, J., Beavis, A., McQueen, J. & Adams, I. (2004) *Evaluation of School-Based Arts Education Programmes in Australian Schools,* Canberra: Commonwealth of Australia.

Bryden, J., Watson, D., Storey, C. & Van Alphen, J. (1997) *Community Involvement and Rural Policy,* Edinburgh: Scottish Office Central Research Unit.

Buikstra, E., Ross, H., King, C., Baker, P., Hegney, D., McLaughlan, K. & Rogers-Clark, C. (2010) 'The Components of Resilience: Perceptions of an Australian Rural Community', *Journal of Community Psychology,* 38, 8: 975–991.

Bulick, B., Coletta, C., Jackson, C., Taylor, A. & Wolff, S. (2003) *Cultural Development in Creative Communities,* Washington: Americans for the Arts.

Bullen, P. & Onyx, J. (1998) *Measuring Social Capital in Five Communities in New South Wales.* www.mapl.com.au/A2.htm. Accessed on 23 March 2006.

Bullen, P. & Onyx, J. (1999) *Social Capital: Family Support Services and Neighbourhood and Community Centres in New South Wales,* Family Support Services and Neighbourhood and Community Centres, New South Wales. www.mapl.com.au/A12.htm. Accessed on 22 June 2016.

Burt, R.S. (1992) *Structural Holes: The Social Structure of Competition*, Harvard: Harvard University Press.

Burton, J.M., Horowitz, R. & Abeles, H. (2000) 'Learning In and Through the Arts: The Question of Transfer', *Studies in Art Education, A Journal of Issues and Research*, 41, 3: 228–257.

Cabrita, M.R. & Cabrita, C. (2010) 'The Role of Creative Industries in Stimulating Intellectual Capital in Cities and Regions', in Rodrigues, S. (ed.) *The Proceedings of the 2nd European Conference on Intellectual Capital*, Portugal: ISCTE Lison University Institute, 171–179.

Campbell, D., Wunungmurra, P. & Nyomba, H. (2007) 'Starting Where the People Are: Lessons on Community Development from a Remote Aboriginal Australian Setting', *Community Development Journal*, 42, 2: 151–166.

Carley, M. & Kirk, K. (1999) *Learning by Doing: Fostering Sustainable Communities*, Glasgow: Forward Press.

Catterall, J.S. (2002) 'The Arts and the Transfer of Learning', in Deasy, R. (ed.), *Critical Links: Learning in the Arts and Student Academic and Social Development*, Washington: Arts Education Partnership, 151–157.

Cavaye, J. (2000) 'Governance and Community Engagement: The Australian Experience', in Lovan, W.R., Murray, M. & Shaffer R. (eds) *Participatory Governance: Planning, Conflict Mediation and Public Decision Making in Civil Society*, Hants, England: Ashgate Publishing UK, 85–102.

Cavaye, J. (2000a) *The Role of Government in Community Capacity Building*, Department of Primary Industries, Brisbane: Queensland Government.

Cavaye, J. (2001) 'Rural Community Development: New Challenges and Enduring Dilemmas', *The Journal of Regional Policy Analysis*, 31, 2: 109–124.

Cavaye, J. (2008) *Stanthorpe 2020: Your Say in Our Future Community Plan*, Toowoomba: Cavaye Community Development.

Caves, R.E. (2000) *Creative Industries: Contracts Between Art and Commerce,* Harvard: Harvard University Press.

Chanan, G., Gilchrist, A. & West, A. (1999) *SRB6: Involving the Community,* London: Community Development Foundation Publications.

Chapman, M. & Kirk, K. (2001) *Lessons for Community Capacity Building: A Summary of Research Evidence,* A Research Review to Scottish Homes, Edinburgh: Scottish Homes.

Charbit, C. (2009) *Regions Matter: Economic Recovery, Innovation and Sustainable Growth,* Paris: OECD.

Chaskin, R.J. (2001) 'Building Community Capacity', *Urban Affairs Review,* 36, 3: 667–709.

Chaston, I. (2008) 'Small Creative Industry Firms: A Development Dilemma?', *Management Decision*, 46, 6: 819–831.

Chenoweth, L. & Stehlik, D. (2001) 'Building Resilient Communities: Social Work Practice and Rural Queensland', *Australian Social Work*, 54, 2: 47–54.

Choi, Y. & O'Brien, S. (2002) 'Aboriginal Art Business Online: Issues and Lessons in Establishment', unpublished paper presented to the Electronic Networks: Building Community, 5th Community Networking Conference, 3–5 July, Melbourne.

Coleman, J. (1990) *The Foundations of Social Theory,* Cambridge: Belknap Press.

Cook, P. (2001) 'Alliances, Linkages and Challenges: the Queensland Heritage Trails Network', unpublished paper presented at the Making Tracks Conference, Making Tracks From Point to Pathway: The Heritage of Routes and Journeys, 23–27 May, Alice Springs. www.aicomos.com/wp-content/uploads/Alliances-Linkages-and-Challenges-the-Queensland-Heritage-Trails-Network.pdf. Accessed on 25 August 2010.

Cox, G. (2005) *Cox Review of Creativity in Business: Building on the UK's Strengths,* Norwich: Her Majesty's Stationery Office.

Craig, G. (2007) 'Community Capacity-Building: Something Old, Something New…?', *Critical Social Policy*, 27, 3: 335–359.

Creative Industries Task Force (CITF) (2001) *Creative Industries Mapping Document 2001,* London: Department of Culture, Media and Sport, London. www.creativitycultureeducation.org/creative-industries-mapping-document-2001. Accessed on 22 June 2016.

Cruickshank, L. (2010) 'The Innovation Dimension: Designing in a Broader Context', *Design Issues,* 26, 2: 17–26.

Culture and Learning Consortium (2009) *Get It: The Power of Cultural Learning,* London: Culture and Learning Consortium. www.cloreduffield.org.uk/userfiles/documents/publications/Get_it_the_power_of_cultural_learning.pdf. Accessed on 22 June 2016.

Cunningham, S.D. (2004) 'From Cultural to Creative Industries: Theory, Industry, and Policy implications', *Media International Australia Incorporating Culture and Policy: Quarterly Journal of Media Research and Resources.* acpculturesplus.eu/sites/default/files/2015/03/26/cirac-cunnigham_fromculttocreativeind.pdf. Accessed on 22 June 2016.

Cunningham, S.D. (2004a) 'The Creative Industries After Cultural Policy: A Genealogy and Some Possible Preferred Futures', *International Journal of Cultural Studies,* 7, 1: 105–115.

Cunningham, S.D. (2005) 'Creative Enterprises', in Hartley, J. (ed.) *Creative Industries,* Malden: Blackwell Publishing, 282–298.

Cunningham, S.D. (2006) 'What Price a Creative Economy?', *Platform Papers: Quarterly Essays on the Performing Arts,* No. 9, July, Sydney: Currency House.

Darling, I. (2008) 'A Human Face for Urgent Social Issues', *Connect,* 8, June, Melbourne: Australian Business Arts Foundation.

Daskon, C.D. (2010) 'Are Cultural Traditions Real Assets for Rural People?: An Analysis from a Livelihood Perspective', *Global Journal of Human Social Science,* 10, 3: 13–23.

Davis, D. (2008) *First We See: The National Review of Visual Education,* Australia Council for the Arts and the Department of Education, Employment and Workplace Relations, Canberra: AGPS.

Deasy, R. (ed.) (2002) *Critical Links: Learning in the Arts and Student Academic and Social Development,* Washington: Arts Education Partnership.

DeFilippis, J. (2001) 'The Myth of Social Capital in Community Development', *Housing Policy Debate,* 12, 4: 781–806.

Dickie, M. (2005) *Lessons from Elsewhere: A Think Piece on Innovation,* Brisbane: Queensland Department of Education and Training. www.vetpd.qld.gov.au/resources/pdf/tla/lessons-elsewhere.pdf (site discontinued). Accessed on 24 July 2008.

Dickie, M. (2005a) *Keys to Successful Change: A Think Piece on Innovation,* Brisbane: Queensland Department of Education and Training. www.vetpd.qld.gov.au/resources/pdf/tla/keys-successf-chng.pdf (site discontinued). Accessed on 24 July 2008.

Dickie, M. (2005b) *Adopting Change: A Think Piece on Innovation,* Brisbane: Queensland Department of Education and Training, www.vetpd.qld.gov.au/resources/pdf/tla/adopting-change.pdf (site discontinued). Accessed on 24 July 2008.

Dolfsma, W. & Dannreuther, C. (2003) *Globalisation, Social Capital and Inequality: Contested Concepts, Contested Experiences,* European Association of Evolutionary Political Economy, Cheltenham: Edward Elgar Publishing.

Duncan, P. & Thomas, S. (2000) *Neighbourhood Regeneration: Resourcing Community Involvement,* Bristol: The Policy Press.

Duncan, P. & Thomas, S. (2001) *Evaluation of the Community Champions and the Community Development Learning Fund,* London: Department of Education and Skills.

Dunn, A. (2006) *Cultural Development and the Arts in Everyday Life,* discussion paper prepared for the Australia Council's Scoping Study Reference Group, Sydney: Australia Council for the Arts.

Dunn, A. (2006a) *Future Directions for the Support of Arts and Cultural Development in Communities Scoping Study,* discussion paper prepared for the Australia Council for the Arts, Sydney: Australia Council for the Arts.

Dunn, A. (2006b) *Creative Communities: Community Partnerships Scoping Strategy,* Sydney: Australia Council for the Arts. static.placestories.com/pool/project/0001/0007950/docs/doc-2E.pdf. Accessed on 22 June 2016.

Edwards, B. & Foley, M. (1998) 'Civil Society and Social Capital Beyond Putnam', *American Behavioural Scientist,* 42, 1: 124–139.

Eger, J.M. (2003) *The Creative Community: Forging Links Between Art, Culture, Commerce and Community,* Californian Institute for Smart Communities, San Diego: San Diego University.

Eng, E. & Parker, E. (1994) 'Measuring Community Competence in the Mississippi Delta: The Interface Between Program Evaluation and Empowerment', *Health Education Quarterly,* 21, 199–200.

Evans, G. (2005) 'Measure for Measure: Evaluating the Evidence of Culture's Contribution to Regeneration', *Journal of Urban Studies,* 42, 5–6: 959–983.

Fagin, G. (1997) *New Ideas in Rural Development No 3: Involving Rural Communities — The CADISPA Approach,* Edinburgh: Scottish Office Central Research Unit.

Fiske, E.B. (1999) *Champions of Change: The Impact of the Arts on Learning,* Arts Education Partnership, Washington: President's Committee on the Arts and the Humanities.

Florida, R. (2002) *The Rise of the Creative Class,* Melbourne: Pluto Press.

Foord, J. (2009) 'Strategies for Creative Industries: An International Review', *Creative Industries Journal,* 1, 2: 91–113.

Fowler, K. & Etchega, H. (2008) 'Economic Crisis and Social Capital: The Story of Two Rural Fishing Communities', *Journal of Occupational and Organizational Psychology,* 81, 2: 319–341.

Freeman, A. (2007) *London's Creative Sector: 2007 Update,* Working Paper 22, London: Greater London Authority. www.london.gov.uk/sites/default/files/gla_migrate_files_destination/wp_22_creative.pdf. Accessed on 22 June 2016.

Fukuyama, F. (1995) *Trust: The Social Virtues and the Creation of Prosperity*, New York: Free Press (Simon & Schuster).

Fulton, A., Fulton, D., Tabart, T., Ball, P., Champion, S., Weatherly, J. & Heinjus, D. (2003) *Agricultural Extension, Learning and Change*, Canberra: Rural Industries Research and Development Corporation.

Gadsden, V.L. (2008) 'The Arts and Education: Knowledge Generation, Pedagogy, and the Discourse of Learning', *Review of Research in Education*, 32, 1: 29–61.

Galloway, S. & Dunlop, S. (2007) 'A Critique of Definitions of the Cultural and Creative Industries in Public Policy', *International Journal of Cultural Policy*, 13, 1: 17–31.

Garnham, N. (2005) 'From Cultural to Creative Industries: An Analysis of the Implications of the Creative Industries Approach to Arts and Media Policy Making in the United Kingdom', *International Journal of Cultural Policy*, 11, 1: 15–29.

Geddes, M. (1995) *Poverty, Excluded Communities and Local Democracy*. London: Commission for Local Democracy Research.

Gemmel, L.J. & Clayton, P.H. (2009) *A Comprehensive Framework for Community Service-Learning in Canada*, Ottawa: Canadian Alliance for Community Service-Learning. www.communityservicelearning.ca/en/documents/AComprehensiveFrameworkforCSL.pdf. Accessed on 6 September 2010.

Gertler, M.S. (2004) *Creative Cities: What Are They For, How Do They Work, and How Do We Build Them?* Background Paper F/48, Ottawa: Canadian Policy Research Networks. www.oldvancouver.com/pdfs/creative_cities_gertler.pdf. Accessed on 4 November 2009.

Gilchrist, A. (1995) *Community Development and Networking*, London: Community Development Foundation.

Gilchrist, A. (2009) *The Well-Connected Community: A Networking Approach to Community Development*, Bristol: The Policy Press.

Goldbard, A. (1993) 'Postscript to the Past: Notes Toward a History of Community Arts', in *High Performance*, 64, Talmage: Community Arts Network. www.darkmatterarchives.net/wp-content/uploads/2011/11/GoldbergCETAsanfrancisco.pdf. Accessed on 22 June 2016.

Goldbard, A. & Adams, D. (2006) *New Creative Community: The Art of Cultural Development*, Oakland: New Village Press.

Goldberger, P. (2011) 'New York's High Line', *National Geographic*, April 2011.

Grams, D. & Warr, M. (2003) *Leveraging Assets: How Small Budget Arts Activities Benefit Neighborhoods*, research report commissioned by the Richard H. Driehaus Foundation, Chicago: John D. and Catherine T. MacArthur Foundation. www2.tulane.edu/liberal-arts/sociology/upload/Grams-and-Warr-2003-Leveraging-Assets-March-2003.pdf. Accessed on 22 June 2016.

Green, G.P. & Haines, A. (2011) *Asset Building and Community Development*, Thousand Oaks: Sage.

Green, M. & Sonn. C. (2008) *Drawing Out Community Empowerment Through Arts and Cultural Practice*, Perth: Community Arts Network Western Australia.

Gregory, J., Hartz-Karp, J. & Watson, R. (2008) 'Using Deliberative Techniques to Engage the Community in Policy Development', *Australia and New Zealand Health Policy*, 5, 16: 1–9.

Greenspan, A. (2005) 'Empowering Communities, Attracting Development Capital and Creating Opportunities', *National Community Investment Coalition Conference*, March, Washington DC. www.bis.org/review/r050322a.pdf. Accessed on 5 November 2009.

Grodach, C. (2011) 'Art Spaces in Community and Economic Development: Connections to Neighborhoods, Artists, and the Cultural Economy', *Journal of Planning Education and Research*, 31, 1: 74–85.

Grodach, C. & Loukaitou-Sideris, A. (2007) 'Cultural Development Strategies and Urban Revitalisation', *International Journal of Cultural Policy*, 13, 4: 349–370.

Grogan, D., Mercer, C. & Engwicht, D. (1995) *The Cultural Planning Handbook: An Essential Australian Guide*, St Leonards: Allen & Unwin.

Guetzkow, J. (2002) *How the Arts Impact Communities: An Introduction to the Literature on Arts Impact Studies*, Centre for Arts and Cultural Policy Studies, Working Paper Series 20, Princeton: Princeton University. www.princeton.edu/~artspol/workpap/WP20%20-%20Guetzkow.pdf. Accessed on 2 July 2005.

Guldberg, H. (2000) *The Arts Economy 1968–1998: Three Decades of Growth in Australia,* Sydney: Australia Council for the Arts.

Haggblade, S., Hazell, P. & Reardon, T. (2010) 'The Rural Non-Farm Economy: Prospects for Growth and Poverty Reduction', *World Development,* 38, 10: 1429–1441.

Hamel, G. & Valikangas, L. (2003) 'The Quest for Resilience', *Harvard Business Review,* 81, 9: 52–63.

Hampshire, K.R. & Matthijsse, M. (2010) 'Can Arts Projects Improve Young People's Wellbeing?: A Social Capital Approach', *Journal of Social Science and Medicine,* 71, 4: 708–716.

Harvey, E. & Shaw, K. (1998) 'Competitive Urban Policy and the Single Regeneration Budget: A Case of Innovation or Frustration', *Local Governance,* 24, 1: 21–29.

Haufman, J.C. & Baer, J. (eds) (2005) *Creativity Across Domains: Faces of the Muse*, London: Psychology Press.

Haufman, J.C. & Sternberg, R.J. (eds) (2006) *The International Handbook of Creativity*, Cambridge: Cambridge University Press.

Hawe, P. & Shiell, A. (2000) 'Social Capital and Health Promotion: A Review', *Social Science & Medicine*, 51, 6: 871–885.

Hawkes, J. (2001) *The Fourth Pillar of Sustainability: Culture's Essential Role in Public Planning,* Melbourne: Common Ground Publishing.

Hawkes, J. (2003) 'Understanding Culture', address to the National Local Government Community Development Conference: Just and Vibrant Communities, Local Government Community Services Association of Australia, Townsville. www.culturaldevelopment.net.au/downloads/Just_Vibrant.pdf. Accessed on 13 August 2009.

Hawkes, J. (2005) 'Creative Engagement', *Artworks,* 54: 10–15.

Hawkins, G. (1993) *From Nimbin to Mardi Gras: Constructing Community Arts*, St Leonards: Allen & Unwin.

Healy, K. (2001) 'Community Capacity Building: From Ideas to Realities', paper presented at the Australian Association of Social Workers Conference, Melbourne, September.

Healy, K. (2002) 'What's New for Culture in the New Economy', *Journal of Arts Management, Law and Society,* 32, 2: 86–103.

Healy, K. & Hampshire, A. (2002) 'Social Capital: A Useful Concept for Social Work?' *Australian Social Work*, 55, 3: 227–238.

Healy, K. & Hampshire, A. (2003) *Creating Better Communities: The Role of Non-Profits in Social Capital Creation*, Sydney: University of Sydney.

Hemlin, S., Allwood, C.M. & Martin, B.R. (eds) (2004) *Creative Knowledge Environments: The Influences on Creativity in Research and Innovation*, Cheltenham: Edward Elgar Publishing.

Henderson, P. & Mayo, M. (1998) *Training and Education in Urban Regeneration,* Bristol: The Policy Press.

Herbert-Cheshire, L. (2000) 'Contemporary Strategies for Rural Community Development in Australia: A Governmentality Perspective', *Journal of Rural Studies*. 16, 2: 203–215.

Hesmondhalgh, D. & Pratt, A.C. (2005) 'Cultural Industries and Cultural Policy', *International Journal of Cultural Policy,* 11, 1: 1–13.

Holden, J. (2008) *Culture and Learning: Towards a New Agenda,* London: Demos.

Holmes, J. (2005) 'Impulses Towards a Multifunctional Transition in Rural Australia: Gaps in the Research Agenda', *Journal of Rural Studies,* 22, 2: 142–160.

Hope, A.D. (1955) *The Wandering Islands,* Sydney: Edwards & Shaw.

Hossain, D., Burton, L., Lawrence, J. & Gorman, D. (2010) *Identifying the Key Factors that Impact on Rural and Remote Students' Participation in Higher Education at USQ*, Toowoomba: University of Southern Queensland. eprints.usq.edu.au/8581/1/Hossain_Burton_Lawrence_Gorman_AV.pdf. Accessed on 14 May 2011.

Hounslow, B. (2002) 'Community Capacity Building Explained', *Stronger Families Learning Exchange*, 1, Autumn: 20–22.

Howe, B. & Cleary, R. (2001) *Community Building: Policy Issues and Strategies for the Victorian Government*, Melbourne: Department of Human Services.

Howkins, J. (2002) *The Creative Economy: How People Make Money from Ideas*, London: Allen Lane.

Hulse, K. & Stone, W (2005) *Housing, Housing Assistance and Social Cohesion in Australia*, Melbourne: Australian Housing and Urban Research Institute. www.ahuri.edu.au/__data/assets/pdf_file/0015/2814/AHURI_Positioning_Paper_No91_Housing_housing_assistance_and_social_cohesion.pdf. Accessed on 22 June 2016.

Hur, M.H. (2006) 'Empowerment in Terms of Theoretical Perspectives: Exploring a Typology of the Process and Components Across Disciplines', *Journal of Community Psychology*, 34, 5: 523–540.

Hutton, T.A. (2008) *The New Economy of the Inner City: Restructuring, Regeneration and Dislocation in the Twenty-First-Century Metropolis*, Abington: Routledge.

Infrastructure Australia (2010) *State of Australian Cities 2010*, Canberra: Major Cities Unit, Infrastructure Australia, Australian Government. infrastructure.gov.au/infrastructure/pab/soac/files/MCU_SOAC.pdf. Accessed on 22 June 2016.

Inglehart, R. (1997) *Modernization and Post-Modernization: Cultural, Economic and Political Change in 43 Societies*, Princeton: Princeton University Press.

Ireland, R.D. & Webb, J.W. (2006) 'Strategic Entrepreneurship: Creating Competitive Advantage through Streams of Innovation', *Business Horizons*, 50, 1: 49–59.

Isaksen, S,G., Dorval, K.B. & Treffinger, D.J. (2011) *Creative Approaches to Problem Solving: A Framework for Innovation and Change,* London: Sage.

Jackson, S. (1999) *Half Full or Half Empty? Concepts and Research Design for the Study of Indicators of Community Capacity,* Working Paper 97, North York: Community Health Promotion Research Unit.

Jacobs, J. (1961) *The Death and Life of Great American Cities,* New York: Random House.

Jaffe, A.B. & Trajtenberg, M. (2002) *Patents, Citations, and Innovations: A Window on the Knowledge Economy,* Massachusetts: MIT Press.

James, R., Wrigley, R. & Lonnqvist, L. (2007) *Investigating the Mystery of Capacity Building: Learning from the Praxis Programme: Praxis Paper No. 18.* International NGO Training and Research Centre. drt.handicap-international.fr/fileadmin/cdroms/Biblio_Renforcement/documents/Chapter-5/Chap5Doc3.pdf. Accessed on 22 June 2016.

Jeannotte, M.S. (2003) 'Singing Alone?: The Contribution of Cultural Capital to Social Cohesion and Sustainable Communities', *International Journal of Cultural Policy,* 9, 1: 35–49.

Jeffcutt, P. & Pratt, A. (2002) 'Managing Creativity in the Cultural Industries', *Creativity and Innovation Management,* 1, 4: 225–233.

Johnson, L.C. (2009) *Cultural Capitals: Revaluing the Arts, Remaking Urban Spaces.* Surrey: Ashgate Publishing.

Jupp, B. (2000) *Working Together: Creating a Better Environment for Cross-Sector Partnerships.* London: Demos.

Kenway, J., Bullen, E. & Robb, S. (eds) (2004) *Innovation and Tradition: The Arts, Humanities, and the Knowledge Economy,* New York: Peter Lang Publishing.

Knoke, D. (2009) 'Playing Well Together: Creating Corporate Social Capital in Strategic Alliance Networks', *American Behavioral Scientist,* 52, 12: 1690–1708.

Landry, C. & Wood, P. (2003) *Harnessing and Exploiting the Power of Culture for Competitive Advantage,* Stroud: Comedia.

Landry, C., Greene, L., Matarasso, F. & Bianchini, F. (1996) *The Art of Regeneration: Urban Renewal Through Cultural Activity,* Stroud: Comedia.

Larson, R.W. & Walker, K.C (2006) 'Learning About the Real World in an Urban Arts Youth Program', *Journal of Adolescent Research,* 21, 3: 244–268.

Laverack, G. (2001) 'An Identification and Interpretation of the Organizational Aspects of Community Empowerment', *Community Development Journal,* 36, 2: 134–145.

Laverack, G. & Wallerstein, N. (2001) 'Measuring Community Empowerment: A Fresh Look at Organizational Domains', *Health Promotion International,* 16, 2: 179–185.

Lebski, S. (2010) *Arts and Heritage Tourism Experiences in Northern Tasmania: A Discussion Paper,* Launceston: Tourism Tasmania and Northern Tasmanian Development. stors.tas.gov.au/store/exlibris1/storage/STORS/2012/06/14/file_10/au-7-0095-03939_1.pdf. Accessed on 22 June 2016.

Lee, R. (2010) *Growing Rural Business: An Innovative Approach to Development,* Createspace.

Li, W.J. (2006) 'Community Decision Making Participation in Development', *Annals of Tourism Research,* 33, 1: 132–141.

Liaw, S-T. & Kilpatrick, S. (eds) (2008) *A Textbook of Australian Rural Health,* Canberra: Australia Rural Health Education Network.

Littlejohns, L.B. and Thompson, D. (2001) 'Cobwebs: Insights into Community Capacity and its Relation to Health Outcomes', *Community Development Journal,* 36, 1: 30–41.

Lowe, S.S. (2000) 'Creating Community: Art for Community Development', *Journal of Contemporary Ethnography,* 29, 3: 357–386.

Lyons, M., Smuts, C. & Stephens, A. (2001) 'Participation, Empowerment and Sustainability: (How) Do the Links Work?', *Journal of Urban Studies,* 38, 8: 1233–1251.

Macadam, R., Drinan, J., Inall, N. & McKenzie, B. (2004) *Growing the Capital of Rural Australia: The Task of Capacity Building*, Canberra: Rural Industries Research and Development Corporation.

MacDonald, A. (2000) *Defining Art in the Community*, Realtime Publishing. www.artshaus.com.au/community/resources (site discontinued). Accessed on 23 June 2008.

MacDonald, R. & Jolliffe, L. (2003) 'Cultural Rural Tourism: Evidence from Canada', *Annals of Tourism Research*, 30, 2: 307–322.

Manley, K. (2001) 'The Challenges Faced by Public Sector Innovators', paper presented at Technology Transfer and Innovation Conference, 26–28 September, Brisbane. eprints.qut.edu.au/7929/. Accessed on 27 May 2003.

Mann, L. & Chan, J. (2011) *Creativity and Innovation in Business and Beyond: Social Science Perspectives and Policy Implications*, New York: Routledge.

Markusen, A. & Schrock, G. (2006) 'The Artistic Dividend: Urban Artistic Specialisation and Economic Development Implications', *Journal of Urban Studies*, 43, 10: 1661–1686.

Markusen, A., Wassall, G.H., DeNatale, D. & Cohen, R. (2008) 'Defining the Creative Economy: Industry and Occupational Approaches', *Economic Development Quarterly*, 22, 1: 24–45.

Martins, E.C. & Terblanche, F. (2003) 'Building Organisational Culture that Stimulates Creativity and Innovation', *European Journal of Innovation Management*, 6, 1: 64–74.

Matarasso, F. (1996) *Defining Values: Evaluating Arts Programmes*, Stroud: Comedia.

Matarasso, F. (1999) *Towards a Local Cultural Index: Measuring the Cultural Vitality of Communities*, Stroud: Comedia.

Matarasso, F. (ed.) (2001) *Recognising Culture: A Series of Briefing Papers on Culture and Development*, Stroud: Comedia (in partnership with the Department of Canadian Heritage and UNESCO).

Matarasso, F. (2002) 'Smoke and Mirrors: A Response to Paola Merli's "evaluating the social impact of participation in arts activities"', *International Journal of Cultural Practice*, 8, 1: 337–346.

Mattern, M. (2001) 'Art and Community Development in Santa Ana, California: The Promise and the Reality', *The Journal of Arts Management, Law, and Society,* 30, 4: 301–315.

Mayo, E. (2005) 'The Northcott Narratives: Big Pictures and Little Things' *Artwork,* 63: 26–32.

McGinty, S. (2003) 'The Literature and Theories behind Community Capacity Building', in McGinty, S. (ed.) *Sharing Success: An Indigenous Perspective,* Altona: Common Ground Publishing, 65–94.

McGranahan, D. & Wojan, T. (2007) 'Recasting the Creative Class to Examine Growth Processes in Rural and Urban Counties', *Regional Studies*, 41, 2: 197–216.

McNicholas, B. (2004) 'Art, Culture and Business: A Relationship Transformation, a Nascent Field', *International Journal of Arts Management*, 7, 1: 57–69.

Mellander, C. & Florida, R. (2007) *The Creative Class or Human Capital?: Explaining Regional Development in Sweden,* CESIS Electronic Working Paper 70. www.infra.kth.se/cesis/documents/WP79.pdf. Accessed on 13 June 2009.

Metropolitan Redevelopment Authority (MRA) (2016) *Claisebrook Village: a case study in urban development.* assets.mra.wa.gov.au/production/b726e3fcb5404575292ba33ed8ae1a24/claisebrook-village-case-study.pdf. Accessed 22 June 2016.

Miller, L.S., Hess, K.M. & Orthmann, C.H. (2010) *Community Policing: Partnerships for Problem Solving,* New York: Delmar.

Mills, D. (2006) *Cultural Development and The Arts In Everyday Life,* discussion paper prepared for the Australia Council's Scoping Study Reference Group, Sydney: Australia Council for the Arts.

Montgomery, J. (1990) 'Cities and the Art of Cultural Planning', *Planning Practice and Research,* 5, 2: 17–24.

Morato, A.R. (2003) 'The Culture Society: A New Place for the Arts in the Twenty-First Century', *The Journal of Arts Management, Law, and Society*, 32, 4: 245–256.

Moscardo, G. (2008) 'Analyzing the Role of Festivals and Events in Regional Development', *Event Management*, 11, 1–2: 23–32.

Mowbray, M. (2005) 'Community Capacity Building or State Opportunism?', *Community Development Journal*, 40, 3: 255–264.

Murphy, C. (2004) *Heartwork: Great Arts Stories from Regional Australia*. Sydney: Australia Council for the Arts.

Murphy, J. & Thomas B. (2002) 'The Role of Business in Community Capacity Building: An Alternative Approach', *Communities Builders*, New South Wales, Sydney.

Newman, J. (2005) 'Participative Governance and the Remaking of the Public Sphere', in Newman J. (ed.), *Remaking Governance: Policy, Politics and the Public Sphere*, Policy Press: Bristol, 81–100.

Niland, C. (2000) 'Capacity, Capacity, Capacity: Communities and Community Services', *The Sydney Papers,* 12, 1: 88–94.

Organisation for Economic Cooperation and Development (OECD) (2007) *OECD Regions at a Glance: 2007 Edition*, Paris: OECD. www.oecd-ilibrary.org/urban-rural-and-regional-development/oecd-regions-at-a-glance-2007_reg_glance-2007-en. Accessed on 22 June 2016.

Peck, J. (2005) 'Struggling with the Creative Class', *International Journal of Urban and Regional Research*, 29, 4: 740–770.

Pennar, K. (1997) 'The Ties that Lead to Prosperity: The Economic Value of Social Bonds is only Beginning to be Measured', *Business Week*, December 15: 153–155.

Peppler, K.A. & Davis, H.J. (2010) 'Arts and Learning: A Review of the Impact of Arts and Aesthetics on Learning and Opportunities for Further Research', in *Proceedings of the 9th International Conference of the Learning Sciences: Volume 1,* International Society of the Learning Sciences.

Peters, M.A., Marginson, S. & Murphy P. (2009) *Creativity and the Global Knowledge Economy,* New York: Peter Lang Publishing.

Phillips, R. (2004) 'Artful business: Using the Arts for Community Economic Development', *Community Development Journal,* 39, 2: 112–122.

Portes, A. (1998) 'Social Capital: Its Origins and Applications in Modern Sociology', *Annual Review of Sociology,* 24: 1–24.

Potts, J., Cunningham, S., Hartley, J. & Omerod, P. (2008) 'Social Network Markets: A New Definition of the Creative Industries', *Journal of Cultural Economics,* 32, 3: 167–185.

Pratt, A.C. (2009) 'Urban Regeneration: From the Arts Feel Good Factor to the Cultural Economy', *Journal of Urban Studies,* 46, 5: 1041–1061.

Pritchard, B. & McManus, P. (2000) *Land of Discontent: The Dynamics of Change in Rural and Regional Australia,* Sydney: University of New South Wales Press.

Proctor, T. (2010) *Creative Problem Solving for Managers: Developing Skills for Decision Making and Innovation,* New York: Routledge.

Psilos, P. (2002) *The Impact of Arts Education on Workforce Preparation,* Washington: Center for Best Practices, National Governors Association.

Psilos, P. & Rapp, K. (2001) *The Role of the Arts in Economic Development,* Washington: Center for Best Practices, National Governors Association.

Purdue, D., Razzaque, K., Hambleton, R. & Stewart, M. (2000) *Community Leadership in Area Regeneration.* Bristol: The Policy Press.

Putnam, R.D. (1993) *Making Democracy Work,* Princeton: Princeton University Press.

Putnam, R.D. (1995) 'Bowling Alone: America's Declining Social Capital', *Journal of Democracy,* 6: 65–78.

Putnam, R.D. (2000) *Bowling Alone: The Collapse and Revival of American Community*, New York: Simon & Schuster.

Queensland Community Arts Network (QCAN) (1985) 'Coordinators Report' in *Notes of Annual General Meeting, June 1985*, Brisbane: Queensland Community Arts Network.

Queensland Community Arts Network (QCAN) (1985a) *QCAN Strategic Plan 2007 to 2010*, Brisbane: Queensland Community Arts Network (QCAN).

Queensland Community Arts Network (QCAN) (2003) *Insights: Community, Culture and Local Government*, Brisbane: Queensland Community Arts Network.

Queensland Government Public Art Policy (2001) *Art Built In*, Brisbane: Queensland Government.

Rabkin, N. & Redmond, R. (2006) 'The Arts Make a Difference', *The Journal of Arts Management, Law and Society*, 36, 1: 25–32.

Rajkumar, S. & Hoolahan, B. (2004) 'Remoteness and Issues in Mental Health Care: Experience from Rural Australia', *Epidemiologia e Psichiatria Sociale*, 13, 2: 78–82.

Reeves, M. (2002) *Measuring the Economic and Social Impact of the Arts: A Review*, London: Arts Council England.

Reid, J., Green, B., White, S., Cooper, M., Lock, G. & Hastings, W. (2008) 'New Ground in Teacher Education for Rural and Regional Australia: Regenerating Rural Social Space', unpublished paper presented at the Australian Association for Research in Education International Education Conference, Brisbane, 30 November – 4 December.

Richards, G. & Palmer, R. (2010) *Eventful Cities: Cultural Management and Urban Revitalisation*, Oxford: Butterworth-Heinemann.

Robinson, K. (2001) *Out of Our Minds: Learning to be Creative*. Oxford: Capstone.

Robinson, J.W. & Green, G.P. (2010) *Introduction to Community Development: Theory, Practice, and Service-Learning*, Thousand Oaks: Sage.

Rojewski, J.W. (2002) 'Preparing the Workforce of Tomorrow: A Conceptual Framework for Career and Technical Education', *Journal of Vocational Education Research*, 27, 1: 7–35.

Rosenfeld, S. (2004) 'Crafting a New Rural Development Strategy', paper presented at Conference on Knowledge Clusters and Entrepreneurship, Minnesota, Minneapolis. theinnofthepatriots.com/Crafting%20a%20New%20Rural%20Development%20Strategy.pdf. Accessed on 30 July 2009.

Ross, D. (2009) 'Urban Youth Cultures and the Re-Building of Social Capital: Illustrations from a Pilot Study in Glasgow', *A Journal of Youth Work*, 1: 7–22.

Ruane, S. (2007) *Paving Pathways for Youth Inclusion: The Contribution of Community Cultural Development*, Perth: Community Arts Network Western Australia.

Saatchi & Saatchi Australia (1999) *Australia and the Arts*, Sydney: Australia Council for the Arts.

Sahlberg, P. (2009) 'Creativity and Innovation through Lifelong Learning', *Lifelong Learning in Europe*, 1: 53–60.

Scott, A.J. (2006) 'Creative Cities: Conceptual Issues and Policy Questions', *Journal of Urban Affairs*, 28, 1: 1–17.

Seifter, H. (2004) 'Artists Help Empower Corporate America', *Arts Business Quarterly*, 1: 1–22.

Shaw, M. (2008) 'Community Development and the Politics of Community', *Community Development Journal*, 43, 1: 24–36.

Shaw, E. & Carter, S. (2007) 'Social Entrepreneurship: Theoretical Antecedents and Empirical Analysis of Entrepreneurial Processes and Outcomes', *Journal of Small Business and Enterprise Development*, 14, 3: 418–434.

Singapore Travel Guide (2012) *Marina Barrage: Singapore's Latest Downtown Icon*, Singapore: AGCGO – Singapore Travel and Lifestyle. sgcgo.com/marina-barrage/. Accessed on 5 November 2011.

Smith, L., Littlejohns, L.B. & Roy, D. (2003) *Measuring Community Capacity: State of the Field Review and Recommendations for Future Research*, Health Policy Research Program, Ottawa: Health Canada.

Smith, R. & Warfield, K. (2008) 'The Creative City: A Matter of Values', in Cooke, P. & Lazaretto, L. (eds), *Creative Cities, Cultural Clusters and Local Economic Development*, London: Edward Elgar, 287–312.

Smyth, J. (2009) 'Critically Engaged Community Capacity Building and the "Community Organizing" Approach in Disadvantaged Contexts', *Critical Studies in Education*, 50, 1: 9–22.

Sonn, C.C., Drew, N.M. & Kasat, P. (2002) *Conceptualising Community Cultural Development: The Role of Cultural Planning in Community Change*, Perth: Community Arts Network Western Australia.

Stace, D. & Dunphy, D. (2002) *Beyond the Boundaries: Leading and Re-Creating the Successful Enterprise*, Sydney: McGraw-Hill.

Stone, G. (2005) *Agribusiness Role in Extension, Education and Training: A Case Study*, Canberra: Rural Industries Research and Development Corporation.

Storper, M. & Scott, A.J. (2009) 'Rethinking Human Capital, Creativity and Urban Growth', *Journal of Economic Geography*, 9, 3: 147–167.

Tambo Teddies (1994), 'Business Plan', unpublished paper.

Taylor, M. (2000) 'Communities in the Lead: Power, Organisational Capacity and Social Capital', *Urban Studies*, 37, 5–6: 1019–1035.

Teaque, M. (2015) 'How MONA Changed Travel to Tasmania', Artworks Awol, Junkee Media and Qantas.

Teece, D. (2010) 'Business Models, Business Strategy and Innovation', *Long Range Planning*, 43, 2–3: 172–194.

Tepper, S.J. (2002) 'Creative Assets and the Changing Economy', *The Journal of Arts Management, Law and Society*, 32, 2: 159–168.

Thomas, C.Y. (1996) 'Capital Markets, Financial Markets and Social Capital: An Essay on Economic Theory and Economic Ideas', *Social and Economic Studies*, 45, 2–3: 1–23.

Thompson, D. & Pepperdine, S. (2003) *Community Capacity for Riparian Restoration: A Discussion Paper,* Canberra: Land and Water Australia.

Throsby, D. (2001) *Economics and Culture,* Melbourne: Cambridge University Press.

Throsby, D. (2008) 'Modelling the Cultural Industries', *International Journal of Cultural Policy*, 14, 3: 217–232.

Throsby, D. & Hollister, V. (2003) *Don't Give Up Your Day Job: An Economic Study of Professional Artists in Australia,* Sydney: Australia Council for the Arts.

Tonts, M. (2005) 'Competitive Sport and Social Capital in Rural Australia', *Journal of Rural Studies,* 21, 2: 137–149.

Totterman, H. (2008) 'From Creative Ideas to New Emerging Ventures: Entrepreneurial Processes among Finnish Design Entrepreneurs', unpublished PhD thesis, Hanken School of Economics.

Verity, F. (2007) *Community Capacity Building: A Review of the Literature,* South Australia Department of Health, Adelaide. www.sapo.org.au/pub/pub10783.html. Accessed on 22 June 2016.

Wakerman, J. & Humphreys, J. (2008) 'Rural and Remote Health: Definitions, Policy and Priorities', in Liaw, S-T. & Kilpatrick, S. (eds), *Textbook of Australian Rural Health,* Canberra: Australian Rural Health Network, 13–30.

Walker, C., Jackson, R.R. & Rosenstein, C.E. (2003) *Culture and Commerce: Traditional Arts in Economic Development,* Washington: Urban Institute.

Wallerstein, N., Sanchez, V., & Velarde, L. (2005) 'Freirian Praxis in Health Education and Community Organizing', in Minkler, M. (ed.) *Community Organizing and Community Building for Health.* New Brunswick: Rutgers University Press, 195–215.

Watkins, K. (2006) 'Agricultural Trade, Globalisation, and the Rural Poor', paper presented at International Food Policy Research Institute seminar, Globalisation and the Rural Poor, Washington DC, 6 December. www.tanzaniagateway.org/docs/agricultural_trade_globalisation.pdf. Accessed on 28 August 2009.

Weiss, D. (2004) *Chimer,* Paris: Association for Art, Education and New Technologies. www.arenotech.org/12mayo2003/actas%2012%20 mayo/chimer.htm (site discontinued). Accessed on 15 March 2007.

West, M. (2009) 'Establishing Community Organisations', in Phillips, R. & Pittma, R. H. (eds) *An Introduction to Community Development,* New York: Routledge, 104–115.

Williams, D. (1995) *Creating Social Capital: A Study of the Long Term Benefits from Community Based Arts Funding,* Adelaide: Community Arts Network of South Australia.

Williams, D. (2000) *The Social Impact of the Arts: How the Arts Measure Up,* Stroud: Comedia.

Williams, S. (2005) 'Fragile Cultures Find Strength in Unity', *Australian Financial Review,* 1 September: 44.

Williams, K & Durrance, J.C. (2008) 'Social Networks and Social Capital: Rethinking Theory in Community Informatics', *Journal of Community Informatics,* 4, 3. ci-journal.net/index.php/ciej/article/view/465/430. Accessed on 15 November 2010.

Wilson, P. (1997) 'Building Social Capital: A Learning Agenda for the Twenty-First Century', *Urban Studies,* 34, 5–6: 745–760.

Winchester, J. (2004) *Measuring the Cultural, Economic and Social Impacts of the Arts in Australia: Audit of Research,* Sydney: University of Technology Sydney.

Wolff, T. (2010) *The Power of Collaborative Solutions: Six Principles and Effective Tools for Building Healthy Communities,* San Francisco: Jossey-Bass.

Wood, M. (2000) 'Community Involvement and Capacity Building', in Carley, M., Campbell, M., Kearns, A., Wood. M. & Young, R. *Regeneration in the 21st Century Policies into Practice: An Overview of the Joseph Rowntree Foundation Area Regeneration Programme,* Bristol: The Policy Press, 12–20.

Wood, P. (2001) 'A Piece of Action: Regional Strategies for the Creative Industries', paper presented at Convergence, Creative Industries and Civil Society: The New Cultural Policy Conference, 28 September, Nottingham, Culture Link Network.

Woodhouse, A. (2006) 'Social Capital and Economic Development in Regional Australia: A Case Study', *Journal of Rural Studies,* 21, 1: 83–94.

Woolcock, G., Renton, R & Cavaye, J. (2004) *What Makes Communities Tick?: Local Government and Social Capital Action Research Projects,* Brisbane: University of Queensland.

Woolcock, M. (1998) 'Social Capital and Economic Development: Towards a Theoretical Synthesis and Policy Framework', *Theory and Society,* 27, 2: 151–208.

Yarnet, M. (2000) *Towns, Cities and Regions in the Learning Age,* London: Department of Education and Skills.

Yigitcanlar, T. (2010) 'A Comparative Knowledge-Based Urban Development Analysis: Vancouver, Melbourne and Manchester vs. Boston', in Yigitcanlar, T., Yates, P. & Kunzmann, K. (eds), *The 3rd Knowledge Cities World Summit,* Melbourne: World Capital Institute, City of Melbourne and Office of Knowledge Capital, 112–117.

Yigitcanlar, T., Baum, S. & Horton, S. (2007) 'Attracting and Retaining Knowledge Workers in Knowledge Cities', *Journal of Knowledge Management,* 11, 5: 6–17.

Appendix A: Chronological Review of CCB Definitions

Date	Author/source	Focal area	Key definitional indicators	Key features and characteristics
1994	Eng & Parker	Community competence	A community can work collectively to solve problems and develop skills and capabilities.	Emphasis on empowerment.
1996	Aspen Institute	Community problems and opportunities	The combined influence of a community's commitment, resources and skills that can be deployed to build community strengths and address community problems and opportunities.	Emphasis on community needs. A shared community awareness of problems, opportunities and solutions.
1999	Jackson	Community health	CCB is a holistic representation of capabilities (those with which the community is endowed and those to which the community has access), plus the facilitators and barriers to realisation of those capabilities in the broader social environment.	One of the first uses of the term in literature — drawn from earlier research on social capital and community development. Building community capability. Recognition of community knowledge and skills. Recognition of the importance of knowledge and skills residing outside the community. Emphasis of barriers and impediments to the development of community capacity.
2000	Cavaye	Government services	Community capacity consists of networks, organisations, attitudes, leadership and skills that allow communities to manage change and sustain community-led development.	Creating a vehicle for local people to express and act on existing concerns. Personal relationships between government agents (public servants) and community members. New roles and understandings of the relationships between government and community.

Date	Author/source	Focal area	Key definitional indicators	Key features and characteristics
2000	Duncan & Thomas	Community development	CCB places greater emphasis on the community itself (rather than professionals or government) identifying its needs and defining desired outcomes — that is, on the community initiating action rather than being mobilised to act.	Strong emphasis on community power and action. A rebalance of the role of external agencies and government.
2001	Healy	Non-profit organisations	Community capacity refers to the capabilities that exist within communities and within the networks between individuals, communities and institutions of civil society that strengthen individual and community capacity to define their own values and priorities and capacity to act on these.	Identification of CCB dimensions including financial capacity, physical resources and assets, human resources, and social resources. Recognition of social resources (networks) and their critical importance to disadvantaged communities.
2001	Littlejohns & Thompson	Health	The degree to which a community can develop, implement and sustain action that will allow it to exert greater control over its physical, social, economic and cultural environments.	Holistic approach to the physical, social, economic and cultural environments of a community. Emphasis on community control and sustainability.
2001	Howe & Cleary	Heath	The ability of individuals, organisations and communities to manage their own affairs and to work collectively to foster and sustain positive change.	Strong emphasis on change management. Collaboration between communities and external organisations.
2002	Hounslow	Overall community development	While the main purpose of CCB is to build a community's capacity to achieve a specific outcome, many practitioners and analysts argue that CCB is a desirable end in itself as it contributes to the creation and maintenance of active citizenship and social trust.	A broad approach removed for specific outcomes. Build on values and trust.
2002	Matarasso	Cultural capacity building	Cultural capacity building focuses on strengthening organisational infrastructure to enable artistic growth. Its goal is to stimulate new practices, policies and approaches through which communities can dynamically adapt to the ever-changing conditions of producing, presenting and preserving arts and culture.	A new focus on the role of the arts and culture in CCB.

Appendix B: Snapshot of Arts-based Community Initiatives (1960–2010)

Name of initiative	Date	Country	Background and purpose of initiative	Positioning of the arts	Outcomes	Issues	Source
San Francisco Neighborhood Arts Program (NAP)	1967	USA	San Francisco Neighborhood Arts Program (NAP) is regarded by some as a founder and exemplar of community-based arts. At a time of social and racial unrest, the US Government was keen to fund projects to occupy young people in constructive pursuits – creating murals, learning and performing music, putting on street festivals, and so on.	NAP provided arts-based services to San Franciscan neighbourhoods – usually the poor and underprivileged neighbourhoods. A key driving principle of the program was that the arts provide new opportunities for communities to grow and learn.	Exposure of the arts to neighbourhoods relatively untouched by art. Channelled government grant money to small-scale community projects like murals and street festivals. Provided arts-based education and training. Accessed government funds to increase employment opportunities for artists.	A key issue for the San Francisco Neighborhood Arts Program (NAP) was its sustainability after government grants subsided. The short-term success on NAP represented an historic moment in time when government agencies saw community arts as a valid tool for engaging communities in self-education and self-activation. It was also a highly visible, often effective and always colourful way to achieve community outcomes. By the mid-1980s, government priorities had changed, funding disappeared and the NAP (and many other community art projects) folded.	Goldbard, 1993

Name of initiative	Date	Country	Background and purpose of initiative	Positioning of the arts	Outcomes	Issues	Source
Jam Factory	1974	Australia	The Jam Factory was established with government funding in 1974 to assist, train, guide, challenge, empower and promote artists locally and nationally. Its name derives from its original location in a disused jam factory. It is one the earliest examples of art and artists reclaiming an abandoned building (well before the trend appears in the literature during the 1990s).	Art is the core activity of the Jam Factory, which has become a major centre for the design, production, exhibition and sale of work by leading and emerging Australian artists and designers.	Has provided income streams for over 400 artists. Has employed and trained more than 360 of Australia's leading makers, artists and designers. Provides over 60 per cent of its annual funding from sales, services and creative business initiatives.	The Jam Factory has been sustainable for more than three decades. While government financial support continues, the factory has moved towards more financially sustainable models. However, the original aims of empowerment and promotion of emerging artists have been challenged as demands increase for sales and returns on investment.	www.jamfactory.com.au (Accessed on 22 June 2016)
Fusion Arts Centre – Oxford's Community Arts Agency	1980	UK	Fusion was one of the first community arts organisations in the UK with a primary focus on supporting community-based arts activities. Originally called Bloomin' Arts, it was established by three committed people who initially developed a program of participative performance events in the local parks. From these beginnings, the organisation grew to offer many arts-based programs at venues across the UK.	Fusion was primarily a community arts organisation dedicated to using the arts to support communities in the UK.	Provided a hub for community artists and community workers through which programs and resources can be communicated and shared. Delivered a program of arts activities for adults and children in communities. Facilitated and supports creative projects within communities.	Fusion Arts Centre has evolved and changed since the 1980s as government support was redirected to other activities. It now operates as company limited by guarantee as well as a registered charity, and fundraising has become a significant part of its operations. The organisation has grown but operates in a much wider environment than community arts.	www.fusion-arts.org (Accessed on 22 June 2016)

Name of initiative	Date	Country	Background and purpose of initiative	Positioning of the arts	Outcomes	Issues	Source
Community Arts Networks (CANs)	1980s onwards	Australia	CANs were established in several Australian states during the 1980s (Western Australia, South Australia, and Queensland). Each evolved from a network of people committed to community arts practice. All CANs were committed to empowering communities through arts and cultural development.	Before 1990, all Australian CANs were focused on supporting communities (urban, regional and rural) through community arts. This was primarily achieved by linking communities with artists who would work collaboratively with community members on a community art project — such projects were usually murals, theatre productions, etc.	During the 1980s, CANS were government funded and provided many community arts programs for Australian communities. Significant outcomes for communities included: • Community involvement in the arts. • Community resources. • Community confidence (new skills).	The CANs built on their early experiences in the 1980s and continued to evolve for the next two decades — their commitment to social justice increased and they developed a philosophical platform of using the arts to address social inequalities. Many CANs began working with Aboriginal communities and disadvantaged communities in urban and regional areas of Australia.	www.canwa.com.au/about/the-organisation/history/ (Accessed on 22 June 2016) and Environment scan/interviews
Avenue of the Arts	1989	USA	The Avenue of the Arts is a mile-long section of South Broad Street in Philadelphia that provided a catalyst for a major downtown revitalisation. The project was a collaboration between cultural institutions, philanthropic organisations, local property owners and Philadelphian civic leaders.	The arts and arts organisations worked collaboratively to create a lively and vibrant arts precinct, which in turn generated the development of other businesses.	The strategy strengthened Philadelphia's position as a major cultural destination generating tourist numbers and the economic spin-offs of increased cultural tourism. Other outcomes include: • An increase in cultural infrastructure — there are now over 11 cultural and educational institutions and over seven individual performance spaces in the avenue; • Increased private sector investment in Philadelphia in general and the arts specifically; • Historic warehouses have been converted to up-market housing; • $157 million is generated annually through the Avenue's cultural organisations, hotels, restaurants and retail businesses; • 2,800 full-time jobs and 1,000 part-time jobs are supported through the project.	The Avenue of the Arts was one of the earliest examples of the arts being used to fuel urban regeneration. The project concept was generated by city planners not by artists or cultural leaders.	Psilos & Rapp, 2001

Name of initiative	Date	Country	Background and purpose of initiative	Positioning of the arts	Outcomes	Issues	Source
The Promenade Ribbon Sculpture	1990	USA	The city planners of San Francisco were provided with an opportunity to unite a downtown area with the waterfront, which had been cut off from the city. The response was the creation of a functional sculpture — a five-kilometre ribbon of illuminated glass. Over the distance the sculpture changes shape to accommodate seating and tables for al fresco dining.	The Promenade Ribbon Sculpture has created a new space that allows people alternatives to driving and encourages people to take time to consider the beauty of the city and its surroundings, especially the harbour.	This project is an early example of the use of public art to create a vibrant public place; it encourages a sense of pride in community and provides an arts-based tourist attraction.		Psilos & Rapp, 2001
Arts West	1991	Australia	Arts West was established as an independent non-profit arts organisation servicing the artists of Central Queensland. The organisation aims to promote the development of the arts as an integral part of small rural communities. A central feature of the organisation is a gallery and shop front for local arts. The gallery/shop has evolved into a successful venture, attracting a good tourist trade and contributing to other cultural tourism attractions of central Queensland.		Arts West is a successful organisation operating for almost two decades. Its future challenge is to grow and evolve to cater for the changing demands and interests of the community. It needs to engage more with young people and identify opportunities for new and emerging artists in the community. Arts West current operations depend primarily on the contribution of established community artists. While well respected, these artists are ageing and are generally very traditional in their approach to the arts. Arts West needs to protect the interests of established community artists while broadening its approaches to engage new participants that reflect the changing nature of the community.		Site visits and interviews

Name of initiative	Date	Country	Background and purpose of initiative	Positioning of the arts	Outcomes	Issues	Source
Tambo Teddies	1992–	Australia	From humble beginnings (three women making teddy bears from wool during a time of drought and record low wool prices), this initiative has grown into an arts-based business enterprise that employs 40 local people. Tambo Teddies sells its product throughout the world and has become a major tourist destination for outback tourists.	Regional identity through the arts. Integration of the arts in community life. Promotion of regional arts. Retail outlet for regional artists resulting in increased sales. Integration of the arts with other community initiatives and cultural tourism events and attractions.		Tambo Teddies is primarily a business enterprise based on an innovative product using local resources and talent. Because each product is handcrafted, the business can legitimately be described as an arts-based enterprise. This is at odds with the perceptions of the owners/proprietors who see themselves as businesswomen rather than artists.	Site visits and interviews
Big hArt	1996	Australia	Big hArt is a non-profit organisation that pilots arts-based projects for marginalised young people with the aim of re-engaging them in community life. Big hArt began work in Tasmania but has expanded to run projects in New South Wales and the Northern Territory. It also has proposals under consideration in other states of Australia.	Big hArt works with young people in communities to develop successful, sustainable, local arts-based projects for rural and regional communities. The projects build skills and capacity at grass roots levels by working with communities on real-life projects. One project allowed Big hArt to work with 250 marginalised young people from five communities in northern New South Wales to produce a film titled HURT. In 2000, HURT was awarded an Australian Film Institute award for Best Concept in a Non-Feature Film.	Community engagement for marginalised youth. Raised awareness of community skills and capacity. New community cultural products. New cultural skills and talents. Skills for youth.	Big hArt primarily relies on project-based funds from government to support its activities. It works with communities and provides valuable opportunities for disengaged youth. Its projects are primarily focused on building social and human capital. If funding becomes unavailable, there are few mechanisms to sustain the activity.	Ainsworth & Ritchie, 2002

Name of initiative	Date	Country	Background and purpose of initiative	Positioning of the arts	Outcomes	Issues	Source
Santa Ana	1998	USA	In 1998, the city of Santa Ana proclaimed itself the 'Arts and Culture City' of Orange County, California. The city aimed to use the arts to revitalise the downtown district to increase commercial activity and improve intercultural relations.	The project focused on the development of infrastructure to support and accommodate the arts, specifically the development of an 'Artists Village' and 'The Bowers Museum'. The new infrastructure houses a range of venues that attract visitors to the areas. However, many of the visitors are from other towns and cities and the majority are white middle-class people. While this generates significant economic activity and impacts positively on property values and other economic measures, it further isolates the poor Hispanic population and thus has failed to achieve its key objective of improving cultural relations.	Improved recreational options. New cultural facilities. New revenue streams. New businesses. New infrastructure. Renovated facilities. Improved property values.	Santa Ana is Orange County's largest and poorest city. There is a deep division between the city's poor Hispanic majority population and its affluent, white minority. While the project has brought considerable economic benefits, the project has not influenced the class divide. In fact, the art infrastructure development and associated projects has further divided the community along class and ethnic lines. In must be noted that the community outcomes described here are related directly to initiatives of the Arts and Culture City Project. The Hispanic population has rich, organic, grass roots arts practices and programs that contribute significantly to their community and quality of life.	Mattern, 2001

Name of initiative	Date	Country	Background and purpose of initiative	Positioning of the arts	Outcomes	Issues	Source
Mowanjum Community Art Project	1999	Australia	Mowanjum is an isolated Aboriginal community near Derby in the north of Western Australia. The community is made up of three tribes: Ngarinyin, Wororra, and Wanambul. This project sought to introduce the unique aspects of the Indigenous art of Mowanjum to a wider national and international audience.	To the Indigenous people of Mowanjum, the Wandjina is their supreme spirit being having created everything on and in the earth and developed the rules by which the people live. Visual images of Wandjina first appeared on rocks and in caves of the north coast thousands of years ago, and some of this ancient artwork is still visible today. This project sought to promote and present the art of the people of Mowanjum to a wider audience. Before the project, Wandjina art was confined to its own cultural landscape in the Kimberley and had not been presented to a wider audience. The result of the project was the first major exhibition of Wandjina art.	Community confidence as artists travelled with the art to tell their stories. Community resourcefulness (artists improvised with available materials and resources to produce artwork). Community cohesion through collaborative art. Community self-determination (as project was planned and funded from within the community). Increased appreciation of cultural heritage by a wide audience. Recognition of local artists and Indigenous art. Continuity of an endangered cultural heritage. New revenue streams contributing to community financial independence. Market development (exhibitions now held in Sydney, Melbourne and New York).	The project has provided some significant outcomes for the community — most significant has been the demonstration of art in contributing toward social cohesion and community self-determination through a shared cultural purpose. Also of significance is the development of community skills in planning and managing the production of art for a wider audience. Much has been made of the revenue returned to the community through the sale of the artworks. This was estimated to be approximately $160,000 during 1999. Despite the claims about the contribution to financial independence for this community, the amount raised would have little impact on the community and its future. The sustainability of the project outcomes need to be revisited to determine its long-term community gains.	Community Wise Programs, Department of Local Government and Regional Development, Western Australian Government

Name of initiative	Date	Country	Background and purpose of initiative	Positioning of the arts	Outcomes	Issues	Source
On the Day	2000	Australia	On the Day was a collaboration between Japanese artist Nakahashi Katsushige and the community of Cowra — represented by individual citizens and corporate and government organisations. The project assembled 25,000 photographs to commemorate Cowra's history in World War II. (Cowra hosted a prisoner of war (POW) camp and, in 1944, 1,000 Japanese prisoners attempted to escape — 231 prisoners died during the attempted escape.)	One hundred and thirty community members worked with Katsushige for two-and-a-half weeks to collect photographs and assemble an installation, They also created a full-scale photographic representation of a section of the POW camp and scattered the ground with 231 eucalyptus leaves inscribed with POW numbers of the men who died.	The collaboration provided the community with a new appreciation of history and the heritage of Cowra. The project also provided a range of social and cultural outcomes for the community: • Increased sense of community cooperation and collaboration; • New sense of community identity; • New community insights into the arts and the role of artistic vision.	The project provides a good example of cooperation between artists, community members and government and corporate organisations. The event of both a celebration and commemoration of Cowra's history. Despite the significance of the event for the community, it remained a one-off event that provided few long-term benefits to the town.	Murphy, 2004
A Regional Cultural Plan for the New Millennium	2001	USA	In the late 1990s, local government authorities in Silicon Valley, California, embarked on a planning process to ensure community artistic and cultural assets were protected and developed in a sustainable way.	A key platform of the planning process was to involve both public and private organisations to develop and connect creative capacity across business and cultural realms. The plan's key aim was to integrate the artistic assets of Silicon Valley into civic life.	The planning process resulted in a 10-year blueprint for development: *20/21: A Regional Cultural Plan for the New Millennium*. The plan included specific recommendations and strategies on: (i) arts and cultural education; (ii) artistic and organisational development; (iii) community and neighbourhood arts; (iv) community artistic leadership; and (v) funding. Cultural Initiatives Silicon Valley was created to implement the plan and develop the cultural and creative aspects of Silicon Valley.	This approach was one of the first examples of civic and business leaders recognising that artistic and cultural assets are essential for quality of life and necessary for sustained growth. The plan proposes that the region's highly successful digital industries work alongside government and non-profit organisations to maximise the integration of the arts into civic life.	Philos & Rapp, 2001

Name of initiative	Date	Country	Background and purpose of initiative	Positioning of the arts	Outcomes	Issues	Source
Alice Springs Beanie Festival	2001	Australia	This small festival grew from a desire to sell excess beanies crocheted by local Aboriginal women. It has grown into a significant festival celebrating traditional women's crafts.	The festival grew from a very utilitarian need to dispose of excess beanies. These were functional clothing items to protect against the cold desert nights. The festival provided a stimulus to become more creative with the beanies and they now are sought-after fashion statements and a central Australian art form. A focus on art and women's craft was a secondary outcome of the festival.	Community networks of Indigenous and non-Indigenous women. New community skills (planning, organising, exhibiting and project management). Strengthening cultural recognition of local crafts. Revenue from sales. Increase in visitor and tourist numbers.	From very humble beginnings, the beanie festival now attracts over 3,000 entries from local Indigenous and non-Indigenous women, as well as attracting entries from fibre artists around Australia. Most items are for sale, the organisers have worked hard to ensure the focus of the festival is nor overtaken by an emphasis on retail. The evolution of the festival demonstrates how real community need drives activity. In addition, the festival is self-funding and has never attracted or sought government or business funds or sponsorships — it is run on good will and friendship.	Murphy, 2004
Desert Uplands Festival	2002	Australia	This festival was the product of collaboration between 14 towns across Central Queensland (covering an area of thousands of square kilometres). Rather than establishing 14 separate arts festivals, the shires of Central Queensland collaborated to produce one major festival in an attempt to increase tourist numbers to the region.	Art was the central feature of the festival, which celebrated the creative achievements of the 14 participating towns, with a focus on performance and exhibition. A feature of the two-week festival was the production of 'Stumping', a work created and performed by young people from across the Desert Uplands region.	By consolidating a number of individual festivals, the Desert Uplands Festival saved money by reducing duplication — there is, however, little evidence that overall revenue from tourism increased across the region.	The region covered by the Desert Uplands Festival represents unique and usual geography that has traditionally provided a platform for tourism to the area. The sustainability of the festival may require a stronger links between the arts and the environment.	Interviews and site visits

Name of initiative	Date	Country	Background and purpose of initiative	Positioning of the arts	Outcomes	Issues	Source
Natimuk Fringe Festival	2002	Australia	The Natimuk Fringe Festival built on the changing population of the Natimuk community. Like many rural communities, the traditional Natimuk population of farmers and business people have increasingly shared their community with an influx of artists and rock climbers, attracted to the beauty and physical challenges of surrounding mountains.	The festival used the skills and experiences of new and old community members to create an aerial dance on the sides of 30-metre wheat silos (rock climbers working with artists and farmers to create and perform).	As well as creating a sense of purpose for the community, the festival: • Involved numerous community groups in the production (schools, community organisation, clubs and businesses); • Created a sense of uniqueness for the town and its people; • Generated visitor interest in Natimuk.	The festival illustrated how the arts can bring various groups in the community together to work for a common good. It should be noted that the festival idea was generated by a rock climber and not an artist. The festival has run for a number of years but its sustainability relies on continuous innovation and novelty to attract community involvement.	Murphy, 2004
Bundaleer Weekend	2003	Australia	The Bundaleer Weekend (Jamestown, South Australia) combined fine art, music, adventure, heritage and local community culture to increase awareness of the need for environmental protection of the Bundaleer Forest. It sought also to promote cultural and environmental tourism in the area.	The program used local artists, musicians, poets and performers to create a three-day cultural event focused on the protection of the environment and the promotion of sustainable eco-tourism.	The Bundaleer Weekend focused on using the arts to successfully increase public awareness of a critical community issue — the protection of the Bundaleer environment. It was successful in: • Generating 10,000 visitors and tourists to promote awareness (as well as stimulate short term economic returns to the community); • Promotion of regional arts and local cultural identity.	This initiative illustrates how the arts can be used to consolidate community interest around significant issues. The arts can mobilise community action and integrate with broader community issues to generate outcomes for specific concerns.	Murphy, 2004

Name of initiative	Date	Country	Background and purpose of initiative	Positioning of the arts	Outcomes	Issues	Source
National Limestone Sculpture Symposium	2003	Australia	This symposium resulted from collaboration between Country Arts South Australia and manufacturer Kimberley Clark Australia. Together they staged a National Limestone Sculpture Symposium, bringing together 36 sculptors from all over Australia to create and display new works created from Mount Gambier limestone.	The 36 invited sculptors worked with regional and local artists to create sculptures from local limestone. Sculptors worked in full view of locals and visitors in a local park that was formerly the Old Mount Gambier Gaol Market Garden. Visitors not only watched progress but were encouraged to interact with the artists to learn more about the medium and the process.	The project was a significant success for Mount Gambier. Outcomes included: • The generation of 300 room nights of accommodation over the eight days of the symposium; • $40,000 of sales of sculptures; • Improved relationships between the town and the manufacturer; • Public appreciation of sculpture as an art form by the community; • Increased sense of community identity through the recognition of the value of local commodity (limestone).	This project was hugely successful and generated local, national and international interest. While further symposia were held in two subsequent years, the project could not be sustained over the long term due to increasing expenses and declining visitor numbers.	Murphy, 2004
Bobcat Dancing	2003	Australia	Bobcat Dancing was a community theatre event staged in the bed of the Leichhardt River in Mt Isa, Queensland. In a tribute to the town's mining history, three three-tonne bobcats 'danced' to a live band playing popular music. The bobcat choreography was created as part of the Queensland Biennial Festival of Music.	The key aspect of the event was a celebration through the arts of the town's mining industry and history, and focused on the strong interdependence between people and machines.	The event attracted an audience of 18,000 people. The event was a collaboration between urban-based arts experts and community members — 155 local people were directly involved in the final show.	While an extremely successful and creative activity, Bobcat Dancing represents a one-off event that stimulates a sense of community cohesion and an appreciation of the uniqueness of the Mt Isa Community. It fails to demonstrate an integration of the arts in community development over the long term.	Queensland Community Arts Network, 2003
Artist Mob	2003	Australia	Artist Mob was a program aimed at delivering professional development to Indigenous and regional artists in Western Australia.	The program aimed to increase the level of professionalism in the creation of artists' portfolios and CVs. It also aimed to better inform artists in marketing, accessing funds and copyright.	The program resulted in a growing number of Indigenous and regional artist achieving exhibitions, commissions and successfully winning grants and project funding.	The project provides an example of a major theme of the decade — the professional development of regional artists. The project provides little evidence of the arts and artists using the arts to contribute to the sustainable development of communities.	Murphy, 2004

Name of initiative	Date	Country	Background and purpose of initiative	Positioning of the arts	Outcomes	Issues	Source
CHIMER	2004	Europe	CHIMER set out to investigate the connection between the arts and new technologies. By capitalising on the natural enthusiasm of children, the project sought to develop innovative approaches to using new technologies to document the cultural heritage of selected European communities.	Children aged between nine and 12 years from different parts of Europe were asked to build cultural digital maps of communities. They used GPS devices with mobile technologies and digital cameras to create digital archives of their own towns or villages, which could be easily shared with other children around the world.	The project developed a sense of community identity among participating communities and helped to share cultural uniqueness with communities around the world.	The project provides interesting insights into the potential role of technology in mapping community cultural heritage and communicating the special identity of communities, thus increasing interest in communities leading to a potential increase in visitor and tourist numbers.	Weiss, 2004
Ulysses Link	2004	Australia	Ulysses Link was a regional arts project that designed and built a creative walkway linking four villages of Mission Beach in far north Queensland. The walkway interwove history and environment through Indigenous and historical stories expressed through mosaics, carvings and ceramic sculptures created by local artists.	Fourteen local North Queensland artists worked collaboratively to design and develop the walkway. The artists worked with fruit farmers, tourist operators, steel fabricators, conservation groups and other members of the local community to ensure the walkway reflected local culture and history, and was built to be practical and sustainable. While many people were involved in providing advice and building the walkway, arts and artists were at the centre of the project.	Community networks and collaboration. New community skills. New community facilities (including facilities built to enhance the walkway, such as playgrounds and a meeting piazza). Public art development (incorporating a sculpture precinct as well as the walk itself). Promotion of regional arts and local cultural identity. New business model combining cultural tourism, conservation and the arts. New business connections and partnerships.		Arts Queensland, 2007a

Name of initiative	Date	Country	Background and purpose of initiative	Positioning of the arts	Outcomes	Issues	Source
Kaltjita/ Kashmir Collaboration	2005	Australia/ India	This initiative is a collaboration between the remote Aboriginal artists of the Aṉangu Pitjantatjara Yankunytjatjara lands and the traditional craftspeople of Kashmir in northern India. Aboriginal artists send their designs to Kashmir where the local craftspeople apply them to their own handmade rugs, cushions and wooden lacquer boxes and then send them back to Australia for sale.	The groups participating in the collaboration have two things in common: • A love of good art and craft; • A determination to improve life for their communities.	The rugs have been commercially successful — the largest rugs are sold as limited editions and retail from $800. A number have been bought by galleries and museums, including the Australian National Museum. The business arrangement has been economically successful for both groups and projections suggest a sustainable future. The intellectual property of the Aboriginal artists is protected and ownership of the designs is maintained by the artists. Socially, the Aboriginal community has a much greater sense of identity and the project has been culturally empowering to both groups.		Williams, 2005

Index

Note: locators in italics indicate tables, figures or other illustrative material. For details of case studies, see the Case Study Index.

Case Study Index

Note: locators in italics indicate tables, figures or other illustrative material.

www.ingramcontent.com/pod-product-compliance
Lightning Source LLC
LaVergne TN
LVHW052350100826
845147LV00013B/799
9781760460525